How the World is Making Our Children Mad and What to Do About It

How the World is Making Our Children Mad and What to Do About It

LOUIS WEINSTOCK

Sourcebooks and the colophon are registered trademarks of Sourcebooks.

This publication is designed to provide accurate and authoritative information in regard
to the subject matter covered. It is sold with the understanding that the publisher is not
engaged in rendering legal, accounting, or other professional service. If legal advice
or other expert assistance is required, the services of a competent professional person
should be sought. —*From a Declaration of Principles Jointly Adopted by a Committee
of the American Bar Association and a Committee of Publishers and Associations*

Published by Sourcebooks
P.O. Box 4410, Naperville, Illinois 60567-4410
(630) 961-3900
sourcebooks.com

Originally published in 2022 in Great Britain by Vermilion, an imprint of Ebury
Publishing, part of the Penguin Random House group of companies.

Cataloging-in-Publication Data is on file with the Library of Congress.

Printed and bound in the United States of America.
POD

To our children, to the child within, to all those children yet to be born, may you experience a deep and abiding sense of 'enoughness'.

CONTENTS

PROLOGUE

We had entered the twilight zone. It was 4.30am, the morning of Halloween. We were in a home-from-home room at the Whittington Hospital, north London, where my wife Laurey had just given birth in a big tub of water to our daughter Rose Gaia.

After four whole years of trying to make a human and four miscarriages – a series of broken promises and broken hearts – this moment was everything. As Laurey got out of the tub, the midwife passed this warm, squidgy creature to me and I held her against my heart. She felt so delicate. I felt so tender.

This was a space between two worlds – the world of the womb where everything was safe and all her needs were met, and this mad world where life can be tough and there is no happy ending. I wanted to build a bridge for her between these two worlds, to help her feel safe. If there is one single lesson all those years of psychotherapy training and practice had taught me, it is the importance of helping children to feel safe.

So, I rocked her in my arms and whispered to her, over and over:

> *'You are safe'*
> *'You are safe'*
> *'You are safe'*

It's eighteen months later now and Laurey and I have turned into zombies. The calm baby I'd held in my arms is still cute by day – though less squidgy, more solid now and she can walk and even talk a bit. But by night, our sweet little angel turns into a sleep-destroying machine.

I'm walking home from work, from the serene red houseboat on Regent's Canal, King's Cross in London where I run my therapy practice. On top of my tiredness, it's been a hard day, with one of my clients in suicidal despair, and I'm really looking forward to a cuddle from my daughter.

Just round the corner from our flat in Stamford Hill, I notice some signs plastered all over the bus stop and on the wall behind it. The signs are in beautiful pastel colours but depict skulls and crossbones. They shout: EXTINCTION REBELLION. Curious, I look online. I find out they're a newly formed organisation talking more radically and creatively about the state of the planet than anyone I've come across before. I then stumble across an article written by a dad questioning the morality of bringing children into a world where humans are facing extinction. A feeling of terror grips me.

That evening as I bathe Rose, her big, brown, innocent eyes seem to confront me with questions about her possible future. When she arrived in this world, I promised her that she was safe, safe, safe. Now this promise appears naive and empty. What kind of safety can I provide my daughter in a world on the brink of collapse? I feel guilty and hopeless.

But, as we often do when we've got deep feelings too painful to address, I put on a smile and continue with the stuff of life – brushing her teeth, reading her a bedtime story with a happy ending, tucking her in and wishing her sweet dreams.

INTRODUCTION

The outside, it bashes us in, bashes us about a bit

– This Is the Kit

This is a book about our children's minds.

And it's a book about the world.

Because our children's minds are affected by this world, and we don't talk about this anywhere near enough.

There are some features of our world that are making our children mad. When I use the word 'mad', I'm not just talking about the epidemic rates of depression, anxiety, self-harm and suicide. I'm also talking about how millions of children are taking their anger to the streets to fight for a viable future.

If you've picked up this book, I know you care about children. Whether you've got your own kids or you look after other people's, you have a deep love for these little humans. You know that their minds are so precious, and that the state of their minds determines the state of their lives. And you want them to feel safe. You want them to grow up in a world without conflict, where people are basically kind to each other. You want them to feel confident in themselves and confident in the world around them. You know that life isn't perfect, that some amount of suffering is inevitable. But, at the very least, you want your children to grow up feeling like there is something beautiful about this world, that this life is worth living. But when you look at what's happening now, when you look to the future, even the near future, you feel a widening gap between what your heart desires for your children and the actual world into which they are growing.

Take a moment now to think about the things in this world that break your heart open.

Perhaps your heart broke open when you saw that picture of the three-year-old Syrian refugee lying with his face in the sand, arms lifeless by his side, his sodden t-shirt and shorts so familiar.* Or perhaps it was the footage of George Floyd gasping for air, a knee on his neck. Or maybe it's the dawning reality of the climate crisis, with wildfires spreading and species dying, when even the sunny David Attenborough warns us that large parts of the earth may soon become uninhabitable. Even if you aren't so alarmed by predictions of apocalyptic futures, perhaps your heart breaks when you see your child trying to engage in a world full of blank faces staring at screens, one in which, even before a virus spread from Wuhan, we were spending more time indoors, more time online, more time alone. You might, like me, feel that human beings are capable of so much love and beauty and joy and togetherness that it breaks your heart when you see families being torn apart by opinions so entrenched and so polarised – like who is vaccinated and who isn't, who has the correct approach to race, gender or sexuality issues – that it can feel ever more impossible just to get along with one another.

Or, you might have picked up this book right now because of more immediate worries. Perhaps your child has what feels like an insurmountable problem, possibly a few. You're at the end of your tether, feel as if you've tried everything and you simply don't know what to do next.

---

* The boy's name was Alan Kurdi.

In my family practice, parents come to me and say things like this:

'We're really struggling with our son's behaviour at home. He's constantly fighting with his sister and refuses to co-operate with us. It feels like our relationship is a constant battleground.'

'My daughter's been having panic attacks and we're worried she is going to fail her exams.'

'I'm worried my son isn't coping well with our divorce. He won't speak to me and he's spending a lot of time in his room playing video games.'

'I've just seen a series of cuts on my daughter's arm as she was getting changed. I don't know how to help her.'

'I've been diagnosed with a stage 4 cancer. I'm terrified and I don't know how to talk to my children about it.'

'I'm worried that my son is going to struggle in life because of the colour of his skin.'

'My daughter is experiencing acute anxiety about all this climate change stuff. Now she can't even leave the house.'

Whatever your own worries, I've created this space for us to explore these worries together. If there is one lesson we really need to learn in the twenty-first century, a lesson that Covid-19 hit us over the head with, it is this: **we are all in this together.** We are not supposed to suffer alone. We need to be confused, together. We need to feel hopeless, together. We need to share our deepest fears about ourselves, about our children and about the things in this world that break our hearts open, together. Because, in my experience, the way we can feel most safe, the way we can find authentic hope for our children and for their future, is by coming together and sharing from our broken open hearts.

So let me tell you a little bit about me. I've devoted my whole working life to protecting vulnerable children from harm. I've done this in my child and family psychotherapy practice, working in a psychiatric unit for teenagers, as a child protection social worker, running a therapeutic school and co-founding a charity called Apart of Me that helps children through loss and trauma. I've also spent many hours supporting adults through some of the most challenging experiences life can throw at us. So whatever worries or problems brought you to this book, please know I've been in the trenches with people just like you.

But I'm not 'the expert'. You are. You know yourself and the children in your care better than anyone else. I'm here as your guide. I believe human beings have access to incredible inner wisdom. My job is to give you a little help to access this wisdom, so you can find your own authentic answer to the question of how best to prepare your children to live in these turbulent times.

I wrote this book because I've been worried about the state of the world and the state of our children's minds, and I see a clear connection between the two. As a dad, a child psychotherapist and a concerned inhabitant of planet Earth, I really wanted to (needed to) figure out how we can support our children to grow in the context of a world that appears to have gone so wrong.

There are already countless parenting books, many of them very helpful. But few address the backdrop to our parenting – a world so full of change and uncertainty that it's getting harder to catch our breath, to find our feet on solid ground.

We don't raise children in a vacuum.

The causes of mental health problems are complex. But we don't focus anywhere near enough on the ways in which this world affects our children's minds.

Just to be clear: my intention in this book is not to heap more blame on social media, politicians or contemporary culture for all our children's problems (OK, maybe a little bit). We tend to hold the modern world responsible for our children's problems – video games, vapes, online porn, ketamine, trap music, woke culture, TikTok, 'the system'. We wag our angry fingers at it, then sigh, shrug our shoulders and keep scrolling.

When I'm talking about how this world affects our children's minds, I want you to remember that their world begins with you. You are the primary filter through which your children experience the world.

So this is the radical idea I invite you to explore in this book ('radical' means getting to the roots): whatever we blame for our children's problems, we can often find the roots of these problems inside our own minds. When we follow these roots, we discover hidden, unloved parts of our self. And when we bring some love to these hidden parts, we have a much better chance of helping our kids *and* having a positive impact in the world. I know this idea might be difficult to accept for some. But please bear with me.

Take social media, for example. It is only powerful because it taps into deep human needs that we struggle to take care of in our modern world – like our need for autonomy, our need to be seen, our need to feel part of a tribe.

When we focus on fixing problems 'out there', just as in the myth of Hydra, as soon as we cut off one head from the monster, two more heads emerge. Banning social media or video games isn't going to solve the root problem that has left our children starving for connection, for autonomy, for validation.

Getting rid of Donald Trump isn't going to solve the root problem that allows leaders like him to get into power.

Using less plastic isn't going to solve the root problems that have led to the climate crisis.

Similarly, a few sessions of CBT or an antidepressant aren't going to solve the root problems that cause a child to feel stressed or depressed.

These things might help for a little bit. But, in my experience, until we address the root cause, these problems just come back in another form later down the line.

To be clear, I'm not saying our problems are 'made up' and that we can solve them just by changing our minds. From my personal experience and clinical work, I have seen the many ways in which issues like trauma, abuse, sexism, racism and inequality can have a very real and painful impact on people's lives. But this is not an either/or. You can work on yourself **and** take action in the world. Gandhi said it best: 'Be the change you want to see in the world.'

One great advantage of this approach I'm offering is that it focuses on the one place we can have a direct and immediate influence – our own minds. We can, for example, take care of the part of us that yearns to be seen, to be in community. When we do that, we grab our power back from external forces like social media.

You might be thinking: 'What difference will it make? Whatever work I do on myself is just a tiny drop in the ocean compared to the big, scary problems out there.'

I will address these concerns throughout the book. But for now, I'll share some words from Indian philosopher Krishnamurti: 'Our relationship to ourselves and one another multiplied by six billion creates the world . . . We are the world.'

Loving relationships with ourselves and then with our children add up to make a loving world. What follows is the best way I know to protect our children from the 'madness' in the world out there.

1

DISCOVERING THE ROOTS

How it all begins with you

NINA: AN ACHE IN THE CHEST

Nina came to see me because her nine-year-old son, Billy, was getting into trouble for starting fights at school. After one fight he got so angry that he punched through some glass in a door. At home, he was increasingly withdrawn and sullen. When Nina tried to talk to Billy about school or homework, or anything that involved her setting a boundary, they'd end up in a fiery argument.

Nina told me, 'I get so furious, I don't know who I am any more. It's like something takes over me.'

Nina's trigger for coming to see me was that, after one particularly intense argument, Billy had taken a bottle of bleach from the kitchen and threatened to drink it because, he said, 'I just wanna die.'

There were some obvious, surface-level explanations for Billy's despair. His parents had been through an acrimonious divorce. And Billy was spending hours playing Fortnite every night and not getting enough sleep. But Nina told me that the divorce had been finalised four years before and, at the time,

Billy had seemed to deal with it pretty well. And anyway, lots of other children were playing Fortnite without falling into such a dark place.

When we dug a little deeper, I discovered that when Nina was nine years old her father had taken his own life. At the time, no one had told Nina how her dad died. Nina's mum and her wider family had dismissed her questions and her feelings, telling her things like, 'He's happy in heaven now.' Nina remembered feeling rage and total despair at the time but she buried these feelings somewhere deep inside because she didn't feel safe to express them.

Can you imagine how confusing that might be for a child? Children are very sensitive to the world around them. They can sense when the stories they are told don't match with the feelings they carry in their body. Nina's body sensed that something wasn't right. But she learned not to trust that sense.

In one session, I helped Nina to access these feelings that had been so deeply hidden in her body. I asked her, 'What's difficult for you to accept right now?' And I suggested she listen to her body, not her mind, for the answer.

Nina noticed an aching in her chest, a feeling – she realised – she'd been aware of for a long time. I suggested she just let that ache be there and that she bring as much tenderness and love to this part of herself as she could. Suddenly, Nina burst into tears. Now, a memory rose up from this ache in her chest – of a time just after her dad had died when she went back to school and felt so deeply alone and terrified. In that moment in the therapy room it was as if a portal had opened to a whole series of hidden feelings and memories. Over the course of several sessions, we kept going back to tend to these feelings in her body and any images or memories associated with them, and each time Nina would bring compassion to these hidden parts of herself.

We didn't run through any specific parenting 'techniques'

to use with Billy. But I did encourage her to see any challenging interactions with him as an invitation for her to heal the parts of her own self that needed healing. After a few weeks, Billy's intense anger began to settle. He started to do better at school. He was getting into fewer fights. And at home, Nina and Billy's relationship had lost its angry edge and was starting to bloom again.

You might find it hard to believe that a child's problems can improve just by the parent working on themselves. But I have seen this happen time and again. And I do not want you to feel like it is all your fault. It is not your fault. But it is your responsibility.

I don't fully understand how this works. But there are some important clues I've discovered on the way. One of those clues lies in the (almost) infinite potential of human beings.

The (almost) infinite potential of children

We have decommissioned natural selection and must now look deep within ourselves and decide what we wish to become – E O Wilson

The human infant is born a paradox: it is both the most vulnerable creature on planet Earth and the creature with the greatest potential. A horse can walk within 20 minutes of birth. But it can't learn Mandarin, coding or how to build an igloo.

Your child is like a little sponge with a very plastic, social-relational brain – which means their brain and nervous system is sculpted by their interactions with you, with other people and with the world around them. This is how a baby – that vulnerable, squidgy little thing that can't feed itself, can't walk, can't even hold its body up for a second – can grow into the most powerful creature on earth, capable of nuking the whole planet or radiating pure love like a saint.

But although human beings are influenced by our environment, we can also transcend it. We can choose what we wish to become. You could say that we have (almost) infinite potential. That's why we love Oprah Winfrey (well, some of us do) because she is living proof of this ability. Born into poverty in rural Mississippi to a single, teenage mum, Oprah was sexually abused by family members from the age of nine and was made pregnant at 14. Her son was born prematurely and died in early infancy. A brutal start to life. And yet she rose to become one of the most beloved people on the planet today.

But is it really that easy to choose what we wish to become?

It seems not. If it was, the world would surely be populated by eight billion Oprahs, or Jesus Christs, or Buddhas or <insert your superhero here>. Instead, about 7 per cent of children in the UK have attempted suicide by the age of 17 and almost one in four say they have self-harmed in the past year. So how does our (almost) infinite potential get so misdirected that we're seeing more and more children like Billy wanting to hurt themselves or even end their lives? How did humans become the most self-destructive species on the planet, even destroying our own ecosystem, our own home?

The forest and the clearing

Adventures don't begin until you get into the forest. That first step is an act of faith – Mickey Hart (Drummer, Grateful Dead)

Without realising it, through thousands of interactions every day we coach, bribe, cajole, threaten and mould our children into behaviours that are the 'norm' for our society. In the Western world, for example, we might want our children to be polite, to sit still and definitely not to burp or fart at the dinner table. We want them to stop being so sad, to sleep independently, to show off less, to stop playing with their private parts, to share more, to work hard and get good grades at school. As these interactions build, the child learns which parts of their (almost) infinite potential it's OK to express – and which parts it's not. Like a fish in water, it's hard for us to be aware we are immersed in our culture and its rules. We rarely question them. What other unquestioned norms might you be moulding your child into?

Of course, we need rules for societies to work. But in this book we are going to investigate whether our current rules are working for our children. And, on a bigger scale, whether they are working for our world.

In *The Crack in the Cosmic Egg*, child development expert Joseph Chilton Pearce came up with a beautiful metaphor for the way we socialise our children: the forest and the clearing. The clearing is the small part of the forest where we've cut down the trees and where we allow our socially acceptable parts to be seen in the light of day. But this clearing only works because all our unacceptable parts get pushed back into the vast, dark, wild forest. What happens to the rejected parts that are pushed out into the forest? Do they go quietly into the night? Nope. They continue to affect our lives but in more mysterious, unconscious ways. As a child psychotherapist, I regularly see how this influence from the 'forest' directly impacts children's lives.

This is how I understand Nina's story. Her rage, her despair, her intuitive sense that something wasn't right about her father's death – all these energies got pushed out into the dark forest. But they insisted on finding a way to come back, through her son Billy. I often find that parents bring their children to see me at the exact same age that the parent had some difficult or traumatic event in their own life.

The dark forest is what the great Swiss psychiatrist Carl Jung called the 'shadow', the region of our psyche where all the rejected, unloved aspects of our selves end up. It's what you might consider your 'blind spot'. What's in there isn't necessarily 'bad'. It's just the bits that aren't acceptable for the family or society we grew up in. Let's say that you grew up being told 'big boys don't cry'. Then the tender, emotional, sensitive part of you would end up in the forest.

One way we keep the uncomfortable, unacceptable parts of our self at arm's length is to project them onto other people, groups or institutions. Imagine your mind as a movie projector projecting images onto the screen. The screen isn't blank; there are already some silhouettes on there. But your mind fills in the blanks with footage it has stored in a special hard drive. This might seem woo-woo to you. But neuroscience experiments have confirmed this to be true. When you 'see' something out there in the world, the image that your brain creates is composed mostly of memories and expectations stored in your visual cortex. As neuroscientist David Eagleman explains: 'You don't perceive objects as they are, you perceive them as you are.'

In the families I work with, I have often seen how difficult-to-accept feelings in a family get projected onto one member, often a child, who becomes the 'black sheep'. The child gets labelled as 'bad' or 'mad'. It's not that anyone is doing this consciously or maliciously. It's just a way that our human minds deal with uncomfortable truths. We split ourselves off from these uncomfortable truths and project them onto another.

So are you willing to try a little experiment now? One of

the best ways to explore your own forest is to think about what it is that really winds you up in other people. Ask yourself now: what bothers me the most about other people? It helps to get specific. If, for example, it's when someone close to you is being 'excessively' emotional, this may point back to a part of yourself – the emotional part – you have cut yourself off from. If it's that you get wound up by people who show off, notice what exactly it is about their showing off that gets you. The loudness? The attention-seeking? The high opinion of themselves? Again, this will point you back to a part of yourself you have sent into the forest. Or, for a very direct path into the heart of the forest, ask yourself: what would I most hate for someone else to think about me?

Doing this work is not easy or comfortable. But we do it for the sake of our children. We don't want our kids to suffer because of psychological wounds we have neglected to take care of ourselves. We don't want them to grow up feeling like they are bad, mad or broken.

Imagine a different scenario where Nina sends Billy for treatment, he is diagnosed with depression and given anti-depressant medication. This may have helped for a while. But it wouldn't have addressed the root cause. And Billy would have grown up thinking there was something deeply wrong with him.

To understand this in more depth, let me introduce you now to Sam.

SAM: TODDLER ON THE ROOF

When I ran a therapeutic school for kids with complex trauma, Sam was one of our most brilliant and most challenging students. Bright-eyed and freckle-faced, when he first arrived at the school aged 13 he bounded straight up to me and gave me a high-five before running past me up the stairs drumming his hands against the walls and singing out loud. He was funny, loving, cheeky as hell and full of energy. Sam had been diagnosed with ADHD when he was younger and had been heavily medicated for many years. Because of his wild energy, he had been kicked out of every other school. We were the last chance saloon.

One day, I was reading through his case notes and discovered something that shocked me. Sam had been given his diagnosis of ADHD after neighbours found him crawling on the roof of his house. He was just three years old.

Unfortunately, nobody picked up at that time that Sam's dad was a violent drug dealer and his mum was a chronic alcoholic. In truth, Sam's wild energy was a deeply intelligent, resilient response to a horrible situation. If you grew up in that environment, you too would find it hard to sit still and concentrate. You too would want to crawl onto the roof. But the ADHD diagnosis and the medication covered up the intelligence of his symptoms.

Sam grew up thinking there was something deeply wrong with him.

Gaslighting children

Imagine going to the dentist with toothache from an infected root and, instead of doing a root canal surgery, the dentist gives you some painkillers and sends you on your not-so-merry way. This is how most child mental health problems are treated today. We focus almost exclusively on surface-level, quick fixes for children's minds instead of getting to the root of the problem.

Child psychiatrist Sami Timimi has dubbed the rapid

growth in child psychiatric diagnoses and the use of drugs to deal with unwanted behaviour or emotions the 'McDonaldization' of children's mental health. In the past five years, there has been a 40 per cent rise in antidepressants prescribed for children in the UK, while in the US, one in ten children are now diagnosed with ADHD and the number of children taking Ritalin (a powerful amphetamine-like drug) is growing all over the world.

This does not mean that all diagnoses are bad. Nor does it mean that taking medication for mental health problems is bad. A diagnosis can help a parent or child feel less shame and open the door for extra support and funding. And psychiatric medication can help someone to get through a difficult time. But the story behind this approach says that mental health problems are primarily a function of faulty brain chemistry. This is what Sam grew up to believe. This story says the 'madness' is to be found within the individual child, excluding the possibility that the 'madness' may be better diagnosed in the world the child is born into. With this story, could we be gaslighting a whole generation of kids?

Questioning 'resilience'

Krishnamurti said, 'It is no measure of health to be well adjusted to a profoundly sick society.' What does it mean for a child to be 'well adjusted' in a society that appears terminally ill?

You may not believe that our society is 'sick'. But I invite you now to question some of the ideas you might carry about being 'well adjusted' or 'resilient'. You might have heard the term 'resilience' used to describe a certain approach to child mental health. There is currently a whole industry built around 'resilience' and other similar factors like 'grit', which psychologist Angela Duckworth describes as the ability 'to fall down seven times and rise eight'. But the problem with these approaches is that they tend to frame the 'resilient' child (or grown-up) as an individual who is barely affected by the world around them, someone who just grits their teeth and keeps going. 'Resilience' tends to include all the behaviours that exist comfortably in the clearing in the forest – happy, obedient, productive, sits still in class. But what if those 'resilient' behaviours are actually part of the problem, not the solution?

Think about Billy's anger, an expression of family trauma. Think about toddler Sam crawling on the roof, all that fiery violence in the house below. To me these responses seem more resilient than grittily clenching teeth as the house burns down.

Perhaps you can think of some behaviours you developed as a child to adapt to your family and the world around you. Maybe you became a people pleaser, sacrificing your own needs because this was the only way you knew to stop your mum and dad fighting. Or maybe you coped with the chaos of your earlier life through behaviours someone else described as 'bad' or 'mad' – getting really angry, developing an eating disorder or a drug problem. However you adapted to your own unique childhood, I'm here to tell you that you are not bad or mad. Those behaviours were an intelligent response to your world.

I used to teach mindfulness in schools at a time when it was just coming into vogue and schools, businesses and even governments were lapping up its promises of increased focus, productivity and resilience. Schools in particular thought this panacea would lead to good behaviour and better academic results. There is a huge pressure on schools to appear 'well adjusted'; a well-adjusted school is one that performs strongly in the academic league tables.

Students who were deemed 'bad' or 'mad' were sent to see

me, so I could fix them. But I knew that fitting into a system that is broken did not help anyone, so I used my mindfulness lessons like a Trojan horse. I taught children the basic skills of mindfulness but I also empowered them to think critically about the world around them and how it was affecting their minds. I helped them to see how their emotions and their behaviours were adaptive, that they made sense.

Canaries in the coalmine

If our dominant way of thinking about our children's minds is limiting, and potentially even gaslighting, how can we change it? Well, first we need to shift our perspective. We need to see that our child's symptoms may be intelligent. They may be trying to communicate something vital to us. They may be unconscious attempts to heal conflicts in the world around them. In this sense, the 'world' means both you, the family, and the wider society.

I'm sure you know the phrase 'canary in the coalmine'? The term came from some high-risk experiments by Professor John Scott Haldane, a Scottish physiologist with a huge, bushy moustache and an interesting approach to parenting. While working at Oxford University, he wanted to find a way to stop miners dying from toxic gases. So he'd lock himself in sealed chambers full of potentially lethal gas cocktails to discover their effects. On one occasion, deep underground in a mine filled with toxic gas, he had his young son Jack recite a speech from Shakespeare's *Julius Caesar* until Jack's legs buckled and he fell unconscious. Fortunately for Jack, his dad soon discovered that canaries made much better gas detectors than children.

This is how canaries became what's known as a 'sentinel species', warning us of danger. I believe our children are a sentinel species. Because they haven't yet built up strong psychological defences (more on this later), they are more sensitive than grown-ups to the social pressures and toxic values of the world around them. Just as the canaries would be sent into the dark realms of the mines, our children are more connected to the darker realms of the forest beyond the clearing. They are canaries in the coalmine. From this perspective, the rise in psychological distress among our children warns us of impending danger and beckons us to a more beautiful world.

You see, the turning point we humans find ourselves in at this time is similar to the twilight zone I experienced when my daughter was born. We are in a space between worlds. We can no longer hold on to the old comforting truths about ourselves and the world. Infinite growth is not possible on a finite planet. While some will surely continue business-as-usual, there is a growing realisation that our way of living is not sustainable and that something new will have to emerge. We are in the birthing suite for humankind's next stage of evolution. Are we about to give birth to a more beautiful world for our children? The truth is: it's up to you.

The place to begin is with YOU.

Like the red-faced, stressed-out teacher who shouts at the children in his class to 'calm down!', it doesn't work when we try to impose on our children something we haven't already accessed within ourselves. It's like Alexander den Heijer says: 'When a flower doesn't bloom, you fix the environment in which it grows, not the flower.' When we realise that we are the environment in which our children grow, we stop pathologising them. Instead, like Nina, we start the deeper work of healing ourselves.

As Nina began to see her son's suffering as reflecting something back to her about the environment he was growing up in, she could begin the work of healing this hidden part of her own psyche. And as she cultivated compassion for these difficult-to-accept parts, her son Billy stopped wanting to hurt himself and started to love himself.

Deep patterns

Maybe you are searching among branches for
what only appears in the roots – Rumi

Over the 20 years I've spent helping people, I've noticed that the things people find difficult to accept about themselves or their children have common, underlying features. There are certain psychological patterns that keep recurring, no matter what the background of the person I'm helping. These patterns form part of the glorious mosaic of being human. And when I help people to see these patterns, it gives them a framework that reduces shame and blame and supports the healing process.

In this book, I'm going to describe the seven patterns that I believe cause the most difficulties for us, for our children and for the world at large. These patterns have both a shadow side, which means we don't like to see them in ourselves, and they have a light side too. I call the shadow side of these patterns 'roots' because they grow beneath the earth, in our blind spots, in the darker places that we struggle to see. And I call the lighter side of these patterns 'fruits' because while roots grow underground and get nourishment from the earth, fruits grow above ground, offering their beauty into the world. These deep and recurring patterns aren't unique to the twenty-first century; it's just that they seem to be reaching a tipping point now.

I'd love to take the credit – and ideally a Nobel prize – for this groundbreaking insight but I'm not the first to notice deep and recurring patterns in human behaviour. The idea of 'patterns' is loosely based on Carl Jung's concept of 'archetypes'. From his interviews with patients and a lifetime studying myths from around the world and across time, Jung discovered these universal patterns that seemed to recur in all human cultures (his archetypes included the Wise Old Man or Woman, the Trickster, the Hero). Our minds, Jung concluded, are not just the sum of our individual experience, we also share in common a psychic inheritance which expresses itself differently depending on the person or the culture. Jung called this the 'collective unconscious'.

Like a psychological DNA, the patterns stored in our collective unconscious are formed over long periods of time and contain concentrated versions of all our ancestors' experiences. Think of it like humanity's black box – a device containing the most important recordings of what can go really badly for us, and what can go really well, too. In a similar way, whether you are watching the latest hit on Netflix or reading Greek tragedy or Shakespeare, you will tend to find the same types of drama, the same types of character recurring.

Have you ever had that feeling that the same dramas keep playing out in your life and in your relationships over and over again? Or maybe you have a recurring dream with symbols and characters that seem somehow personal and also from another time or place? Until we become aware of these recurring patterns, they tend to shape our lives in unconscious ways. And this is why we find the same dramas recurring in our own lives, in our dreams and in the world at large. Jung called the archetypes 'inherited potentials' that silently shape not only our lives but also our world: 'the archetypes are . . . the roots which the psyche has sunk not only in the earth in the narrower sense but in the world in general'.

It might feel strange for you to think of your unique life problems or our chaotic world as being underpinned by universal patterns. But consider fractals – a discovery of modern science. Fractals are patterns that recur at both a micro and macro scale, in fields as diverse as economic markets, the behaviour of earthquakes and broccoli florets. If you zoom in or out on fractals you find exactly the same patterns. Fractals demonstrate that a hidden order can be found within the seeming chaos of complex systems, like our 'minds' or 'the world'.

Seven roots and seven fruits

In this book, the seven roots we will be exploring together are:

1. Victimhood: we feel helpless.
2. Virtual reality: we want to escape our bodies and live in our heads.
3. Narcissism: we crave to be seen and loved.
4. Scarcity: we fear not having or being enough.
5. Anaesthesia: we push down our 'negative' emotions.
6. Chaos: we are addicted to stress.
7. Hopelessness: we sometimes want to give up.

And their corresponding fruits are:

1. Victimhood – Empowerment. We are stronger than we realise.
2. Virtual reality – Bodies in nature. We can find a home in our bodies and in nature.
3. Narcissism – Compassion and co-operation. We are born to help each other.
4. Scarcity – Abundance. We are enough.

5. Anaesthesia – Feeling. We can learn to tune in to and learn from all of our emotions.

6. Chaos – Peace. We can find acceptance and stillness in the madness of this world.

7. Hopelessness – Hope. We can imagine and co-create a more beautiful tomorrow.

In the modern Western world, we tend to want to focus only on the fruits. Some call ours a culture of 'toxic positivity'. But if we ignore the health of a tree's roots, it won't produce healthy fruits above ground. For example, it is only once we have tended to the root of narcissism that the fruit of compassion can grow in a sustainable way. Untended, these seven roots are destroying our children's mental health. And they are the defining themes behind the climate crisis and most problems of the modern world, too. Think about the feeling of scarcity, of never having enough, and how it drives consumerism.

It's really important to say that there is no blame here. None of this is your fault. But once you begin to see these patterns and how they play out in your own life, it is your responsibility to do something about it.

For example, perhaps you recognise that you tend to avoid painful emotions, to ignore them or push them underground, the pattern I've called 'Anaesthesia'. In the twenty-first century, this manifests as a world that prioritises happiness above all other emotions. And so we ignore other emotions, or pathologise them. When we do this, it makes us feel 'mad' – and our children, too. But, like Nina, we can tend to these roots, we can see how their patterns get revealed in our own lives and in our world at large. All that is required is a willingness to look with loving eyes at the parts of ourselves that are difficult to accept. When we do this, we are less likely to project these difficult-to-accept bits of ourselves onto our children or the world. And our children will grow up more grounded, more courageous and more confident.

I also believe these roots contain huge amounts of creative energy, waiting to be channelled in the right direction. We forget how much energy it takes to twist ourselves into the socially acceptable shape that gets us access to the clearing.

You may not see how working on yourself could possibly have such a big effect, or you may feel you don't have the time or resources and you just want some quick solutions for your child's problems. I totally get it. Sometimes, I too wish I had a quick and easy fix for the suffering I experience in my own life. But I have seen time and time again that when parents work on this stuff, face and heal their shadows, whatever problems their children are having dissolve. And parents and their children become less vulnerable to some of these shadowy patterns in the world, too.

All it takes, at this point, is to be open to this possibility. Even by picking up this book, by reading these words, you've begun your journey.

How to use this book

I know, I know. I too normally skip over this section. I skim through most non-fiction books looking for the single treasure, the one golden nugget that is The Answer. It's a sign of the times; we are all attention and time poor, overwhelmed with content, anxious to get parenting right. But I would love you to have a different, slower experience of reading this book. To notice the space between the words. After all, speed-reading is a symptom of the world that's making our children mad. That said, this book also welcomes a casual dipping in and out if there's a chapter that speaks to you first.

Throughout this book, you will find a simple practice woven

throughout the stories and exercises. This practice is the best way I know of helping us face uncomfortable truths. Because, let's face it, if we want a better world for our children and their children, we need to get better at facing uncomfortable truths. As a child psychotherapist, my most important job is to create a space where a child and those who care for them can be with uncomfortable truths. I'd love you to feel like this book is a safe space where we can explore these uncomfortable truths together.

What makes a truth 'uncomfortable'? It's the feeling behind the truth that no one taught us how to bear – the grief, the shame, the loneliness, the terror. For example, I have worked with a child who wished their dad was dead after he left their mother for another woman. His anger was difficult for him to bear. I've worked with a teenager who couldn't get out of bed when he realised the world was heating up because of human greed. His grief was difficult for him to bear.

Below is a short version of this core practice just to give you a taster of how simple it really is. I have learned so many different healing techniques over the years and I have tried them all on myself, and later with my clients. But of all these techniques, this practice below is the simplest and the most effective healing tool I know.

A SIMPLE PRACTICE FOR FACING UNCOMFORTABLE TRUTHS

Facing reality is an empowering act – it can liberate our mind and heart to discern how best to use our power and influence in service for this time – Margaret Wheatley

1. **Find the feeling in your body:** Bring to mind just for a moment an uncomfortable truth (it might be about yourself, your family, about death, or the climate crisis).

Gently bring your attention into your body and find the place in the body where the uncomfortable feeling beneath this truth is most alive. If this doesn't appear easily, notice if there is any tension in your body. Often tension is a sign there is something we are struggling to accept. Don't overthink this. This is your body's wisdom, not your thinking mind. If you notice the mind coming in with judgements, just notice these thoughts and let them float away like golden leaves on an autumnal breeze.

2. **Let the feeling be there:** when you have settled on a place in your body, give the sensation or feeling a space to be there just as it is. Let go of any wish to fix or change anything about this experience. Put a nurturing hand on this part of your body and let the feeling know it's OK for it to be there, as though you were comforting a scared child.

Most people when they use this simple practice feel a sense of relief, a lightness, and often the feeling in the body will transform into something else. Please don't worry if it doesn't quite make sense to you now. It's a practice that we need to . . . well, practise. And we will keep revisiting variations on this throughout the book.

If you are guiding your children through uncomfortable truths, you can use the same practice. But, in my experience, as long as you are able to be with these uncomfortable truths yourself, you will naturally be able to guide your children. In fact, children are much better at handling uncomfortable truths than we give them credit for. What can cause problems is when they notice that adults aren't being honest with them. So trust your child's capacity a little bit more. If a discussion arises about an uncomfortable truth, help them to follow the steps of this exercise. Let them ask as many questions as they need to. Don't sugar-coat the answers.

I recommend treating yourself to a lovely notebook (or use that one collecting dust, the one you've been saving for a special occasion) so that you can take notes as you read, do some of the exercises and generally give yourself a space to reflect.

At the back of the book I have suggested ways for you to work through this book with other people. We are not meant to do this stuff alone.

Of course, there will be some of you reading this book who may need professional help. If you want or need to explore any issues that come up for you as you read this book, there are so many amazing therapists, coaches, healers, support groups and communities out there.

Please, please don't feel guilty if you don't have time to do all of the exercises. We parents – we humans – already have enough guilt. There is no right or wrong way to use this book. Do the exercises if you want. Underline words that mean something if that works for you. Meditate on it. Stick it under your pillow. Light a candle on it.

I am sure you will still have reservations and doubts. All of this is welcome here. I am bringing my doubt and my faith in equal measure to the questions in this book. I don't have an absolute answer. Poet David Whyte says, 'Wanting soul life without the dark, warming intelligence of personal doubt is like expecting an egg without the brooding heat of the mother hen.'

Lastly, I want to say, as a human being and a parent, you are enough. May this book serve as a reminder of your enoughness, for you and for the children in your care. May each word, each space between the words, remind you that you are loved.

2

ROOT ONE: VICTIMHOOD

How we learn to be helpless

*You are in prison. If you wish to get out of prison, the
first thing you must do is realize that you are in prison.
If you think you are free, you can't escape*

– George Gurdjieff

A mature elephant can grow up to 13 feet tall and weigh up to seven tonnes. The strongest animal on land, they have been known to crush humans and even rhinos with their feet. They can topple buses and uproot trees with their trunks. How could such a powerful creature ever be tamed?

The tradition of training elephants goes back around 4,000 years, as depicted by some of the oldest paintings and statues found in the Indus Valley (modern-day South Asia). The traditional practice begins with the trainer tying the baby elephant to a tree by its leg with a rope. At first, the baby elephant will fight and fight to break free. But eventually, it gives up fighting and accepts it cannot escape. The trainer then replaces the rope with a heavy cord. Again, the elephant fights against the rope but, by now, the elephant's attempts to break free have grown half-hearted. It still can't break free, so it gives up.

Finally, the cord is replaced by a silk ribbon. At this point, the elephant doesn't move anywhere until the trainer unties the ribbon. The elephant has learned to be helpless.

Why do we so easily give up?

In psychology, the term 'learned helplessness' describes the process where humans and other animals give up trying to improve their situation. It was coined by psychologist Martin Seligman in 1967, after he led a series of experiments – which from a modern viewpoint seem extremely cruel – that involved giving electric shocks to dogs.

In part one of the experiment, dogs were put into boxes and given electric shocks. Half of the dogs were given a lever that allowed them to stop the electric shocks. The other half had no lever. In part two, the dogs were put in a bigger box divided by a small fence over which they could easily jump to escape. Again, they were given electric shocks. But this time, the dogs that had been given a lever to stop the shocks in part one of the experiment simply jumped over the fence and escaped the pain. The other dogs passively lay down and whined, letting the electric shocks continue. They experienced the shocks and the stopping of the shocks as random events over which they had no control. These dogs had been conditioned to feel there was nothing they could do to avoid their pain, so they gave up trying to improve their situation.

Reviewing a whole series of similar experiments on learned helplessness in humans (thankfully not using electric shocks) biologist Robert Sapolsky concludes: 'it takes surprisingly little in terms of uncontrollable unpleasantness to make humans give up and become helpless in a generalized way.' Like the dogs, all it takes for our helpless button to be switched on are a series of unpredictable, negative experiences over which we are made to believe we have no control.

Why am I sharing this? Because I believe that this mad world is conditioning us and our children to feel helpless. I see people giving away their power every day without even realising it. And it breaks my heart. You have forgotten how magnificent and powerful you are. And I don't mean crushing rhinos with your feet. I mean that no matter what is going on for you, no matter what is going on in the world around you, you have an innate ability to find creative solutions to your problems. You always have a choice. You can be free. And when you claim back your power, you can make the world a better place for your children. But first, you need to get to know what is pushing your helpless buttons.

How our culture pushes our helpless buttons

As you probably know, depression is on the rise globally. Figures reveal that people born after 1945 are ten times more likely to have depression and that there was an almost 50 per cent increase in clinical depression from 1990 to 2017, while a recent study from the UK showed that now a quarter of girls and one in ten boys are depressed by age 14. If you know anyone who suffers with depression, you will probably (like me) feel heartbroken that so many of our beautiful children are getting lost in this darkness.

So how can we explain this epidemic? The rise in depression is a paradox, according to Martin Seligman, because 'every objective indicator of well-being – purchasing power, amount of education, availability of music, and nutrition – has been going north, while every indicator of subjective well-being has been going south.'

One factor we must seriously consider is learned helplessness. There's a strong correlation between learned helplessness and depression. Rats in electric shock experiments (similar to those described above) spend long periods of time lying immobile. They stop grooming themselves and lose interest in sex and food: i.e. they display typical signs of depression. Even when they're put in a totally new situation, with no electric shocks and more fun or tastier options on offer, such as sugar-water or play, the rats don't attempt to improve their situation. Their learned helplessness button has been switched on.

In the twenty-first century, we have our own version of electric shocks: the 24/7 bad news cycle. We are bombarded with fear-based content, scary headlines such as *The Robots Are Coming for Your Jobs* and *Human Civilisation Coming to an End by 2050*. As Tristan Harris, one of the biggest whistleblowers on the workings of the tech industry, says: 'Our Palaeolithic brains aren't built for omniscient awareness of the world's suffering. Our online news feeds aggregate all of the world's pain and cruelty, dragging our brains into a kind of learned helplessness.'

We also fall into a kind of learned helplessness when we rely too much on experts or devices to tell us things we may already know. We check the weather on an app instead of looking at the sky. As parents, we might lean heavily on expert advice and we might try to stick to that advice even when somewhere inside we know it's not working for our kids. It's not that experts are bad but that we are losing touch with our own instincts, our own wisdom, our own power.

And we may be unwittingly teaching our children to be helpless. Think about how our culture's attitude to children has changed in just 60 years, as family sizes have shrunk radically since we started using contraception. With fewer children, we tend to become more protective, sometimes overprotective, treating our children as though they need insulating from all suffering, whether at home, at school, in playgrounds or in the wider world. In the words of David Lancy, an anthropologist who studies childhood, 'Our few, irreplaceable offspring are now treated as precious treasures rather than future helpers.'

Young people are now being called 'snowflakes', too easily triggered or offended, too delicate, too precious. I don't like this name; it's judgemental and I see so many young people with levels of courage I never had at their age. But I can also see how, more broadly, our efforts to protect our children are disempowering them, teaching them to be helpless, lowering their capacity to handle the inevitable suffering that's guaranteed to every human being.

LISA: LOOKING FOR ANSWERS

Lisa was a single mother who had been struggling with depression, and her two children (aged six and eight) were really playing up, especially at bedtimes when, instead of listening to Lisa, they would run around the house, eating sweets, fighting each other, refusing to sleep. Lisa tried so hard to find solutions to her children's behaviour. In the evenings, when the kids were finally asleep, she would google things like 'how can I get my children to behave?' and 'does my child have ADHD?' and 'tips to get your children to sleep'. She listened to hours of parenting podcasts. And she paid for some consultations with a 'supernanny' behavioural consultant. But despite her best efforts, the kids' behaviour didn't change. Understandably, Lisa reached a really low point. She felt like giving up.

A few months before I met Lisa, her psychiatrist had doubled her dose of fluoxetine (antidepressant medication). But she still felt incredibly low. And this made her feel even more broken – because, if even a strong dose of antidepressants wasn't working, there must be something deeply damaged about her brain, she thought.

In our first sessions, as we explored Lisa's childhood, I shared some of the research on learned helplessness with her. It was a lightbulb moment. She recognised how as a child she'd become conditioned to feel helpless, particularly by a very critical father who was never happy with her. He was especially disparaging of her schoolwork, which she struggled to keep up with – it was only later in life that Lisa realised she had dyslexia. There were also lots of big changes in Lisa's family, changes that she found difficult and had no control over, such as moving to Italy aged nine to a new school where she was bullied. And then, when she was 14 and feeling particularly low, her parents took her to a psychiatrist where she was diagnosed with depression and prescribed Seroxat, an antidepressant medication. I helped Lisa to see that the story she had been told about her low moods – that they were due to having faulty chemistry in her brain, as opposed to being a natural reaction to the world around her – was another element that probably made her feel helpless.

To start to break this pattern, I encouraged Lisa to really notice with compassion the helpless part of her. I also used coaching-type questions to get Lisa to trust in her own strength and wisdom. And I encouraged her to start paying attention to all the good moments with her children and all the good things she was doing as a mum (more on these techniques below). Slowly but surely, Lisa rediscovered her power, and as she respected herself more, her kids began to respect her more too.

The thing is, no matter what you have been made to believe, you are way more powerful than you realise. So are your children. In the next chapter, we will look at ways to remember that power. But before you can truly access that power, you need to get to know the deep and recurring pattern beneath learned helplessness. It's time to meet your inner Victim.

The magnetic power of the Victim

A few years ago, I went to a meditation retreat in the Rhodope mountains in Bulgaria. I had never been to this place before but had heard they used some unconventional methods to help people 'wake up' from suffering, so I arrived curious. On the third night, the teacher announced it was 'drama night', which meant we'd be doing a role-play exercise. 'Role-play' – these words can cast fear into the hardiest of souls. Even the veterans of this retreat seemed anxious at this news. As for me, I put on my invisibility cloak and it worked a treat – two women and a man were chosen and set up at the front of the room with a chair, a table and a lot of space. One was told to play the Victim, one was given the role of the Rescuer, the third was to be the Persecutor. The teacher gave them no further instruction.

The idea of this kind of role play is to reveal deep psychic patterns – unconscious driving forces that govern our life. So they can be pretty confronting.

Each actor began by nervously, self-consciously acting. The Persecutor would say some bossy or mean thing to the Victim. The Victim would cry and the Rescuer would try to make the Victim feel better. But then something happened. The best way I can describe it is that the three people on stage fell into a trance, directed by a force much deeper than their conscious minds.

I found the rest of the role-play excruciating to watch. I couldn't help identifying with the Rescuer (therapists tend towards being Rescuers, often having been Victims at some point, hence the cliché of the 'wounded healer'). I could see how the Rescuer kept being pulled to rescue the Victim. Whatever the Rescuer and the Persecutor tried (and they threw everything into this drama), ultimately nothing was as powerful as the Victim. When the teacher stopped the drama, the three actors collapsed to the floor, seemingly exhausted.

What I was most struck by here was that, contrary to what you might expect, the strongest, most magnetic energy in the room had come from the Victim. By the end, she was sitting back in the chair, almost regally, as if all the power was in her.

The triangle of disempowerment

This trio – Victim–Rescuer–Persecutor – is a deep and recurring pattern in human relationships, as we will explore below. The pattern was given a specific shape when, in the 1960s, psychiatrist Stephen Karpman created 'the drama triangle'. In addiction recovery work, this pattern is now known as the Triangle of Disempowerment – because when we are in the pattern, we are operating unconsciously and no one gets what they really need. It's the triangle that's the boss.

Have you ever played or seen the improv game Sit, Stand, Lay? Each person occupies one position at a time. When one changes, everyone else has to shift position, too. The triangle operates in a similar way in real life, except we slot into our role unconsciously and certain people tend to gravitate more towards certain positions. In most families I've worked with, there is only room for one main Victim, one main Rescuer, and one main Persecutor. And these roles are co-dependent: a Rescuer needs a Victim to rescue; a Victim needs a Persecutor, etc.

Having said that, the distinction between roles is not

always so clear. For example, in the role play described above, I was surprised to see the Victim commanding so much power in the room. I also realised that the role of heroic Rescuer can often appear powerless and at the mercy of the Victim. Every Victim also has the capacity to be a Persecutor. Many bullies were once bullied and many child abusers were abused as children.

How these roles operate might be obvious to an outsider but for those on the inside of the triangle, we are usually deeply unconscious of these patterns, as we will see in Katie's story in the next chapter. These deep patterns get exiled into the forest where they continue to shape our behaviour in ways that make us suffer.

It's important to say that there are real victims and real persecutors out there. What I'm describing are the deeper, largely unconscious patterns that we can get stuck in, sometimes for our whole lives.

The deep roots of the drama triangle

Like all the deep patterns I describe in this book, the pattern of the Victim is so fundamental to being human that it's found in many of our stories, both old and new. In Charles Perrault's version of *Sleeping Beauty*, published in 1697, when the princess wakes up she says, 'Are you my prince? You've kept me waiting a long time.' The story goes on: 'The prince, charmed by her words . . . did not know how to express his joy.'

Can you see the similarity between Sleeping Beauty, a victim lying passively waiting for a hero to rescue her, and the learned helpless dogs lying passively in their box? Prince Charming is charmed by this Victim and feels an indescribable joy at having his role as Rescuer validated.

Wherever there is a damsel in distress (Victim), there is a prince (Rescuer) and a wicked stepmother (Persecutor).

Even today, the world is still hooked on stories about princes and princesses, about rescuers and victims. As I write, Oprah's interview with Prince Harry and Meghan Markle has just aired. In essence, the Oprah interview was telling the story of how Meghan and Harry were the Victims of a cold and racist Persecutor, the institution of the Royal Family. Oprah, of course, was the Rescuer. To date, the show has been watched by over 50 million people around the world. (By the way, I'm not saying here that the Royal Family aren't Persecutors and that Meghan and Harry weren't Victims. I'm just highlighting our fascination with these deep and recurring patterns.)

ALICE: SLEEPING BEAUTY

When Alice first walked into my therapy room, she shook my hand firmly in spite of her thin frame. Through her orthodontic braces, she gave me a broad, radiant smile. In this moment, it was hard for me to separate the person I saw before me from the story I'd heard about her. I wondered how this 13-year-old girl – who seemed so confident – could be having such troubles with her mental health.

About a year before she came to see me, Alice had woken up one school morning and refused to get out of bed. When Clara, her mum, spoke to her, she answered in the voice of a very young child. This wasn't an act or a joke. No matter what her mum tried, Alice couldn't snap her out of it. It was if she was in a trance.

This pattern continued for weeks. Alice would wake up, refuse to get out of bed, speak in a baby voice and even crawl around her room like a baby. Nothing could rouse her. Whenever she did eventually wake from this trance, she couldn't remember anything. It was an almost total amnesia.

Frustrated and anxious, Alice's parents took her to a clinic where she was diagnosed with a rare sleeping disorder called Kleine-Levin syndrome, also known as Sleeping Beauty syndrome. This is a rare condition that mainly affects adolescents. Symptoms can include excessive sleeping for up to 22 hours a day, lack of energy and regression to child-like voices and behaviours. The clinic treating Alice tried a number of different psychological approaches but none worked.

By the time Alice's mum, Clara, contacted me, things had got desperate. Alice had been refusing to go to school for weeks on end. The psychiatrist at the clinic had recommended Alice start taking lithium, a powerful mood stabiliser prescribed most commonly to adults for bipolar disorder and acute psychosis. Alice's mum did not want her 13-year-old daughter to take lithium. So Alice and I began our therapy sessions, with her strong handshake and radiant smile.

Clara had told me that Alice was the oldest of three children. After she was born, Clara had a series of miscarriages which left her in a state of depression. It was only when Clara gave birth again that her depression finally lifted. Clara also told me that Alice's symptoms had begun just after she had her first menstrual period and that the symptoms seemed to get worse before each cycle.

During the first few sessions with Alice, it became clear that she had developed an unconscious belief that only babies could make her mum happy, only babies could get her mum's attention. And so, just as Alice was entering her biological adulthood, something pulled her back into this child-like trance.

I see this kind of pattern often. There are key stages in our development, like puberty, and often at these critical points in life something pulls us back to earlier stages if we still have wounds we need to take care of. Psychotherapist Michael Washburn calls this 'regression in the service of transcendence'.

So I decided to take Alice on a series of hypnotherapy regressions to see if we could access the younger versions of her that had been frozen in time. She told me about a time when she was around five years old and felt sick but the baby-sitter didn't believe her. Her dad came home from work but he was busy and stressed and had to keep working. Alice remembered feeling alone and powerless.

After a few more sessions with Alice, she learned to make a more conscious connection to these frozen parts of herself. She learned to listen to their needs and she learned she could meet those needs herself as a maturing woman, without regressing. She was able to transform her helplessness into a source of empowerment. I also supported Clara to spend an hour of focused, quality time with Alice once a week. This is based on the idea that, in the same way plants need the right amount of sun and water to grow, children need the right kind of attention from us to thrive.

A few months after I stopped working with Alice, she sent me a short and lovely email in which she wrote: 'I'm doing brilliant now. No bad days at all. Enjoying school. Thank you.'

Which roles do you play?

Clients often find it really helpful to understand their family dynamics in terms of the triangle of disempowerment. We often find that the role we identify most with is shaped by our family of origin. If you lean towards being a Victim, it may be that you've been conditioned to recognise the power you have in staying small, vulnerable and persecuted. You haven't been shown a healthier form of power. Below, I'll explain how the different roles typically show up.

What can the Victim look like?

If we're in Victim mode, we might find ourselves blaming other people and things – excessively – for what's not working in our lives. The people we blame can be family members, partners, children, but we can also blame bigger 'systems' for all that is wrong with our lives – like Facebook, the government or the Illuminati. Now obviously, our lives can be made really difficult by bigger institutions or systems – I'm so grateful I don't live in Nazi Germany, for example.

But mostly, when we are in Victim mode, we get so stuck blaming others that we don't notice there is something we can do to improve our situation. We might find ourselves constantly seeking reassurance and validation, or always looking for the answers to our problems outside of ourselves. Like Sleeping Beauty, we might be waiting for a knight in shining armour to come and rescue us – a partner, a therapist, a boss, an expert, a doctor, anyone in fact who might be able to save us. And if we don't get rescued in the way we hoped, we can then spiral into rage or a sense of worthlessness and loneliness.

And in Victim mode, we want those around us to know that we are suffering. When we tell a story about our suffering, we might unconsciously amp up our pain because a part of us senses that we might gain more status or support or power by doing so. When two or more victims come together, it can become a competitive race to the bottom to prove whose pain is worse, aka the Suffering Olympics. And sometimes we want to let people know about our suffering indirectly – when we are doing something we find hard or time-consuming, we might let out a loud sigh or a huff.

Many believe we now live in a culture of victimhood where we get more likes by letting our inner Victim run the show. I once worked with a teenage girl who was in a lot of distress and would self-harm regularly. But because she could see so many of her friends posting on social media about their own mental health struggles, my client began to doubt herself. She said to me: 'Maybe I'm just making it all up because all this mental health stuff just seems so fake.' I know this example might stir up feelings and questions for you, but please know that I will guide you through this tricky terrain in more detail in later chapters.

What can the Persecutor look like?

It's not the world that was my oppressor, because what the world does to you, if the world does it to you long enough and effectively enough, you begin to do to yourself. – James Baldwin

I am yet to meet a person who self-identifies as Persecutor. The Persecutor is usually that other person or thing we blame for our problems. Or you might be the Persecutor in someone else's Victim story. And there are real Persecutors out there who we need to be aware of and protect ourselves and our children from. However, more often than not, in my experience, we tend as Victims to create Persecutors by projecting all the bad stuff into someone – a boss, an ex-partner, a current partner, our child, even. We say: 'It's all your fault!' But, if we slow down and pay enough attention, we will usually find that we have our very own Persecutor inside our heads. This inner Persecutor can be the critical inner voice that judges us so harshly for being overweight, for having a badly behaved child, for not being successful enough. Our inner Persecutor is often the mirror image of the outer Persecutor we blame for our difficulties. If you had a particularly critical parent, for example, see if you can notice their energy next time you are criticising yourself.

Often the Persecutor develops as a psychological defence against feeling helpless, perhaps because we have been bullied or victimised in the past. It can feel like the choice we have is either to be vulnerable and let ourselves be criticised or bullied, or to bully ourselves and other people. In this way, the Persecutor can become a form of internalised oppression. External oppression is the prison walls you can't escape from. Internalised oppression is the elephant's silk ribbon, the inner voice that keeps you trapped, small, helpless.

What can the Rescuer look like?

One recurring pattern I see in families is the parent as Rescuer. If you are doing this, you might hover over your child – if you see them upset or suffering in some way, you swoop in to take care of it. When parents get stuck in Rescuer mode, they sometimes think they have to sacrifice their whole life to their children. And then they can become resentful. This is when the Rescuer can turn into the Martyr, a type of Victim. The Martyr thinks things like, 'After all I've done for them, they don't care about me.'

Sometimes, we have to rescue for expedience – helping your frustrated five-year-old get his school shirt on to get to school on time, for example. But if this becomes our unconscious habit, we disable our children from being able to tolerate frustration and to figure things out for themselves.

Of course, it's our parental instinct to want to protect our children from harm. I remember watching Rose aged two trying to play with some older kids in a woodland. She ran after them, desperately trying to join their game. But she didn't know the rules and was clearly not welcome. She kept asking in her innocent voice, 'Will you play with me?' whilst chasing after these kids, but they completely blanked her. One of them then called her a 'silly little baby'. I could see this was breaking her little heart. And mine too! I felt the urge to scoop her up, call the parents of these little shits and have them severely punished. But I reminded myself that my child has an inbuilt capacity to grow through difficult experiences. She just needs someone by her side.

That doesn't mean your child should have to endure bullying. But as well as having boundaries against bullying, it is also important to empower your child to deal with hard situations without rescuing them.

Rose will get bullied again, at school, by people she knows, maybe even by her friends. And, let's face it, this incident pales in comparison to the challenges she'll face later in life. We need to empower our children if we want to help them flourish.

WHERE ARE YOU DISEMPOWERED?

We find it hard to step out of our usual patterns of behaviour because, like a prisoner who offends just to get back into the safe walls of a prison, we find some comfort in what feels familiar, in knowing our place.

Pick up your notebook and use the following questions to guide you as you write down whatever thoughts come to mind, not worrying about how it reads. Reflecting on these journaling prompts will allow you to turn your unconscious role in the drama triangle from being a toxic force to a conscious, integrated part of your psyche.

1. Do you have any areas in your life where you tend to feel helpless? Can you think of any 'electric shocks', crises or

---

difficult experiences, earlier in your life that, like Lisa or Alice, might have left you feeling helpless? It might have been a depressed or very critical parent or teacher, an undiagnosed learning difficulty or any significant moment when your life felt unpredictable and out of control. (Of course, if you have significant trauma or abuse in your past, you may need some professional support.)

2. Are there areas of your life (career, parenting, relationships, money) where you automatically look for solutions outside of yourself? It's not that it's bad to seek help, it's just good to notice with compassion the areas where we don't trust our inner wisdom.

3. What role do you typically identify with? Are you a Rescuer, a Persecutor or a Victim? Which other 'actors' are usually with you in the triangle? If you aren't sure, pay attention to the people in your life that you feel the most resentment towards.

4. How do these roles play out with the children you care for? One sign a child might be in Victim mode, for example, is when they say they can't do something – such as tying their shoelaces, brushing their teeth, solving a homework problem – that you know they can.

5. Is there anything you secretly like about your role? Does it give you any kind of comfort or feeling of safety to be in this pattern? If you are often in Victim mode, is there a Persecutor you might secretly be punishing by taking this role? (Think here about individuals and situations, like a mean boss or lack of time, but also people in power, institutions, systems.)

6. Can you give your inner role a shape, a character? What do they look like? Give them a name. You can even draw

them. The more exaggerated the better. Can you find a place in your heart to love this character and the ancient dramas they play out in our lives?

7. If you are ever in Victim mode (and who isn't?), use these sentence starters to go deeper into your helplessness:

   I know I am in Victim mode when . . .
   In the past, my Victim has helped me by . . .
   My Victim can also be a Persecutor when . . .
   I habitually look for a prince charming/Rescuer in these situations . . .
   Five ways I give away my power are . . .

Magic button

I remember pushing Rose in her buggy one day on our way to nursery. We created a game. When she pushed the magic button the buggy would go faster. She loved this.

Strangely, magic buttons can even help us grown-ups feel empowered. In studies on human learned helplessness, there was one consistent finding: the people who had a button to give them some control over the outcome were more confident and capable in the follow-up tasks, even when they never used the button. For example, in one experiment, two groups of participants were exposed to a very loud noise but one group had a button that stopped the noise and the other group had no button. After this stage, the participants were again subjected to a loud noise, and this time both groups were given an option to stop the noise. But the group that had no button in the first part of the test didn't even bother to control the loud noise in the second, even though they had an option to do that. In other words, to go from helpless to empowered we need to remember that we have a button – that we have some agency.

It's true that there are many scary things in the world right now. But how we feel about them and how we respond to them, and how we role-model our response to our children, depends on what psychologists call our 'locus of control'. When we are locked in Victim mode, when we blame other people or things outside of ourself, we have an 'external locus of control'. But when we are empowered, when we know that even when faced with the most frightening things, we always have a choice, we always have agency, this is an 'internal locus of control'.

In one study on childhood trauma, Frank Infurna and Crystal Rivers discovered that children who were supported to a) discover areas of their life they could control and b) take small, positive actions in these areas, recovered from their trauma more quickly and saw mental health gains.

We will explore the how of empowerment in more detail in the following chapter. For now, the lesson that we need to learn for the sake of ourselves, our children and even their children is this: we do have a button. We can stop the electric shocks, especially when we realise we are administering most of them to ourselves. We can step outside the triangle. We can wake ourselves up from this deep sleep and set ourselves and our children free.

3

FRUIT ONE: EMPOWERMENT

Why your children are stronger than you realise

Your children don't need you to be perfect.
They just need you to believe in them

– Colette Marchant, from the movie *Dumbo*

John Ssebunya was born in the village of Bombo, Uganda, in the 1980s, a time when Uganda was embroiled in a brutal civil war. He was just two years old when he witnessed his father kill his mother and then hang himself. And so John ran off to the jungle near his village, a move that probably saved him from becoming a child soldier. He had somehow survived a few days alone in the jungle when a troop of green vervet monkeys approached him. At first, the monkeys were cautious. It's not often you find a little human wandering the jungle on their own. But the monkeys soon realised that John posed no threat. So they began offering him food – nuts and sweet potatoes. They let the boy join them as they travelled around the jungle, teaching him how to climb trees and find food. John was in the jungle for three years before he was

48

discovered, aged five, by a woman from a nearby tribe who brought him back to civilisation.

I'm sure you have heard similar stories, like Mowgli from *The Jungle Book*, about feral children raised by wild animals. But these stories are just fiction, aren't they? John Ssebunya's story is real. How could a toddler – such a vulnerable creature – survive on his own in the jungle?

Perhaps our children are more resilient than we might think. According to Dr Alastair Sutcliffe, senior lecturer in paediatrics at University College London, children are more likely to survive even extreme physical trauma than adults. There are so many stories of children surviving where adults died – babies being pulled alive out of collapsed buildings after an earthquake, children surviving falling out of high windows. Dr Sutcliffe says: 'It's simple physics. They have chubbier bodies, they are more flexible, their lungs are healthier, so they are more robust to injury.'

We'd never wish any of these events on any child. And as I said in the introduction, in some ways, human children are the most vulnerable creatures on planet Earth. But in a world that is pushing us into states of helplessness, we each need to ask ourselves: could our children be stronger than we realise?

Playing with knives

A few years ago, my wife Laurey and I went to visit a Peruvian shaman living in London called Don Oscar Davila, who was known for helping couples with fertility issues. We were struggling after a series of miscarriages and prepared to try all kinds of routes to conceive.

Don Oscar sat us down in a room adorned with huge, exotic feathers and filled with the sweet scent of palo santo wood. He told us about his wife back in Ecuador, who at 48 had given birth to a child, a daughter. There was no IVF, no medical intervention. We lapped up this information. But the story that really stuck in my mind after this visit was the one where Don Oscar gave his four-year-old daughter a machete so she could learn to make her way through the forest on her own. He told me this was normal practice in his village. How could a four-year-old ever be trusted with a machete?

Well, it turns out to be more common than you'd imagine. In an article called 'Playing with Knives', anthropologist David Lancy describes the surprising (to us Western folks) level of trust and autonomy that children in some tribes are given from a very young age. He shares an anthropologist's description of a Pirahã child, from an indigenous tribe in the Amazon rainforest of Brazil, who 'was playing with a sharp kitchen knife, about nine inches in length. He was swinging the knife blade around him, often coming close to his eyes, his chest, his arm and other body parts. When he dropped the knife, his mother – talking to someone else – reached backward nonchalantly without interrupting her conversation, picked up the knife and handed it back to the toddler.'

Can you imagine this happening in your house?

Or what about this? By the age of four, children from the Maniq in Thailand can easily skin and gut small animals.

These cultures are grounded in a child-rearing philosophy that strongly emphasises the child's innate capacity to figure things out. After spending many years in Inuit society in Arctic Canada, celebrated anthropologist Lee Guemple observed that the Inuits, 'do not presume to teach their children what they can as easily learn on their own.'

In case you're wondering, I'm not recommending you leave your child alone in the jungle with a machete, hoping a few kind monkeys will take care of them. But if we want to raise children who can thrive in our uncertain world, wouldn't it help to hover over them a little less, to trust them a little more?

PRACTISE STRENGTHS-BASED PARENTING

One of the best ways to empower children is to nurture their strengths – in trauma work this is known as 'resourcing'. Strengths can include things like determination, creativity, patience or in fact all the fruits in this book. These strengths provide essential balance in a world where there is so much focus on what we can't do and what is wrong with us.

In her book, *The Strength Switch*, psychologist Lea Waters recommends strengths-spotting – being very specific about your child's strengths. So, for example, your child shows you her picture and instead of saying 'Well done', you say, 'I noticed how focused you were when you were drawing.' Like a flower in sunlight, the more regularly you spot strengths, the more they grow. Author and parenting expert Peggy O'Mara has this beautiful quote: 'The way we talk to our children becomes their inner voice.' If you shine a light on your kids' strengths, over time these strengths will bloom into their inner voice.

For this approach to work, we grown-ups need to start with ourselves. Take a moment to write down five strengths you know you have and can feel confident about. If you struggle with this, what would your friends or loved ones say are your top five strengths? Be aware of the voice of your inner critic popping up here. Know that you have the power – you can tell that inner critic to step to one side.

Now, try doing the same with your children. Ask them what they think their five strengths might be and/or share what you think they are. If they are younger, you may need

---

to explain using examples from real life. You can also write down five strengths that you or your kids don't have confidence in yet but that you can work on growing together.

Waters recommends using coaching type questions, where you are not the expert but instead you ask empowering questions that help the child find their own answers. For example, perhaps your child is worried about something. Instead of rushing in to give advice and to fix it, you ask: 'What do you feel you need?' 'How can I help you with this?' To make it even more specifically about strengths, try: 'What strengths do you have that could help you with this?'

Real risk vs perceived risk

The other day, I went to a four-year-old's birthday party. The parents had hired a bouncy castle. As we walked to the party, I thought to myself, 'This is going to be relaxing. The kids can have a great time bouncing while we adults kick back and drink wine.'

Unfortunately, the bouncy castle turned out to be less a place for fun and more of a treacherous minefield of potential broken bones or worse. Or, at least, that's the only explanation I can find for why the parents spent most of the afternoon on guard at the castle doors, constantly intervening in the children's play. I tried really hard to achieve my party goal (sit back drinking my wine) but I could see thought bubbles arising from the other parents' minds – 'What an irresponsible parent!' 'Hasn't he read about those bouncy castle tragedies?' So I reluctantly shuffled over to the gates of the dangerous castle and earnestly stood guard.

In the previous chapter, we looked at how we've been conditioned into a constant state of helpless anxiety by the 24/7 news cycle and the fear-based content filling our feeds. This fear makes us overprotective of our children – even when it comes to things that are supposed to be fun, like a bouncy castle. The facts are that in the past 21 years, on average one child a year dies while playing on a bouncy castle, worldwide. Most were due to faulty set up and strong winds. It is a tragedy that these children died. The truth, however, is that your child is much more likely to die from a bee sting or a dog attack. But the bouncy castle stories make for shocking headlines and so they get a lot of exposure. We read these horror stories and add bouncy castles to the long list of things we think of as dangerous for our children. And then we spend the day anxiously hovering over our bouncing children. (Meanwhile, in other parts of the world, four-year-old children are cutting their way through the jungle.)

Now let's look at a scarier example. I apologise in advance as I'm about to write about every parent's worst nightmare: abduction. The idea erupted into our public consciousness in the UK in 2007 when Madeleine McCann was taken while her parents dined in the restaurant just the other side of the swimming pool from their holiday apartment. As you have likely read, the adults were going back to check on the kids every half an hour. But when Madeleine's mother Kate did her check at 10pm, Madeleine was gone.

Madeleine's became the most heavily reported missing person case in modern history. Why? Because it tapped into our deepest fears. This is the ultimate way to capture our attention, especially when we feel it could have happened to us.

Hooked on 'safety'

In their book, *The Coddling of the American Mind*, Jonathan Haidt and Greg Lukianoff explore how our well-meaning attempts to protect children from physical harm have undergone a mission creep over time, as parents have become less and less tolerant to any risk. They call this 'safety-ism'. They pinpoint the beginning of safety-ism to an abduction in Florida in 1981, when a six-year-old boy named Adam Walsh was abducted outside a shopping mall. Adam's father, John Walsh, channelled his grief into a huge campaign. He made a movie about what had happened, called *Adam*, watched by 38 million people. He launched a true crime show, *America's Most Wanted*. And he developed a new concept that went viral: printing pictures of missing children on milk cartons, under a big, all-caps headline MISSING. Soon these MISSING ads were placed on grocery bags, billboards, pizza boxes and even utility bills.

What was the effect on the minds of American parents? 'Norms changed, fears grew and many parents came to believe that if they took their eyes off their children for an instant in any public venue, their kid might be snatched. It no longer felt safe to let kids roam around their neighbourhoods unsupervised.' A shocking story can press our protective parental buttons, trigger our deepest fears. And then we make a universal rule that allowing our child to do that thing – be left in a hotel room, climb a tree, use a knife, play unsupervised on a bouncy castle, go out without an adult – must be dangerous at all times and in all places.

In reality, it is extremely rare for a child to be abducted by a stranger. In the UK, according to the latest in-depth review into police figures, 50 children are abducted every year, the majority by a parent who doesn't have custody. And the vast majority of the children abducted by strangers come home.

Of course, we can and should minimise the risks our children face. We put them in car seats. We teach them to stop at the kerb. We book them swimming lessons. We give them scooter helmets. We make sure the bouncy castle is properly set up. For our teenagers, we support them to be streetwise, we advise them on safe drinking, safe sex. But there is also a real risk when we overprotect our children. Evidence is building that over-involved and over-controlling 'helicopter' parenting is bad for our children's mental health, triggering their learned helplessness. One 2014 US study found that college students with helicopter parents were significantly more likely to be depressed. The authors blamed this on the parents violating their children's 'basic psychological needs for autonomy and competence'. Add to this a recent finding that three-quarters of children in the UK spend less time outdoors then a prison inmate.

To put this into crucial perspective: your child is 140,000 times more likely to get a mental health problem than to be abducted, the same number of times more likely to self-harm, 38,000 times more likely to attempt suicide and eight times more likely to commit suicide. They are also 80 times more likely to die in a road accident and more likely even to be struck by lightning.

I don't want you to read these stats and go and construct a lightning-proof bunker. The fact abduction happens at all is horrendous and terrifying. But broken bones can heal. Suicide can't. I admit this is strongly worded but I want you to keep in mind the trade-offs between protecting your children from imagined harm and the very real risk of them developing serious mental health issues if they aren't exposed to an appropriate level of risk and stress.

You don't have to be ruled by fear. You have a choice.

Antifragile – the upside of risk

A 2021 study showed that the average age parents in the UK will let their child go out to play unsupervised is 11 years old.

How much freedom did you have as a child? If you grew up in the 1970s or 80s, you probably had a lot more.

When I was aged five, I was allowed to play in the streets near our house in a suburb of Manchester with other kids, unsupervised. When I was six, I was allowed to explore the fields behind my house with my sisters, unsupervised. When I was seven, I was climbing a tree in the fields behind a friend's house unsupervised, I fell and cut my head open. My friend ran back to the house to get help. I needed stitches . . . but I was fine.

When I look back, the moments where I really learned and grew were during unsupervised play. Do you have similar memories? Are you, like me, glad your parents allowed you to explore and take risks?

For our children to thrive, they need exposure to certain environments and certain risks. This is what risk analyst Nassim Taleb calls being *antifragile*. Unlike china teacups, individuals or systems need exposure to stress and risk for them to grow stronger. Human children are antifragile. We are born with (almost) infinite potential but our potential will never grow unless we are allowed to explore and develop away from the protective gaze. There is always another risk your child is ready to take that will help them to grow. Our job as parents is to provide the environment which will allow them to take that risk.

RISK ASSESSMENT

When you're assessing whether to allow your child or teenager to do something, weigh up the worst-case scenario against the longer-term mental health consequences of over-protection. Ask yourself: is there a way my child can take the risk? And what are the minimum safeguards required?

For example, if your child is under 11 years old and wants to travel to school on their own, you can make sure they are with someone. (It's worth noting that in 1971, 80 per cent of seven- and eight-year-olds travelled to school without an adult.)

If they want to go and play in the fields behind your house, make sure they know the boundaries of where they can go and how to find their way home.

For more help and guidance, check out Free-Range Kids, a website dedicated to 'Fighting the belief that our children are in constant danger from creeps, kidnapping, germs, grades, flashers, frustration, failure, baby snatchers, bugs, bullies, men, sleepovers and/or the perils of a non-organic grape' www.freerangekids.com. And LetGrow.org, which contains great resources on children's resilience and the need to give them more autonomy.

KATIE: THE GOOD STUDENT

Katie was sent to me when I was working as a therapist at a school in north London. She was 17. Her English teacher asked me to give her some one-to-one sessions, in the hope of reducing her acute anxiety. In our first session, I noticed Katie's face was tightly crinkled, like an empty crisp packet someone had scrunched up and thrown away. She told me that for two years whenever she felt really stressed she would pull out big chunks of her hair, a condition called trichotillomania. Katie's school and her parents desperately wanted her to be 'fixed' so she could get the incredible A-level results she was predicted. But, after two years getting help from mental health services, Katie was still tightly crinkled, still pulling out her hair.

Remember from our opening section: our children's symptoms are unconscious attempts to heal conflicts in the world around them. If a child feels disempowered in their family, in their school, in their world, symptoms often develop as a way for them to re-establish some kind of power. And hair-pulling is an ancient response to feeling helpless that goes as far back as Aristotle in the fourth century BCE. In the Old Testament, the prophet Ezra discovers that the Israelites had been taking pagan wives after escaping Babylonian captivity and this is how he responds: 'When I heard this, I tore my tunic and cloak, pulled hair from my head and beard and sat down appalled.' It's hard to make sense of the reactions of Ezra, or of Katie, unless you can imagine what it feels like to be so disempowered, so full of despair.

By the end of our third session, it had become clear that Katie's anxiety was largely coming from the unrealistic level of academic pressure her parents were putting on her. They were hovering over her, micro-managing her time, and not giving her any space to do her own thing. And Katie was scared to stand up to her parents and speak her truth – namely, that their ideal of academic success felt too much. I decided to help Katie realise that she did have a choice, that she could say no.

Katie was, understandably, afraid to do this. A child's biggest fear is being rejected by their parents. When parents reject a child, even if it's just by showing disapproval with 'that look', it can be as painful to them as an electric shock. Of course, sometimes we need to disapprove of our children's behaviour. But too much disapproval without encouragement can trigger a child's helplessness. Katie, like the dogs giving up in the electric shock experiment, had experienced so many moments of disapproval that she felt helpless. But her unconscious mind had found a new, more symbolic way to express her disempowerment – hair-pulling.

Katie agreed to role play some of the difficult conversations. We took turns being Katie, her teacher and her parents. Eventually, she felt confident enough to go off and have these conversations for real. She managed to negotiate with her teachers and her parents to reduce the amount of homework she was getting and to take the pressure off her academic results.

Two weeks later, there was a knock on the door of my counselling room. It was Katie's teacher. She said, 'What have you been doing with Katie? She seems so different, so relaxed. And her hair-pulling has almost completely disappeared.'

Empowerment

Just as we are born vulnerable, we are also born with a drive to mastery. Have you watched an infant learning to walk? I remember watching Rose falling over and repeatedly hurting herself, then repeatedly getting up again. Why didn't she just give up? There was an unshakeable drive to mastery inside of her that just had to figure this out.

Inside your child, there is a natural intelligence that wants them to survive at the very least and at best, it wants them to realise their potential. Some people call this intelligence, spirit or soul, or if you feel uncomfortable with those terms, you can call it will or life force or whatever works for you. When we hover over our children, when we swoop in to rescue them from any suffering, we block this natural intelligence. To empower our children, to bring out this deep intelligence from within, we need to trust in it, to trust in our children a little more.

This deep intelligence often works in harmony with the same deep intelligence in the parent. In his book *Nurturing Natures*, Graham Music describes the foetus in the womb as like a 'cosmonaut in charge of a spacecraft'. The most striking example of this comes from research done over the last three decades that has shown how the foetus sends stem cells into the mother and so can heal parts of the mother's body that are damaged. This is called feto-maternal chimerism, 'chimera' being a mythical creature that has a lion's head, a goat's body and a snake's tail. Even more striking is that long after the baby is born, these foetal cells continue to have a positive effect on the mother's body.

Our children are stronger than we realise. They have a power within – the foetus sending stem cells into the mother to heal her; the toddler learning to walk, no matter how many times they fall down. Inside your child is a natural impulse to evolve, to figure things out, to realise their fullest potential.

What I did with Katie, what I try to do with the children I work with, is not rocket science. I trust the deeper intelligence that's guiding them. I try my best to respect it, to respect them. I ask them empowering questions and I listen with a quiet mind and an open heart to their answers. I help them to express thoughts and feelings that they haven't felt safe to express. I give them a voice. I help them to recognise that they have agency, that they can access their own inner strength. This is empowerment.

These four principles will help you to empower the children in your care

1. **This child is stronger than I realise**

    Find a way to trust your child, even just a tiny bit more than you do now. Notice your reactions when they are trying to do something and they get frustrated or anxious. Maybe it's putting on their shoes, doing their homework, going to play without your supervision, getting ready for their first date. See if you can trust a little more in their capacity to figure this out without you needing to swoop in and rescue them.

Practise letting them take small risks that are on the edge of your comfort zone. You will probably notice (as I do) a powerful Rescuer energy brewing up when you do this, so you'll need to tolerate these feelings. If you're unsure about a risk, ask yourself: what is the worst thing that can happen here?

Look for signs of your child's resilience and reflect them back. A few years ago, I was working with a 14-year-old girl, Priscilla, who was self-harming. The standard techniques that I suggested just didn't work (to be honest, the standard, googleable techniques rarely do work, in my experience). So, instead of focusing on the cuts on her arms, I began to pay attention to even the smallest signs of her resilience, such as how she was getting up every morning and taking care of herself by having a shower and eating breakfast. The more I focused on her strengths, the more she began to trust in herself, until eventually she developed her own solutions to stop self-harming – and guess what? They worked much better than the standard techniques you can find online.

2. **There are lots of good people in the world**

It's easy to fall into the trap of believing that headlines are a true representation of a world full of paedophiles and murderers. Balance out this fear-based perspective by actively looking for the goodness in people. There are way more people who are essentially good then there are people who are evil.

Today, actively look for those moments when strangers are kind to one another. Not dramatic, save-the-world type of actions, just small moments like someone holding the door open or thanking the bus driver, or a smile from a passer-by. This will help you regulate your fears. And your child will learn to trust the goodness of people a bit more too.

3. **Symptoms are unconscious attempts to heal the world**

If your child is struggling with some issue, whether it's eating, sleeping, schoolwork, anxiety or depression, instead of trying to 'fix' them, ask yourself these questions:

- What might my child's symptom be trying to communicate or heal in the world around them? (And be prepared, the 'world' might include you!)
- What blind spot in our family or in the world might my child's 'undesirable' behaviours be shining a light on?
- How might their emotions or behaviours be an attempt to regain some power in a situation where they feel powerless?
- How can I help them express this in a healthier way? (It may be just listening to them, or finding someone else to listen to them, or helping them to write or draw it out. You know what works best for your child.)

It's not easy to open to the possibility that our child's 'unwanted' behaviours may be giving voice to an uncomfortable truth about our family or about the world. But if you want your child to heal, if you want your child to grow up in a world where they don't feel permanently broken, then you have to be willing to hear this truth.

I've worked with many families where a child developed a symptom because their parents were in conflict or because there were some really uncomfortable, unspoken truths, like a dad with a drinking problem or a mum who had an affair. Whatever the uncomfortable truths in your family, please remember it's not your fault but it is your responsibility. Can you imagine how much better your family and indeed the world might be if all of these unconscious communications were given a space, a voice; if all that energy expended in hair-pulling and other symptoms was channelled into making positive changes in the world?

If you do have a sense of some uncomfortable truth that your child might be sensing, like that canary in the coalmine, it is appropriate sometimes to name it to them. Just naming the issue can go a long way to relieving the symptoms and to helping the child feel like they are not broken. For example, you might say, 'I know that Mum and Dad have been arguing a lot recently and you might be worried that we don't love you . . .'

4. **With great power comes great responsibility**

Yes, Spiderman was right. Empowering our children only works if we can also teach them responsibility. And the only way to do this is by modelling it. If we say one thing and do another our children know.

Responsibility means the ability to choose how we respond to any situation. Jack Canfield's principle of '100 per cent responsibility' has been life-changing for me and many people I work with. Canfield says when things don't go our way, we tend to blame other people (aka Victim mode). But we should act as if we have 100 per cent responsibility for our life experience – whatever happens to us, we can choose how to respond. It's not always easy to realise we have a choice, especially if we have experienced complex trauma. But we do. The first choice you have is to act as if you are 100 per cent responsible. Notice which person or thing you have been blaming for a problem you are having. Now, see what happens if instead of blaming, you assume 100 per cent responsibility. Notice how this changes things. Most importantly for this chapter, you are 100 per cent responsible for empowering your children. Below are some practical ways to empower them.

- Give your children jobs to do in the house. If they make a mess, it's their job to clean it up. You don't have to be harsh or draconian. Just explain this is how things work – not just in this house, or school, but in the world. As soon as your child can work, support them to get a job.

- If you have a teenager, do you ever still treat them like a younger child? For example, if you wake them up in the morning, can you help them figure out how to do it? I can hear you thinking, 'If I don't get him up he will never go to school . . . he won't ever get up, he won't pass exams or get a job and then he will have a terrible life.' There is a section on natural consequences in Chapter 9 that will help you here.

- Instead of barking orders, ask your child empowering questions. 'What do you need to do next?' or 'What's one thing you could do that would be helpful in this situation?' If they make mistakes, get things wrong, your role is to help them take ownership of that mistake without blame or shame. Ask: 'What could you have done differently?'

This world so full of fear will keep pulling you and your children back into the triangle of disempowerment. But please remember this: every time you empower your child, even in the smallest of ways, these small acts build up a reservoir of self-trust within your child, a deep feeling that they can handle challenges in life, that they can figure things out.

4

ROOT TWO: VIRTUAL REALITY

How we fell out of love with our bodies

So many of us are not in our bodies, really at home and vibrantly present there. Nor are we in touch with the basic rhythms that constitute our bodily life. We live outside ourselves—in our heads, our memories, our longings—absentee landlords of our own estate

– Gabrielle Roth

When I was 21, I fell in love with a library. It was the National Library of Wales on Aberystwyth University campus. The building is over 100 years old, built from white Portland stone, surrounded by plush gardens and has endless views over Cardigan Bay. It has a copy of almost every book you could imagine, millions of them. It was a wet dream for a bookworm like me. With my head in a book, I find peace, solace and – now I think about it – safety from the world out there. I spent long, happy days in this sacred, silent space, discovering obscure books and obscure ideas and weaving them together into my own thinking and writing. Then one day, I got a jolt.

I was walking along the seafront at sunset, surrounded by the most exquisite views, when suddenly I realised that for the last ten minutes or so I hadn't noticed a single thing in the world around me. Why? Because I was so trapped in my own mind. I'd lost touch with my senses. I'd lost touch with reality. This realisation hit me hard. I was flooded with fear, like a panic attack, a question searing through my nervous system: *What is real?*

Stuck in our heads

Only a creature that lives in its head could ask a question like: *what is real?* Animals are naturally embodied. Dogs don't need yoga classes. Monkeys don't need cuddle workshops. Pigs don't need lessons in how to stay grounded. There is something different about us human animals.

A Harvard University study showed we spend nearly half our waking life on autopilot, thinking about something other than what we are doing. To some extent, this disembodiment is normal. It happens every time we daydream and every night as we sleep. But when we get stuck in our heads we suffer. Why?

It's difficult to answer this question with more words because words tend to take us into our heads. Perhaps you remember a time where you felt at home in your body, connected to the world around you. A time when you felt the cool grass kiss your feet, when you gazed at a beautiful sunset or you received a loving hug and your shoulders dropped. These are times when you inhabited your body. When we don't inhabit our bodies, we lose touch with reality. And the stories that loop in our minds tend to be full of fear. We get so lost in these fearful stories that we forget they are not real.

My jolt of panic in Aberystwyth was followed by weeks of angst. Then one morning I remembered the meditation practice I'd learned in India. I used my attention to tune inwards, feeling the sensations in my body, and I gently but firmly let go of the part of my mind that wanted to tell stories about what was going on. I instantly felt more grounded, more connected to reality, more sane. I came to a conclusion: the body is real. I realised that whenever I felt overwhelmed or disconnected from reality, I could ground my attention back in my body. Working with the body has since become a cornerstone of my therapeutic work.

SOLOMON: OLD, FAMILIAR STORIES

Solomon was a father of three from Manchester who worked as a secondary school teacher. When I met him, he had been suffering from depression and anxiety for ten years. As is usual in therapy, we spent the first few sessions exploring the story behind his symptoms. Solomon's own father had suddenly left the family home when Solomon was five years old, leaving his mother to raise five children on her own. His mother became understandably very stressed and shouted a lot at the kids. Solomon would protect himself from this anger by burying his head in books and rich fantasy worlds, such as Dungeons and Dragons.

As we continued to meet and talk, I noticed that Solomon had a lot of stuff going on in his mind – looping, anxious stories about his past, his present and his future. One session, I asked him if we could try something new. I guided him to bring his awareness from his mind into his body, to see if he could find the source of his anxiety. He sat quietly for a few seconds, then he said, 'I can feel the anxiety in my throat, like someone is strangling me.'

I asked him to put a gentle hand where he felt the anxiety

and to just let that sensation be there. The energy then shifted to his stomach, where we did the same thing – gentle hand, let the sensation be there. When Solomon came out of this mini-meditation, he told me he had felt a huge relief as his anxiety dissolved for a moment. However, I also noticed a look of disappointment on Solomon's face. I asked him about this and he agreed – he felt strangely annoyed but wasn't sure why.

This may seem like an odd reaction, to feel annoyed when we experience relief from suffering. But the truth is, our minds get very attached to the old, familiar stories about ourselves and about the world. These stories, the identities we cling to, may have helped us navigate difficult times. And we fear the uncertainty of what lies beyond. Even when we can see it would benefit us, it can be hard to step out of well-worn grooves. We need a gentle but firm persistence if we want to let go of some of the old stories in our heads and guide our minds back home into our bodies.

In the therapy world right now, there is a big shift from talking therapies to body-centred work. This is a response to a world reaching peak disembodiment, where the average adult in the UK will spend 34 years of their life staring at screens, a world that is also disconnected from nature. It's no wonder we are seeing so much psychological distress. When we are disconnected from our bodies, we suffer.

So just how did we end up so lost in our own virtual reality? What are the deep, recurring patterns that drive us to escape our bodies and nature, and how can we find our way back home?

In this moment, I invite you to pay attention to your body. Can you notice the feeling of your bum on the chair? Your feet on the floor? Look around you. What's one thing you can see with your eyes? What's one thing you can hear? Bring your loving, curious attention to one part of your body that you wouldn't normally notice. And, as you read on, see if you can notice what sensations come up in your body as your eyes move over the words and your brain digests their meaning.

Skinship

You were born a sensing, crying, shitting, vomiting, feeling being. But a baby does need some help to come more fully into their body, and this happens through loving touch. Touch is a critical parenting behaviour shared by all mammalian mums. If you were blessed to be born into what the great British psychoanalyst Donald Winnicott called a 'good enough' environment, you would have been regularly picked up, held, stroked, patted on the back, cuddled. He explained that this kind of holding allows the mind to be at home in the body.

After birth, in what's known as the 'fourth trimester', the mother and the infant are really but one body. Skin-to-skin, the mother can perfectly maintain the baby's body temperature, a biological marvel that my former supervisor Graham Music describes as a 'two-person homeostatic system'. This deep, embodied connection – also known as 'skinship' – helps us human beings to grow. Distressed babies who are picked up, held and soothed in their first year cry less after this first year than other babies. Premature babies who receive massage grow more than those left in incubators. Cultures with more positive touch in infancy have even been shown to have less violence. And touch heals both ways: contact between a baby and a parent can also reduce cortisol (the stress hormone) in parents.

What happens when this primal need for touch goes unmet in an extreme way? You may remember the shocking news reports in 1990 of Romanian orphans lying in rows of cots. Communist dictator Nicolae Ceauşescu had banned abortion and contraception because he believed that upping the birthrate would help grow the economy. He hadn't predicted that when families had more babies than they could afford, they would feel forced to abandon them. By the 1980s, it's thought there were about 65,000 children living in orphanages, often from the first month of their life. Some of these babies were left unattended for up to 20 hours a day. Now, as adults, they have been studied extensively. They struggle to make eye contact. They don't talk. And they don't smile. Their capacity to relate to other people, to other bodies, is frozen.

You might have had a difficult experience around touch as an infant. Perhaps you weren't held enough. Whatever your experience, I am sending as much love and holding as I can from this page to that infant within you. You are not alone. You will find a number of exercises throughout this book that will gently guide you back into your body. And, of course, you may need professional help. In the Resources section, I include some links for those who feel they may need more help to repair difficult early life experiences.

Out-of-body experiences

Even if you had the most optimal level of 'skinship' in your early years, there are so many elements in our culture that seem determined to sever our minds from our bodies.

As a child, you were probably taught to eat and sleep according to social rules, not hunger. You might have been forced to sit at the table and eat up all your dinner. Or, if you said you were hungry at the wrong time, your parents might have said 'you can't be hungry now!' You might have been put to bed at a set time, whether you were tired or not. And so you learned not to trust your body. At school, you were told to sit still, to wait for permission to go to the toilet. And you might (as I did) have had the shameful classroom experience of a warm, yellow puddle spreading around your chair. These were early, often painful lessons in putting the needs of our body second.

And we increasingly listen to external, artificial cues, not our body or its senses. We trust the sell-by dates on food, not our noses. And have you ever used an app to tell you how well you've slept? We're like Steve Carrell in an episode of the US version of *The Office*, where he follows his satnav, ignoring the road signs . . . until he drives into a lake.

And then there are the screens, of course. According to a recent survey, US teens spend seven hours a day on their screens, and that's not even including school work. But before we blame the screens, I don't consider technology to be the dark force it's often made out to be. The human tendency to separate mind from body began earlier than the invention of the iPhone 11. As you've read, I was quite capable of being disembodied just by filling my head with books.

What do you use to disembody? Wine, podcasts, Instagram, Netflix, retail therapy? We are surrounded by opportunities to disembody. The richest people in the world today have built their fortunes by luring our minds out of our bodies into virtual spaces. And it doesn't take much for a tendency to escape our body to become a compulsion or addiction – throwing ourselves into work, into extreme exercise, into drink and drugs.

Just as we disconnect from our bodies, we also disconnect from nature. As children, we may have been told not to get dirty or muddy or make a mess. We may discourage our own kids from running outside with their feet on the ground, with the result that their bodies don't get to feel that primal connection to the earth. (And as we will see below, our bodies really need that connection.)

Journalist Richard Louv coined the term 'nature-deficit disorder' to describe our increasing alienation from the natural world. What are the symptoms? Attention difficulties, low mood and depression. Autism is also much more common in urban environments, where we live separate from the seasons and cycles of nature. And it's on the rise. In the US in 2009, 1 in 91 children had autism. By 2017, the rates of autism had risen to 1 in 40 children. If these rates continue, then by 2041, 1 in 10 children will have autism.

I realise some of the words I'm sharing here may feel negative, scary or upsetting to you. But my intention is to remind us of how precious our bodies and their connection to nature are. Take a moment to come back into your body now. Wiggle your fingers and your toes. Put your hands on your belly or chest and feel your breath moving in and out of your body. Can you find one thing about your body that you can feel grateful for right now? It might be as simple as this breath that gives you life. Say thank you to this part of your body and whatever it has allowed you to do or to be.

PERRY: THE BIG FREEZE

Perry was a brave, funny, passionate 16-year-old who was referred to me because he'd been having intense panic attacks and had fainted at school. His parents were also worried he was anorexic as he'd been restricting his calories and had lost a lot of weight over the past year.

During our first conversation, Perry told me very quickly in what felt like one violently expelled breath that his best friend had died in a car accident, also a year before. Perry had been in the car. Since then, he felt like the world wasn't real and he was questioning if even he was real.

After this first session, Perry did not want to talk about the accident. In truth, he could not talk about it. If we ever came even close to the subject of his best friend's death, Perry stopped speaking and stared into space. He wasn't doing this on purpose. His system shut down, as if someone had pressed the emergency OFF button. He became unreachable.

This is dissociation. We have an inbuilt system that disconnects us from painful feelings in our body and painful realities in the world. It's a biological defence that protects us in situations where we can't physically escape. It's sometimes called 'the escape when there is no escape'. It can help children survive the most abusive, neglectful and traumatising situations, like growing up a Romanian orphan or seeing your best friend die in a car crash.

Dissociation is a form of the freeze response, an evolutionary survival mechanism that many animals have too. In the David Attenborough series *Planet Earth*, a baby iguana hatches on Fernandina Island in the Galapagos, only to find that it is surrounded by snakes that want to eat it for breakfast. There's a chase. At one point, the baby iguana is cornered and it plays dead – the freeze response in action.

In its most extreme version, dissociation leads to what used to be known as a split personality (now known as dissociative identity disorder). You may recognise this from characters like the Incredible Hulk, Dr Jekyll and Mr Hyde, or the narrator of the *Fight Club* movie. But there are more everyday forms of dissociation too. Have you ever been so scared that you froze, a rabbit in headlights? Maybe you saw somebody being bullied and stayed silent? Or you were shouted at in a meeting, your throat tightened and you couldn't respond, as your attention shrunk inwards like a snail retreating in its shell? We also dissociate by having overactive minds – overthinking is a way of holding ourselves when we don't feel held, according to Winnicott.

In the Galapagos clip, once the snake passes by, you see the iguana get up, quickly shake itself off and run to safe ground. This is how the body naturally releases trauma. The iguana does not need a therapist. But we human beings, living in our disembodied world, can struggle to free ourselves from trauma in this natural, embodied way.

For Perry, even though the original trauma had long passed, the slightest trigger – a word, a smell, a noise – could activate his freeze response. And on top of this, each time he dissociated he would beat himself up for not being tough enough, for not just 'getting over it'. These cycles of self-criticism and shame can affect us just as deeply as the original trauma, turning a single painful event into an entrenched mental health problem. This is a tragic aspect of being human. If only we could just naturally shake it all off, iguana-style.

In the end, I taught Perry about the freeze response, normalised it for him, and helped Perry to bring a loving awareness to the cycles of shame and self-criticism he felt about his body's trauma response. I guided Perry to find a number of body practices – including yoga and street-dance – that slowly helped him come back home into his body. And once we had cut through these layers of shame, Perry was able to work through the memory of the trauma so that it had less of a grip over him. With great courage and self-compassion, Perry was able to 'un-freeze' his trauma response. He learned to feel safe in his body again.

Are we all traumatised?

If dissociation is a symptom of trauma, could collective trauma explain our disembodied lives?

I am hesitating as I write this. I want to answer yes . . . but with a *very* big caveat. Today there's a huge amount of trauma-talk. Trauma is on trend. Trauma has become a big business. Now everyday experiences like getting shouted at by someone in the street or nearly missing a meeting, or getting a bad haircut might be called 'traumatic'.

But, as psychologist Lucy Foulkes says, 'If we call all stressful events traumas – originally only used to describe events like war and torture and terrorist attacks – and call all resulting distress PTSD, what words are left for the people who lose a limb in a terrorist attack, say?' We need to be aware, as we discuss trauma, that we don't talk ourselves into victimhood.

But for now, let's start with the possibility that we may all be carrying some unresolved trauma. Trauma can be understood as a stressful experience that overwhelmed the capacity of our bodies and minds to cope. However, it is important to distinguish trauma from everyday adversity. Even events that we might think of as traumatic, like war or being violently attacked, don't automatically turn into trauma symptoms for many people. The truth is that most people are exposed to at least one violent or life-threatening situation during the course of their lives. And most people recover from these experiences without any professional intervention.

So what turns adversity into trauma? One crucial factor is loneliness. As trauma expert Peter Fonagy says: 'Adversity becomes traumatic when it is compounded by a sense that one's mind is alone.' We humans are not designed to bear our trauma – of any kind – on our own. Over thousands of years and across many different cultures, we have used collective rituals to guide us through it. Yet, in modern societies, we have largely lost these. As I write, we have just had the Easter weekend and the Jewish festival of Passover – festivals that in different ways honour the suffering of our ancestors. But the power of these rituals has become a little lost among the Peppa Pig Easter eggs and the chocolate matzoh.

As well as trauma from our own lives, there is inherited

trauma. This is when the trauma of our ancestors is handed down to us. It's been shown that traumatic experiences, for example the Holocaust, famine, slavery, war, or personal traumas like abuse can be passed down through at least three generations via epigenetic changes.

CHECKING IN WITH YOUR ANCESTORS

We are born with a unique set of psychological adaptations based on our ancestral history, encoded in that winding DNA staircase we emerge from. This does not mean we are in any way broken. These adaptations are intelligent, keeping the memory of our ancestors alive. Inherited trauma does not equal our destiny. We just need to find better ways to honour and integrate these memories. As Rafiki the mandrill in The Lion King says: 'Oh yes, the past can hurt, but the way I see it you can either run from it or learn from it.'

- Find some time to research your family history. This can shed light on certain present emotional, psychological or behavioural patterns in you or your children that may seem hard to understand. What significant events or traumas have happened in your family up to three generations back? Look for both personal and collective events. For example, did your grandparents and great-grandparents live through the First and Second World Wars? What roles did they have?

- Can you see any 'symptoms' in you or your children that might make sense through the lens of ancestral trauma? Remember, there is a lot of strength and intelligence here.

- Find a way to listen to and honour these ancestral memories. You may have seen the Disney film *Coco*, in which Miguel's family has a beautiful altar to honour their ancestors. If you have pictures of your ancestors, it can help to gather them in one special place. If this isn't too out there for you, you can imagine asking your ancestors what they need you to do for this trauma to heal. Very often, these inherited traumas need your loving attention and forgiveness (see Chapter 13, Fruit Six for more on this).

And then there is what is known as secondary or vicarious trauma – where we develop trauma-like symptoms from witnessing suffering in the outside world. I can be sat in my peaceful office listening to my 'peaceful piano' playlist feeling nice and zen when I happen upon a tragic news item from a country I may never visit about people I may never meet. When I watched David Attenborough's climate change documentary, I could feel the apocalyptic future rattle my nervous system. A recent neuroscience study showed that some children are particularly vulnerable to developing Post Traumatic Stress, just from watching news stories about disasters that don't even happen near them.

Greta Thunberg first heard about climate change when she was eight years old. She was so horrified by this reality that she stopped talking and eating. She was later diagnosed with selective mutism. Most of us won't have such a strong response to bad news. But having our nervous systems continually triggered by terrible events out in the world prevents us from processing personal or inherited trauma. The reality of suffering in the world can be overwhelming, especially if we don't have enough space or community support to process these feelings. Can you imagine how it feels for our children?

So yes, it is likely we are all in some way traumatised and that this may be feeding our virtual reality world. But please do not feel disheartened. While some of us do need professional help to resolve trauma, for most of us, we can be assured that the trauma pattern we carry is ultimately our body's way of keeping us safe. These patterns will become parts of our personality that we can grow to love and accept. Craig Chalquist is a colleague and a psychotherapist with a special interest in ecology. He told me this recently: 'When severely wounded, trees do not heal from their injuries so much as contain them, keeping them as permanent reminders and making them part of an ever-growing structure.'

You are not broken. You are beautiful and whole. And your body is deeply intelligent. If you take one thing from this section, then please take this and place it somewhere deep inside your heart where you won't forget it: alongside the histories of trauma carried by all of our bodies runs an equally powerful current of resilience, of empowerment, of hope.

SOME WAYS TO WORK WITH DISSOCIATION

If you find yourself regularly feeling disconnected from your body or reality, even feeling frozen, these are some ways to help you come back into your body. For all the suggestions below, it will help if you do them in a place where you feel safe, supported, grounded. Many clients I work with feel grounded when in nature. Some clients like to hold or smell objects that help them feel safe – a toy, a blanket, an old jumper, a crystal, an essential oil.

NB: there are many different techniques out there and everyone is different, so find something that works for you. If you do have a strong trauma response, or you really struggle to connect with your body, you may need to seek professional help.

1. **Befriend your freeze response.** If the part of you that shuts down and dissociates was a character or a symbol, what would it look like? Draw it if you like. Try doing it with your non-dominant hand, as this can help you connect with memories held in the body. Ask it: what are you protecting me from? Usually, it is from a memory or emotion that at one point felt potentially overwhelming. Find a way to accept this part of you. Thank it for protecting you.

2. **The 4-7-8 breath.** Breathe in through your nose for four seconds, hold your breath for seven seconds, breathe out through your mouth for eight seconds. And repeat. Four times is the minimum to notice some benefit. This breathing technique activates the parasympathetic nervous system, the part of us that comes online when we feel safe.

3. **Shake and move.** Because dissociation is the freeze response, moving any part of your body can shift you out of this state. Tap your fingers in a gentle drumbeat on different parts of your body. Wiggle your toes. There is growing research that yoga can help with trauma healing, too. Moving with others is even better: social connection is key here. Dancing and shaking your body can really help. If you are open to it, look for a Five Rhythms or Movement Medicine class – movement classes designed to help release trauma from the body.

Sail away into fantasy

You've likely read the classic children's book *Where the Wild Things Are* (possibly many times!). The boy, Max, dressed in a wolf costume, causes havoc around his house, so is sent to bed without supper. Stuck in his room, Max watches as the walls of his bedroom become thick, lush forest. He gets on a boat and sails to the fantasy land of the Wild Things, where big, scary-looking monsters live. Max discovers he can use tricks, like staring them in the eyes, to submit them to his power. And so he becomes the king of the Wild Things. Then, after a wild rumpus, he eventually gets bored of this world and sails back home to find his supper waiting for him in his room, and it is still warm.

Our ability to fantasise allows us to sail away to new lands, especially when times are tough. We can see how Max might have wanted to sail away from painful feelings, to reassert a sense of control in a situation where he felt powerless. Fantasy can be understood as a mild form of dissociation. It allows us to have our desires met in our imaginations when it's difficult or impossible to have them met in the real world.

In the twenty-first century, there are so many options for us to escape painful reality and live vicariously in virtual worlds. There is porn, 'reality' TV, gaming. While games can give young people a sense of agency and autonomy, it's a problem if this is the only place they experience these things. And sometimes we can get stuck in fantasy land and never come home, especially if home or the body feel too painful to return to. Where do you find yourself getting stuck in fantasy?

Darius, a client who was married, became stuck in imagining a sexual relationship with a work colleague. Nothing concrete ever happened and it wasn't clear if the colleague felt anything at all for Darius. But Darius' fantasy meant he didn't face the very real problems in his marriage. I helped him to accept the need to face uncomfortable truths about how he was showing up in his relationship. Our fantasies tend to have common features and deep roots. One of the most enduring fantasies is that of immortality. *The Epic of Gilgamesh* is one of the oldest recorded stories ever found and it is essentially a story about the eponymous hero's quest for immortality. And this age-old fantasy lives on today. Google recently pumped millions of dollars into an immortality project called Calico whose stated mission is to 'solve death'. In fact, a number of the Silicon Valley elites are investing heavily in immortality, using money they earn by extracting our attention away from our bodies.

Why does this fantasy have such deep roots? Because one of our deepest fears is the fear of death. That this body will ultimately return to maggot-ridden dust is a deeply uncomfortable truth – it terrifies us. We can find this fear in our bodies. I can feel it right now – it feels like a scrunched up, hunched up kind of sadness across my face and shoulders. Can you feel it in your body too? Let this fear know it's OK for it to be there. (If you want to explore the fear of death more deeply, you can find an audio course on this topic on my website.)

Here we have arrived at the deepest root of our disembodiment: it's hard to accept that our bodies and our lives come with real limitations.

Attention! Your body needs you

I have a confession. While researching this chapter, I got lost in my head, just as I did once in the Welsh library. Google is a blessing and a curse, a dusty library on steroids

This is where I am, 20 years after my jolt forced me to ask, 'What is real?' It set me on a course I am extremely grateful for, to learn to live more in my body, to trust its wisdom and to help others do the same. But still, I find myself pulled into virtual reality on a daily basis. It's really hard to stay in your body. But it's so important. If we want our children to find a loving home in their own bodies, then we really do need to tend to the roots of our disembodiment. If we don't inhabit our bodies then, as Jung said, we end up living like 'a pressed flower in the pages of a book, a mere memory of yourself'.

So, I invite you now to pay some more loving attention to your body. Take a moment to marvel at it. Look at your fingers. Five on each hand. Move those fingers around. Bend them. Stretch them. How amazing are your fingers? They have allowed you to stroke, to type, to dance, to stitch, to write, to pick your nose, to draw, to strum, to tickle.

Now take your hand and find a place in your body that you sometimes don't like or feel insecure about. Touch it tenderly.

Now see if you can find an energy inside you that doesn't want to be in your body, the part of you that sometimes wants to just sail away on a boat to a magical island where you are king or queen. Bring your loving touch to that part of you. Often, I find this energy trapped in my head. Touch this energy, stroke it with great love. Let this touch remind you of how hard it can feel to be in a sensing, feeling body, especially when this body has so many limitations and when there is so much suffering in the world that is hard to digest. Perhaps as you reflect on this you, like me, can feel a warm, sad, tender feeling in your heart.

Now place your fingers tenderly on the centre of your chest, your heart. Let this touch awaken a long-forgotten memory that this heart, this body is your home.

Now imagine standing before you are anything and anyone who has conditioned you and your ancestors to lose contact with the wisdom of your body. Take your middle

finger, turn it around and give them the bird. See how powerful your fingers are!

While the roots of our desire to escape our bodies run deep,
we must remember that our bodies, along with all their limitations, are our home. Your job is to make this home feel safe
for yourself and for your children.

5

FRUIT TWO: BODIES IN NATURE

How we can set our wild bodies free

Sometimes Kit would look at the veins in his own hands and think, All these little rivers flowing through my body, keeping me alive. Thank you, little rivers. Thank you

– David Arnold, *The Electric Kingdom*

Bogies. Farts. Burps. Wee. Poo. Willies. Vaginas. Bottoms. Just a few things about the body that kids naturally love. Do you remember the thrill of pulling a moonie? Have you seen the joy on a child's face when they tell yet another joke about 'pumps' or 'poo-poo'?

As children, we are fascinated by bodies, we enjoy exploring them, the things that are in them, on them and the things that come out of them. Then, at some point, we develop shame. We begin to dislike parts of our body. We begin to want to cover up or even radically change parts of their body. While some level of shame is certainly normal, our children are growing up in a world where they are falling madly out of love with their bodies from ever earlier ages, as these figures show:

- 24 per cent of childcare professionals have seen body confidence issues in children aged three to five. By the age of six to ten, this figure almost doubles.

- 42 per cent of girls wish to be thinner by the time they reach Year 4.

- Dr Jacqueline Harding, PACEY advisor and child development expert, comments: 'By the age of three or four, some children have already pretty much begun to make up their minds (and even hold strong views) about how bodies should look. There is also research evidence to suggest that some four-year-olds are aware of strategies as to how to lose weight.'

- And for our teenagers, the drive to change their bodies is becoming more aggressive: in 2020, in the UK, 41,000 cosmetic treatments such as botox and lip filler were given to under 18s. TV shows such as *Meet the Kardashians* and *Love Island* have been blamed for teens seeking 'tweakments'.

- A 2019 US study found 22 per cent of 18–24-year-old men reported muscle dysmorphia, a compulsive drive to get bigger muscles.

We might think it's vanity that drives these body changes but it's not. It's self-loathing. Because the way we feel about our bodies is the way we feel about ourselves. A rise in self-loathing is the painful truth behind these statistics.

And the antidote to self-loathing? Acceptance. Hidden inside the bulging biceps and the lip filler is a deep, painful, unmet longing for acceptance. This is the key: we really need to help our children feel accepted, so they can fall back in love with their bodies.

How does body shame begin?

Shame is the feeling that there is a part of us – our bottoms, our bogies, our bellies – we need to cover up from the world. Think of our biblical origin story: Adam and Eve lived in paradise, at one with their bodies and with nature. Then they got kicked out of Eden for being a bit too curious and were told to cover up their nakedness. This story is on one level about the origin of shame, about how we came to be ashamed of our naughty bits, of our wild side and our instinctual nature.

There is nothing wrong with shame, per se. We all have it. A healthy level of shame helps us to fit in, to belong. Sticking out too much from the tribe was, in our evolutionary past, so risky – you might let the sabre-toothed tiger know where you're hiding – that we evolved a deep, powerful emotion to keep us aligned to the group. If we were too exposed there was a risk of death, which is why we use words like 'mortified' or 'mortally embarrassed' ('mort' meaning 'death'). And when we feel the full force of shame we might want the earth to swallow us up.

We humans are a social animal – our survival depends on other people. So shame is a deeply social emotion – we don't mind picking our nose or doing a wee in the bushes, so long as no one else is looking. Shame develops in children when they become more self-conscious about other people's judgements.

Of course, there is a spectrum of shame, from mild embarrassment to toxic shame. If you have a small child, their embarrassment will probably be obvious to see. They might cover themselves up, blush, hide their face, hug onto your leg. But at some point, we learn to cover up our signs of shame. We may still blush but we don't want people to see it. We fear being judged for our shame, like it's a weakness. And so we develop shame about our shame.

That is why shame can be such a slippery emotion. I have tried many times to track the feeling of shame in myself and with my clients. As quickly as it arises, it slips back underground. But we don't need to be ashamed of our shame. Shame is normal. It helps us keep our wild side in check. And anyway, what would a human society look like without shame? Everyone naked, shitting wherever they liked, not giving a shit about anyone else!

How does shame turn toxic?

Here's a rhetorical question for you: have you ever scrolled through a social media page and felt inadequate?

Thought so.

Now imagine being a young person on social media, exposed to hundreds of images a day, mostly of faces and bodies. These images are guaranteed to leave them feeling inadequate. And this pain of inadequacy drives them to desire a different body, so that their body will 'belong' in the imaginary tribe they align to. Depending on the latest trends, they might think they should be smaller, smoother, more muscular, curvier, skinnier, have bigger lips, bigger boobs, a bigger bum. And their body fantasies can now become a reality – through a voracious market of diets, steroids, exercise regimes, nips and tucks.

Where shame was once an emotion that kept us safe, delivered through the critical gaze of a small number of people in our tribe, we are now exposed to the critical gaze of the whole world. Our children feel that they need to contort their bodies and selves to fit into a straitjacket that is constantly shape-shifting. It's exhausting, and really bad for their mental health.

This is how healthy shame can turn into toxic shame. Toxic shame is the intense, painful feeling that there is something fundamentally bad or wrong or broken about us. Toxic shame is becoming normalised in a world where our kids have endless opportunities to compare their private selves to people's public selves. This shame pulls our kids away from a more beautiful world where they can inhabit and enjoy their amazing bodies.

Sadly, and unsurprisingly, I am seeing ever more children with body-related issues. A girl, aged nine, was exercising obsessively. A boy aged 11 was picking his skin until it bled. A girl aged 13 would only share filtered images of herself on social media because she hated her body. She developed acute social anxiety about being seen in real life.

Our bodies are where we feel we can re-establish some sense of control when the world inside us and around us feels out of control. This is one reason why we are seeing so many young people turn to self-harm these days. Self-harm can give a young person a sense of control and can help them feel their suffering is real. Where shame is an invisible pain that forces us to hide parts of our bodies and our selves, a cut on the leg or bruise on the arm makes the pain visible, real.

Carl Jung described shame as a 'soul-eating emotion'. I would add that shame can become a soul-and-body-eating emotion. Healthy child development means that the child's soul (or you can say 'mind' if you prefer) feels at home in the body.

So what's the antidote to shame?

Acceptance.

The more we can help our children to accept themselves, the less shame they will feel and the more at home they will feel in their bodies. It's particularly important to help them understand their shame as a normal part of being human. We can teach them about shame, how it shows up in our bodies, how it makes us want to fit in. And with this acceptance, this loving awareness, they can feel less driven to cover up or radically alter parts of themselves and more empowered to love themselves. If I want to help my daughter feel safe in this mad world, I need to help her feel safe in her body, to remember that her body is her home.

So where do we begin? Well, as always, it begins with us.

LET THE SOFT ANIMAL OF OUR BODY LOVE WHAT IT LOVES

In her beautiful poem 'Wild Geese', Mary Oliver says:

> *You do not have to be good.*
> *You do not have to walk on your knees*
> *for a hundred miles through the desert repenting.*
> *You only have to let the soft animal of your body*
> *love what it loves.*

Can you think of areas or times in your life where you don't give yourself or your children permission to let the soft animal of your bodies love what they love? Can you imagine giving that soft animal just a little bit more permission? What are some simple pleasures you could let yourself or your children enjoy tonight, tomorrow, in the next week? It might be having a really lazy day at home, taking extra time in the shower or bath, having a really good stretch (as opposed to a rigid yoga routine) like dogs and cats do. Give it a try. You might well like it!

Rediscovering a home in the body – a guide

*What is the body? That shadow of a shadow of
your love, that somehow contains the entire
universe* – Rumi

Your body is amazing. Not the six-pack or thigh-gap type of amazing. Across millions of years of evolution and through billions of tiny experiments your body has developed an exquisite wisdom. This bodily wisdom is constantly speaking to you, if only you would listen. It's like having a 24/7 therapist or guru. When you smell off milk, your guru says, 'Don't drink it, it will make you ill.' You didn't need a sell-by date to tell you that. When your eczema plays up again, or that nagging pain in your stomach, it might be your body telling you that you are stressed. As famous trauma therapist Bessel Van Der Kolk says, *your body knows the score.*

In this mind-over-matter culture, we tend to override our bodies. If we feel tired or ill we try to push on through. If an energetic child can't sit still at school, we may give them pills so they can override their body and focus their minds. We need to help our children listen to the wisdom of their bodies.

To help your child have a loving relationship with their body, you need to create a loving field of awareness in which shame can be met and metabolised and a deeper appreciation of our incredible bodies can be cultivated. Remember, where there is no judgement, there is no shame. Acceptance is key. It can help to remember a time when you felt totally at ease in someone's presence, when you didn't need to look down or away because you felt safe, accepted for who you are. For some people, this feeling may arise when with a pet.

Below is a rough guide to the development of shame in

children and how you can help them keep a loving connection to their bodies at each stage. Feel free to skip to the relevant section for your child.

Pre school

Shame comes into view when a child begins to be curious about their own bodies, especially their genitals. At some point, our children will naturally start to explore these. It's important we don't shame them for this. It's natural, normal and healthy, not 'dirty', to explore what feels nice and what doesn't. When children are told touching themselves is 'dirty', this can create shame, disgust and sexual hang-ups that can last a lifetime. What we can be clear about is that playing with their genitals in public is not OK. And we can tell them there are private parts – mouth, breasts, genitals and bum – that no one is allowed to see or touch without their permission.

School

When our children go to school, they begin to compare their bodies to other bodies. At this point, we will need to help our children to keep coming back home to their bodies. In an age of constant social comparison and virtual reality, the pressure to fit in starts early and is greater than it has ever been before.

If your child begins to dislike a part of their body, don't just tell them how beautiful it is. Think about how you feel about your own body. Do you have parts of your body you don't like? Children learn way more from your body language and your behaviours than from your words. Do they see you enjoying food, enjoying your body? Or do they see you controlling your food or your body?

Your child will feel less shame if they know they are not alone in disliking part of their body. Depending on the child's age, you could make cultivating body appreciation into a game to play together.

- See if you can both find parts of your own body that you can appreciate. It can be as small as an ear, an eyebrow or a toenail. Can you be curious together about why this body part even exists? Eyebrows, for example, evolved to help keep rain and sweat out of our eyes. They also help us to communicate our feelings. Eyebrows are amazing!

- A second stage is to look for parts of the body that are neutral, parts of the body you neither love nor hate. Can you find a way to appreciate even the neutral parts? It could just be thanking the neutral part for being there and doing whatever it does.

- For the final stage, you can both look for parts of your body that you don't like. Remember from the previous chapter, a root cause for our disembodiment is that our bodies come with limitations that can be hard to accept. Be curious together about the feeling of shame that arises in the body when you look at these parts. What is the inner voice saying about this part? What judgements or ridicule is your brain predicting you will receive about this part of the body? Write these judgements down or draw a picture of your inner critic. Reflect on where these judgments came from, and how these judgments represent only a very narrow, limiting perspective on what is acceptable, or beautiful. Such reflections can stop the judgements wielding so much power over you.

- Finally, can you find a way to send some gratitude or even love to these body parts? You may not find this easy (because it's not!) but in an age of toxic shame, it's really important to practise. Perhaps reading these words from Ram Dass about trees might help you and your children appreciate that body part:

'When you go out into the woods, and you look at trees, you see all these different trees. And some of them are bent, and some of them are straight, and some of them are evergreens, and some of them are whatever. And you look at the tree and you allow it. You see why it is the way it is. You sort of understand that it didn't get enough light, and so it turned that way. And you don't get all emotional about it. You just allow it. You appreciate the tree.'

Social media

When our children begin to use social media (hopefully not until they are teenagers), shame around the body gets magnified. As I write, a whistleblower from Facebook has just revealed internal research showing that time on Instagram makes body issues worse for one in three teen girls. Facebook hid this research, just as the tobacco industry hid research on the cancerous nature of their products for years.

There is a wonderful movement now towards body positivity on social media, which I celebrate. But I have seen with my clients how shame still lurks here. I've worked with teenage girls who began posting no-make-up selfies and unfiltered pictures of their imperfect bodies. But they still felt shame that they weren't being quite body-positive enough, or weren't getting enough likes for their body-positive posts. Our job as parents is to help our kids disconnect from that online world every day and find ways to come back into their bodies.

The most important thing we can do is to give them a safe and non-judgemental space to talk about their relationship to their bodies and how social media might be affecting that relationship. You can use simple questions to gently guide children or teenagers back into their bodies. For example, 'What do you notice in your body when you do that?' or 'What is your body telling you in this moment?'

Of course, some teenagers will be more up for this kind of conversation than others. Ultimately, you need to think about social media as a potential harm. You might let your 15-year-old have a glass of wine but you wouldn't let them sit in their bedroom drinking vodka all night. Strong boundaries are essential but every family is different.

ERICA: SHAME IN THE BODY

'It's taken me three years to find the courage to write this email . . .'

Thus began my first email from Erica. There was only one other sentence in that email, explaining that she was looking for therapy. It would take six months before I even met her. She would email to arrange a time, then she would go quiet. I'd follow up. She would send an email a few weeks later apologising for how bad she was and ask, 'Can we try again please?' Normally, I would have given up after a couple of rounds of this. But that first email's opening line kept the door of my heart ajar.

When Erica finally arrived for our first session, she was one minute late, frantic, and couldn't stop apologising: 'I'm so sorry I'm late. I'm so sorry I'm late.' I told her not to worry, that I was glad she had finally made it. She came into the room and sat down right on the edge of the couch. She couldn't have been any more on the edge without falling off. It was as though she was giving herself the option to run out at any moment. For most of the session, she looked either at the floor or her hands, her thick, dark brown hair covering most of her face. I found myself mirroring her, sitting on the edge of my chair and turning my body so I wasn't directly facing her.

Erica told me a bit about her life, how she had grown up in a small fishing village about an hour outside of Naples, how her parents had separated when she was seven years old, how her dad had moved to Rome and she lived with her mum and her older sister

Our conversation went around some safe houses for most of that first session. It was only right at the end that she said: 'There is something I want to say but I've never said it to anyone and I just don't know if I can say it to you.' I reassured Erica that there was no rush. And I meant it.

It took ten sessions before Erica felt safe enough to tell me that when she was 17, she had been raped by a man from her village. As she told me the story her body contorted, each word emerging from an epic embodied struggle between the part of her wanting to cover up her shame and the part of her wanting to be witnessed. I kept reassuring her that she could take her time. She told me that one winter's evening she had gone out to the local shop to buy some groceries. As she returned, a man with a knife jumped in front of her, dragged her to a dark and secluded part of the beach and raped her. No one heard her screams. Both during and after the event, the man said to her that if she ever told anyone about this, he would find her and kill her.

In the months that followed, this dark secret smouldering inside her, Erica's body revolted. She would wake up in the night, often after a trauma nightmare, and gorge on sweet foods until she was ready to burst. And then she would make herself sick. If she noticed her naked body in the mirror as she dressed, she would dig her nails into her skin until she bled. And then she developed a stomach condition, ulcerative colitis. It was as if Erica's shame was metastasising in her body.

Now that Erica had finally felt safe enough to share this secret that felt so shameful, we were able to begin the healing process. Because so many of her symptoms were related to her body, I decided to focus on the body. Working with the trauma of rape is complex but the body is understandably a critical element of the work.

Each session, I gently encouraged her to see if there was a part of her body that she could find a way to accept. We began by looking for 'neutral' sensations in the body, like the feeling of her feet planted to the ground. Other body sensations, especially sexual ones, had too much fear, shame and disgust around them for her to bear. During this process, we created a field of loving awareness around her body so that the toxic shame had permission to leave. The work felt like a deep exorcism. I could see how painful it was for Erica and I felt a deep respect for her courage, her willingness to heal her trauma and rediscover the home that is her body. As Erica was gradually able to reduce the shame in her body, her bulimia began to subside too.

After a few months working together, Erica met a boy at college. And slowly, she found she was able to let her body feel safe and be in 'skinship' with another caring body. Shortly after, our work ended.

I hope and pray that the children in your care never experience what Erica did. But I am seeing in my clinical work a rise in toxic shame, even without any precipitating trauma. Our culture violently intrudes into our children's minds and bodies, leaving them wanting to escape from or harm or radically alter that one place (their body) that should feel like home. Which is why helping our children feel less shame and more acceptance of their bodies is so critical in these times.

MY BODY IS MY HOME

This meditation exercise will help you and your child tune into your bodies and create loving awareness there, especially if there are parts that feel difficult to turn towards.

Begin with where you are right now. This is the key to dissolving shame. If you come preloaded with a judgement about what should or should not happen, you are already bringing shame in. So, begin by noticing what is going on in your mind. Is it busy or quiet or somewhere in between? Whatever you notice, just allow it to be exactly as it is. Let go of any part of you that wants to fix things or judge things, or says that some part of your experience shouldn't be there.

Now bring the same loving attention into your body. How does your body feel in this moment? Again, whatever you notice, simply allow it to be.

Now see if there is any tension or stress anywhere in your body. Imagine that place in your body is a small, frightened animal and you are David Attenborough, quietly observing that animal without scaring it off. What does the energy feel like in your body? For me, I'm noticing my heart beating in my chest, a slight sense of constriction in my throat, and an ever-so-slightly sick feeling in my stomach. I have one hand on my chest and one hand on my belly. I'm letting the feelings know it's OK for them to be there.

Whatever is present in your body, use your loving touch – your own 'skinship' – to welcome these sensations. And use your breath to breathe into parts of your body that might feel tense or scared. As you do this, try saying '*my body is my home*'. Notice what it feels like as you breathe this energy in. It might help to look for a place in your body that does feel like home. It could be anywhere – forehead to feet. *My body is my home.*

Rewilding our selves

Now we have found our way back into our bodies, it's time to bring ourselves and our children back to the garden, back into nature.

The other day after nursery, Rose and I went for a walk in the woods. It had been a stressful day. I'd been glued to my computer screen for hours, flicking from one task to another, my head full of work problems. I was not in the mood to play. If you're a parent, I'm sure you've felt the same thing too, distracted from your child by the to-do list in your head.

Rose found some branches on the ground and asked, 'Will you play sticks with me, Daddy? Daddy, this is mummy stick, this is daddy stick and this is baby stick. Here, you can be baby stick.'

I tried to be present with her but my attention kept seesawing. Thoughts of work kept on buzzing into my mind like annoying flies. I swatted them away but soon enough they were back. I knew I should fully commit to being with Rose, commit to being in my body and being in the moment with her (I talk about the importance of this all the time). And I knew that all those things I was worrying about and carrying in my mind were Not Important, compared to this moment.

Eventually, I managed to wrestle my mind away from those annoying flies in my mind to being present with Rose and her family of sticks. Rose pulled up a piece of bark from the ground and, with great joy, showed me the industrious community of woodlice living underneath it. She smelled a red campion flower. I suggested that she gently hold the stem and notice what it feels like in her body as she touched it. She asked to pick the flower and I told her we must always ask the flower if it's OK to be picked. And then if we feel like the flower says yes, we thank it.

When we left an hour later to get some tea, I noticed how much better I felt, how much more peaceful, connected to my body, to Mother Earth and to Rose, too.

Our bodies in nature

It's no coincidence that our bodies feel better when we spend time in nature. Nature doesn't judge us. And our bodies are not separate to nature – they are nature. Our bodies evolved to expect trees and birds and soil and worms. When we aren't exposed to these things, our minds and bodies rebel.

I'm sure you know this already but the research is solid – being in nature is seriously good for our mental health, better than most medications and, dare I say it, therapies. A lot of the best studies on this have come from Japan and South Korea, where *shinrin-yoku*, which translates as 'forest bathing', has been used since the 1990s as a treatment for psychological and physical wellbeing. Studies have shown that spending time in a forest can reduce levels of the stress hormone cortisol, depressive symptoms and feelings of hostility as well as bringing down blood pressure and improving sleep quality. The global Association of Nature and Forest Therapy Guides has a simple slogan: 'The forest is the therapist.'

Mother Nature has specific effects – in a 2019 US study, a 20-minute walk in a park improved children's ADHD symptoms as effectively as taking a dose of prescription stimulant medication. And she has general effects too – a 2015 UK study even showed that more exposure to nature led to more community feeling and lower crime rates.

It's amazing; no pill or policy could ever achieve these effects.

So how much time is enough? A 2019 study from the

University of Exeter of 20,000 people showed a clear number: people who spent 120 minutes a week or more in nature reported much higher levels of wellbeing. It didn't matter if it was a park or a forest, if it was all in one go or spaced out over the week. The result held no matter the age, ethnic group, or occupation. That's 20 minutes a day or two hours on a Sunday. That feels doable, doesn't it?

GROUNDING

When you've spent a day at a screen or in a classroom, grounding is a fast and simple way to connect back to your body and nature. Research shows a variety of benefits, including feeling less stressed and reduced inflammation. Grounding can be done in a garden or a local park – in fact, anywhere there's earth. You and your child simply take off your socks and shoes and feel your feet (or any part of your skin) on the ground. Your kids may, like mine, already know this – as soon as they're in the park, they want to take their shoes off. Their bodies know what they need. Their bodies know the score.

Respect Mother Nature

While spending time in nature is vital for our children's mental health, there is a deeper truth about our bodies in nature that we need to teach our children: Mother Nature is alive and intelligent and we need to treat her with respect.

In our culture, we have tended to treat the natural world as an object that we use for our own purposes – trees exist to give us paper, fuel and cheap therapy; animals exist to give us food or company. We treat our bodies in a similar way. But many indigenous cultures have a different relationship to the natural world, one in which they show deep respect to plants, trees, animals and even the mineral kingdom. This respectful relationship to nature is contained in a worldview we call 'animism', a belief system that sees nature and all its creatures as holding an essence or spirit, a gift or a unique story offered into the world. Inuit people, for example, always take time to thank the soul of the animal they've hunted for offering itself up to them. And when Maori tribespeople are digging up sweet potatoes, they will always say their thanks and blessings (*karakia*) to the spirit of the potato. Such practices may feel strange to us in the West but we talk to our houseplants and to our pets, and have even more intimate relationships with our devices. 'Hello Alexa!'

Fortunately, science is now providing our rational minds with evidence that plants, trees and animals are intelligent in their own way, and that they communicate and co-operate with each other. Trees, for example, communicate through their roots and mycelial networks, sending life-saving nutrients to other trees. Jeremy Lent calls this the original AI – animate intelligence.

I love the work of scientist Robin Wall Kimmerer, whose book *Braiding Sweetgrass* weaves biology with a deep indigenous perspective. In that book, she writes: 'This is really why I made my daughters learn to garden – so they would always have a mother to love them, long after I am gone.' If we can help our children build a respectful relationship with Mother Nature, they will feel less alone.

In fact, our children are natural born animists. They arrive into this world with a taste for the wilderness and a deep affinity to nature, what the great biologist E O Wilson called *biophilia*. It is our job to help them deepen that connection. When Rose was playing in the woods, she pretended the sticks were alive. My job is to show her how to relate to the aliveness of nature – to the red campion flower for example – with reverence and respect.

Healing our relationship with nature is also essential for our children's future. Research shows that positive environmental attitudes come from positive time spent in nature and from a shared understanding that a child is part of nature – that the world's body is our body. Sir David Attenborough summed this up nicely: 'No one will protect what they don't care about; and no one will care about what they have never experienced.'

So, it's not only our job as grown-ups to help our children inhabit their bodies but to help them create this embodied relationship to Mother Earth.

A GRATITUDE PRAYER FROM THE NATIVE AMERICAN HAUDENOSAUNEE PEOPLE

We are all thankful to our Mother, the Earth, for she gives us all that we need for life. She supports our feet as we walk about upon her. It gives us joy that she continues to care for us as she has from the beginning of time. To our Mother, we send greetings and thanks.
Now our minds are one.

6

ROOT THREE: NARCISSISM

How we want to be special (but end up feeling lonely and unloved)

I wanna be adored

– The Stone Roses

I'm on holiday in southern Spain and as the sun is setting one evening I go for a walk along the shoreline. I see Spanish families dotted along the beach, parents sitting on their portable reclining chairs drinking wine and eating crisps, and children playing in the soggy sand with their buckets and spades. I smile as I think to myself: 'Life doesn't get any better than this. Kids playing in nature. Everyone living a simple life, free from the worries of the world.'

Then I see something that broadens my smile. Ahead of me there's a girl, aged around nine, shaking her arms, her head and her hips in a freestyle dance. 'How delightful,' I think, 'this girl is just following her own groove, dancing on the beach like no one is watching.' I walk closer. I notice the girl is looking at something on the rock. I get closer still and I see what she's looking at. You've probably already guessed it: a mobile phone, in selfie mode.

Narcissus is 'winning'!

I'm sure you've already read many articles about how our young people are becoming ever more narcissistic. 'Generation Me', as psychologist Jean Twenge calls it, are apparently more entitled and more obsessed than ever with image than previous generations. And there is some good research to back up this claim.

It has become normal for us to make our most precious or private moments into posts that could get us likes from an impersonal and potentially infinite audience. And our children are growing up in this mad world where the possibility of being centre stage is open to all, where 'influence' or celebrity is dangled in front of us like a grotesque, golden carrot.

The word 'narcissist' comes from the ancient Greek myth of Narcissus. He was a handsome boy who fell in love with his own reflection and got sent to the underworld. Now, let's imagine that after 21 centuries, Narcissus gets a pass out from Hades to come and visit us in today's world.

He is pretty pleased that people are using his name so much. He sees it's even an official psychiatric diagnosis – narcissistic personality disorder (NPD). 'Winning!' he thinks, 'I got really famous.' He grabs a copy of the newspaper and reads that rates of NPD are increasing in the UK and the US. And that in the US, rates are nearly three times as high for those in their twenties as for the over sixty-fives. 'I'm seriously trending with the millennials,' he thinks.

He buys a selfie stick and goes to visit the ancient ruins of Greece, where he grew up. There he takes loads of stunning pictures of himself, masterfully using the stick to get his best angle. He immediately uploads these selfies to Instagram, uses a filter to make his pecs look bigger and, in less than ten minutes, he gets 10,000 likes. He's living the dream.

But one morning, Narcissus wakes up with bad hair, bad

breath and a volcanic pustule on his nose. He feels totally deflated: the bubble has burst. He looks again at his reflection (aka his Instagram posts) and the stunning image he sees there does not match how he feels inside. Inside, he feels deeply alone. So he decides to close the curtains and stay indoors, to spend the day looking at other people's reflections. They all seem so much happier and prettier and more buff and more popular than him.

Eventually, Narcissus decides he is going to fix himself. He buys some make up to disguise the pustule. He visits the GP and gets some happy pills. And he goes to the gym to pump up his pecs. This works for a short while. His posts are getting more likes. He is winning again.

But one day, he collapses from exhaustion. He just can't keep up this pretence anymore. He gets a bottle of paracetamol and . . .

OK, OK, so I know this feels a bit dystopian. But in the earliest versions of the Narcissus myth, he does end up killing himself.

You see, for thousands of years humans have recognised the dark side of self-love. Like a cancerous tongue on the side of a packet of cigarettes, this myth contains a serious health warning. And it reads: *Being obsessed with your own self-image seriously harms you and others around you.*

Understanding narcissism

I hear people use the word narcissist or 'narc' all the time to describe a self-obsessed friend, their boss, their nightmare ex-partner. It's become a popular term for someone who's fixated on themselves. Psychiatrist Gillian Russell gives a helpful definition of narcissism as 'self-adoration with an aloofness that denies a need for another person.' And there is a scale psychologists use to measure levels of narcissism called the narcissistic personality inventory. Statements on the scale include things like:

'I have a natural talent for influencing people.'

'If I ruled the world, it would be a better place.'

'I think I am a special person.'

'I want to amount to something in the eyes of the world.'

'I can live my life in any way I want to.'

'I wish somebody would someday write my biography.'

I just took the test online. I scored 15 out of 40. Apparently, I'm only slightly more narcissistic than the average. I'll take that. But I wonder what my score would be if I'd grown up with a smartphone?

People who score more highly on the narcissism test tend to have unrealistic expectations about the future, are more likely to become angry when threatened, take more resources for themselves and leave less for others, and value money, fame and image over family, helping others and community. You can begin to see here the broader ways in which too much narcissism is bad for our world.

Narcissism lies on a spectrum. At the top end, there are the most pathological forms of narcissism; think *American Psycho* or *Zoolander* – 'I'm pretty sure there's a lot more to life than being really, really good looking. And I plan on finding out what that is.' Pathological narcissism often begins as a mask to cover up vulnerability. For these people, there is usually significant trauma or difficulty in their early childhood. They may be diagnosed with narcissistic personality disorder.

Around the middle, there is healthy narcissism, a positive sense of self that is in alignment with the greater good (more on this shortly).

Then at the other end, there is echoism, named after the nymph Echo, who in the myth has no voice of her own and can only repeat what Narcissus says. Echoism is the personality type that is so self-conscious about being seen, so afraid of appearing narcissistic that they keep putting themselves down until they lose their own voice. Echoists will often team up with more narcissistic characters. Like the drama triangle where Rescuers need Victims, echoists needs narcissists and narcissists need echoists

Echoists can be just as self-absorbed as narcissists. But in their case, they're lost in loops of self-criticism. Again, there is often trauma here. The great Scottish psychiatrist R D Laing captured echoism perfectly in his classic book *The Divided Self*: 'In a world full of danger, to be a potentially seeable object is to be constantly exposed to danger.'

In my work with children and families, I see both ends of the spectrum. At one end are children who struggle to adapt to the real world because they have grown up with an expectation that the world will revolve around them. In these cases, the parents are often like Echo. Then there are those children whose parents are so focused on their own success that they don't give their children the loving attention they need – here the children become like Echo.

Whatever you have diagnosed yourself with by this point (and we all love a little self-diagnosis), please know that there is no judgement here, only love. It's time to tend to those deep, dark roots.

In praise of self-love

I grew up in Manchester in the 1980s when the Stone Roses were bringing their melodic, searing, bittersweet sounds to the world. One of their most famous songs is called 'I Wanna Be Adored'. Really, we all do. Who hasn't in some fleeting moment had a passing thought of playing the headline act at Glastonbury and crowd-diving into a sea of millions of adoring fans? Oh, is that just me?! What's your secret fantasy of being adored? Come on Echo, I know you have one.

Children tend to have little shame about their narcissism. If you have a child under the age of around eight, you may have noticed how competitive and boastful they can be. They might demand your attention when they do a somersault, a new dance move, or complete that 20-piece jigsaw. When Rose rides her scooter down the ramp in our local playground, she sticks one leg up in the air and shouts 'Look at me! Look at me!' You could call this showing off but it's normal, healthy narcissism.

Why do we need narcissism? Well, a child needs to develop a sense of themselves as a separate being who has a will, who can master skills and who can command the attention and validation they need from the world around them. When a child gets enough consistent loving attention, they grow to believe that they are an important and valuable person. And they are more likely to get through life's challenges intact. This is healthy narcissism.

So how does our innocent need for love get so distorted, so lost in the forest? And what can we do to protect our children from this worrying trend?

I WANT TO BE ADORED

In his beautiful and wise book *Care of the Soul*, Thomas Moore says that 'the healing of narcissism is giving the ego what it needs: pleasure in accomplishment, acceptance, and some degree of recognition.' If we ever find ourselves worrying about narcissism out there in the world or find ourselves diagnosing it in someone we know, it is wise to let these concerns first guide us back inside, towards a more loving acceptance of these traits in ourself.

Can you find the part of you that wants to be seen, recognised, adored? Perhaps you can remember a time when you were younger and loved showing off. If you notice any resistance to this idea, or struggle to find this part, perhaps you can acknowledge that your inner Echo may be present now.

What comes up for you when you say hello to this part of you that wants to be adored? Perhaps a tenderness for yourself. Perhaps a sadness that these parts haven't received the love they need. How cruel it is to want to be adored and yet to never be able to get the reverence we so desire.

Take a moment to think about the ways in which you might not have received the right kind of attention growing up. Maybe you were the Echo, your parents so caught up in their own self-image. Or maybe your parents projected their disowned narcissism into you, telling you that you were special, gifted, destined for glory. In this moment, see if there is a sense of grief in your body, a place that carries that wound. Just place a loving hand on whatever feelings are coming up for you in your body. Let those feelings know it's OK for them to be there.

Now, take a moment to reflect on how our mad world hijacks our desire to be adored, makes us and our children believe we can only be successful if we fall in love with our own reflection. Perhaps you can connect to a sense of anger or grief here. Let these feelings guide you back to the innocent child within you that simply wants to be adored. Now, can you please send that child a little love?

The red spot test

*Why are you unhappy? Because 99.9 percent of
everything you think, and of everything you do, is
for yourself – and there isn't one* – Wu Wei

There's a test scientists use to determine if a creature is self-aware or not. It's called the 'red spot technique' and it was developed in 1970 by a psychologist called Gordon G Gallup. In the test, an animal is put to sleep and an odourless red spot is placed on their forehead. When the animal wakes up, they find a mirror in front of them. If the animal touches or in any way shows recognition of the mark on their forehead, it means they are aware that the creature they see in the mirror is them. Animals that have passed this test include bottlenose dolphins, killer whales, various monkeys, elephants, magpies, some fish – and human beings.

By the age of 18 months, most children in Western cultures recognise their reflection. Rose is four and when her grandma calls her on WhatsApp, she has worked out that if she presses the picture of herself on the phone, her reflection will take up most of the screen. She likes this. And there is an innocence to Rose's curiosity about her own reflection.

At least, that's what I thought, until I learned that the results from the red spot test vary hugely across cultures. In one study from the Cameroonian Nso farming community, only three per cent of infants recognised themselves in the mirror. This doesn't mean these children are less intelligent or psychologically developed. It means that the kind of self-awareness we prioritise and study in our Western culture – the kind where you recognise yourself in the mirror – is not the universal benchmark we once thought it was. Other studies have shown that children who grow up in more interdependent cultures develop a different kind of self-awareness first, one that's based more on relationships with others.

When I came across these studies, it made me wonder: could the roots of our narcissism begin in infancy? Could we be unwittingly conditioning our children from an early age into a specific version of self-awareness, one zoomed in our own reflection? In India, the red dot on the forehead has a completely different meaning. This red dot, known as a *bindi*, is used to signify the underlying unity of everything in the universe. Next time you look in the mirror, imagine there is a red dot on your forehead, just between your two eyes, and see if you can let the boundaries of yourself dissolve a little. After all, it gets lonely in these four walls sometimes, doesn't it?

Attention, special child!

Remember the anthropologist of childhood David Lancy, from whom we learned about those children in indigenous tribes playing with knives? I had a great conversation with him that helped me to really unpick some of the ways in which we might, unwittingly, tip healthy narcissism into unhealthy narcissism. He told me of other cultures where parents do not focus on their children in the same way we tend to in the West. For example, in rural Liberia, Kpelle mothers carry their babies on their back most of the day while they work and socialise but they hardly pay them any attention. Meanwhile, children in Fiji from as young as four are expected to bow very low and avoid eye contact when passing an adult and may get a clip round the ear if they don't show enough respect. In contrast, Lancy calls modern Western cultures 'neontocracies', where we plough so much of our time, energy and resources into our children, leaving parents as Echo and the elderly getting a particularly rough deal (off to the care home for you).

I thought back to Rose's first year. Wherever we went, whether I was pushing her around the reservoir, or walking to Sainsbury's with her in the baby carrier, I'd give her a lot of attention – talking to her, imitating her, making her laugh. I wanted her to feel special. And for sure, this constant interaction felt good, the right thing to do. Rose would respond, laugh a lot, make a whole range of noises, wave to the people we passed. I would see other parents pushing their kids in their buggies, eyes glued to their phones, and I'd feel smug. 'I'm a really good dad,' I'd think to myself.

But when I learned from Lancy about the different type of attention some children got in other cultures, the almost obsessive energy and attention we at times poured into Rose suddenly seemed strange, laughable even. Hearing about these other ways of parenting, I felt as if someone had taken my heavy sack of parental guilt, laid it down by the side of the road and said to me: 'It's OK, Louis. You can focus on you without feeling guilty.'

Now, it's really important to say that the mothers I learned about in other cultures did not completely ignore their children. They were still responsive to them, fed them on demand and kept them in close physical contact ('skinship'). But, importantly, their lives didn't bend to the every whim of their children. This is not to say that some of the popular parenting models in the West, such as attachment parenting, have got it all wrong. If we want our children to develop a secure attachment, we need to be warm and responsive. But there is a clear risk that in spending so much energy on our children, we parents become the Echo to their Narcissus. An article in the *Atlantic*, called 'The Perils of Attachment Parenting', put it like this: 'When parents begin a pattern of meeting their child's every need at the expense of their own, it sticks. It's hard to pop out of that mindset when your six-year-old wants another cup of milk even though you've just sat down for dinner or when your 10-year-old is eager to add yet another activity to his schedule that would require you to drive across town at rush hour.'

Small fishies, very big pond

So why does there seem to be such a marked difference in the type and level of attention we give our children across cultures? We can't just blame 'selfies' or Instagram.

As we saw in earlier chapters, in some cultures, families are bigger and the children are economic assets, working and looking after younger siblings. But in many parts of the world now, birth rates are declining and we are more likely to be in a 'beanpole' family: investing our time and energy into fewer children who are protected as long as possible from the challenges of the world. When you have only one child, the spotlight can shine particularly bright.

The problem with raising children who have too much of a sense of being special is that at some point their sense of specialness comes into contact with the real world. In my primary school, I was really good at swimming. I easily won the breaststroke races. I thought I was the bomb – Michael Phelps in disguise. But then I went to a much bigger secondary school and there was a boy who was miles better than me. Bastard. For a while, that really dented my pride. In my practice, I often see children who've developed quite bad mental health issues after the transition to secondary school. They aren't prepared for becoming a smaller fish in a bigger pond.

Now, let's extend this reality to a very big pond – the world of social media. Here, a child comes into contact with billions of other potentially 'special' people. And this contact reveals a fundamental and painful truth: 99.9 per cent of the time there is no special treatment awaiting them.

A self-image based too much on specialness is fundamentally fragile. We need to prepare our children for a world where the spotlight simply won't be on them all the time. And even when it is, spotlights can burn and blind; pop stars are up to seven times more likely than the general public to commit suicide.

And there is a parallel process for our human species right now. Our sense of specialness is melting beneath the dawning truth of the climate crisis. You may have heard the term 'Anthropocene' – used to describe the geological period during which human beings have had a significant and, in many ways, destructive impact on the Earth. If there is one underlying belief that has been driving the Anthropocene then it is 'human exceptionalism', the belief that we are by far the most important and special creatures on this planet. Some trace this belief back to biblical times and the creation story in the Old Testament in which God made man in his image, giving us dominion over 'every creeping thing that creepeth upon the earth'.

The Anthropocene and narcissism arise from the same untended root: both are about having an exaggerated sense of one's own specialness while ignoring the needs of others, taking more resources for ourselves and valuing image over community. We humans with our big and complex brains are certainly unique. But there is a difference between being unique and being better than.

If you, like me, would like to create a better future for your children, then we need to break out of the spell cast by our own reflection. We can still love all the things that make human beings special – many of which we are exploring in this book, like our capacity for compassion and co-operation. And similarly, we can still love all the things that make our children so special. But for their own sake, we need them to grow up knowing this world will not bend over backwards for them. Meanwhile, we can help them to get their need for attention and validation met in healthy, sustainable ways. And, as always, it begins with us.

TIME TO LOOK IN THE MIRROR

You may feel like you focus too much on your child's needs. Or you may feel you (or your partner) focus too much on yourself. Or you may feel like both are true. I know I do. There is no judgement here. We don't need more guilt. And finding balance is an ongoing process.

If you ever find yourself feeling resentful towards your children, at the end of your tether, it may be time to look in the mirror. Are your own needs being met? Is there one area of your life where you are harbouring resentment because an important need isn't being satisfied? What step could you take to address this? Are you getting enough validation from the people close to you, from work? Be direct – ask people what they appreciate or love about you. How might you let yourself take some time in the spotlight? Give yourself permission to show off a bit more.

On the other hand, if you feel you are spending too much time on your own needs, your own projects, inside your own head, it's also time to look in the mirror. The solution here is to find a regular (ideally weekly) slot where you spend quality focused time with your child(ren), doing something that they really want to do. Let go of your own needs, your own interests, and focus fully on them.

Into the looking glass of loneliness

The myth tells us that Narcissus becomes lonely because the only thing he cared for was his own reflection. His parents kept telling him he was so special and so his sense of self became a fragile bubble that could be popped at any moment. The only place he could sustain this inflated sense of self was on his own, by the pool.

Narcissism and loneliness go hand in hand. The word 'narcissus' is derived from the Greek word *narke*, meaning numbness. If we become too absorbed in our own self-image, if the boundaries between our self an others become more rigid, less permeable, then we grow numb to the outside world. When you think only of yourself – whether it's that world-changing project you've been planning or a dark feeling the world would be better without you – you can't connect to other people.

In the UK, young people now feel more alone than any other age group, including the elderly. (Imagine a topsy-turvy near future where elderly people visit teenagers in their bedrooms, playing bingo with them to help them feel less alone.) And loneliness, it turns out, is a health hazard. In fact, scientists showed recently that it can be as bad for your physical health as smoking 15 cigarettes a day. I'm sure that you would be horrified if you discovered the kids in your care were smoking so many fags.

The reason loneliness is so bad for our health is because we are biologically wired, evolved for connection, for being in community. When we don't get that need met, it triggers a feeling of pain from the part of our brain responsible for our social needs, called the dorsal raphe nucleus (DRN). You might find it helpful to know that the pain of loneliness is a biological reality, a deep, intelligence within that calls you back into connection.

116

JAMES: THE POWER OF CONNECTION

When James came to see me, he had deep bags under his eyes and looked dishevelled. He told me that he spent hours locked in his bedroom playing video games. Gaming met a need that James was struggling to have fulfilled in the outside world. It gave him a sense of being in control, a sense of belonging. But it wasn't improving his mental health. He had recently been diagnosed with depression.

One day, he came in and told me that he'd stayed up playing *Grand Theft Auto* with loads of friends from around the world. He said that during the game he felt really good, buzzy, on account of being connected to so many people, together on their virtual adventure. But, he told me: 'as soon as I came off the game, I felt like I had this dark cloud of loneliness hanging over me.' And he couldn't shake it. 'Why did I feel so lonely after being with so many friends?' he asked.

We talked about different kinds of connection and how they might make us feel. I suggested that connecting with his friends playing *Grand Theft Auto* was like a Big Mac meal: it filled him up for a short while but he'd soon feel hungry for more. I asked him to reflect on times when he had experienced a more nourishing type of connection with others.

Often, people come to therapy in order to meet their deep need for connection; it's what I hoped James was experiencing with me. But a world where we depend on a professional for this does not sound like a good world to me. My ultimate goal with James and all my clients is to empower them to find that connection beyond the couch.

We all carry a wound of loneliness. It's the place inside us that has felt excluded, abandoned, disconnected, misunderstood.

We tend to avoid tuning into this place because it's painful. Instead, we reach for superficial solutions, including surface relationships that lack meaningful connection. The trouble is, these can only ever give us a temporary hit of 'false belonging', a brief high that soon leaves us feeling empty and socially malnourished, as James found.

As you now know, our children are mirrors, reflecting back parts of ourselves that need our loving attention. Their loneliness is showing us something important that needs our attention and our care. If we want to protect our children from the loneliness epidemic, the place where we can begin to make a difference is within ourselves. There is a meditation on tending to the roots of loneliness on my website. But for now, the most important thing is this: whenever you feel a pang of loneliness, it does not mean there is something wrong with you. The feeling of loneliness is guiding you into connection.

The Sufi poet Hafez says:

Don't surrender your loneliness
So quickly.
Let it cut more deep.
Let it ferment and season you
As few human
Or even divine ingredients can.
Something missing in my heart tonight
Has made my eyes so soft
My voice
So tender,
My need of God
Absolutely
Clear.

LOVE IS ALL AROUND YOU

If you experience loneliness and sometimes struggle to believe that connections and community are available to you, try this exercise. It was inspired by a conversation I once had with a man on a meditation retreat. We were discussing loneliness and community, and he told me that although he lived on his own, he never felt lonely. Every morning, he got up opened the window and said hello to the birds that landed on his windowsill. Then when the postman arrived, he would take time to chat to him. And so his day would continue. He saw and felt and created community all around him. In this exercise, we are going to connect to the field of love that surrounds us at all times but that we forget to notice because we can get a bit lost in our own self-reflection.

1. Take a big piece of paper and write your name in the middle.

2. Now in a circle around you, you are going to write the names of your ideal support circle. This circle can include the following:

   a. People you know who are alive today who have in the recent past shown you some kindness.

   b. People who aren't alive but that you can still sometimes, somehow feel supported by. This could be a parent or grandparent or a friend who has died. Even if you don't feel supported by them, if there is a person no longer alive who you really wish you could still feel supported by then write them down.

   c. People who you have never met or who you couldn't just call up but you feel you have a connection to. This could be a deity, like Jesus or the Buddha; it could be a wisdom teacher you feel connected to.

   d. Elements of nature that you feel supported by. In many indigenous traditions, they honour their relationship with natural elements. Do you sometimes feel supported when walking in a forest or by the ocean? Or with a pet or animal?

3. Once you have some beings in this support circle, take a moment to imagine that you are standing in the middle and that each and every being in this circle is holding you in a warm, loving gaze. Enjoy this feeling of being surrounded by love and support. And then imagine thanking each and every one of them for being there, for supporting you.

   Know that this support circle is always available to you. Love is all around you.

At the end of the myth of Narcissus, he either dies or goes into the underworld, depending on which version you read. In the place where he dies, a flower with white petals surrounding a yellow heart blooms. Today you can buy the *narcissus* flower, or daffodil, as it is more usually known, from your local garden centre.

We all at want to feel special, to be adored. And the world will continue to break our hearts open, to make us feel like small fish in a big pond. In honouring this painful truth, something beautiful can grow.

7

FRUIT THREE: COMPASSION AND CO-OPERATION

Why we need to help each other more

Unless someone like you cares a lot, nothing is going to get better. It's not

– Dr Seuss

One blustery morning in June 2012, father-of-two Delroy Simmonds arrived at Van Siclen Avenue station in Cypress Hills, Brooklyn. He was on his way to a job interview. Simmonds had been looking for work for over a year and was really hoping to get this role as a maintenance worker. The train was coming around the corner when Simmonds noticed a baby boy in a buggy being blown onto the track by a strong gust of wind. The baby hit the steel tracks. There was blood coming from his skull and the train was approaching fast. The baby's mother was frozen on the platform, three other children by her side. With no hesitation or thought, Simmonds jumped onto the tracks, grabbed the nine-month-old boy in his buggy and pulled him to safety.

Hailed by the local media as a hero, Simmonds said, 'Everybody is making me out to be some sort of superhero but I'm just a normal person. Anybody in that situation should have done what I did.' Simmonds missed his job interview but you'll be pleased to know that after the story of his altruism went public, he received multiple job offers.

On another blustery morning in September 2019, I took my daughter to a youth climate march in central London. It turned out to be the biggest environmental protest the UK had ever seen. Some 100,000 people took over the streets of Westminster. On the bank of the Thames near the Houses of Parliament, I found an Extinction Rebellion family spot, art materials laid out for kids on a big blanket. We sat down and Rose, who was just short of two years old, started painting by dipping her hands in the paint, smearing it over some paper and, mostly, over her face. I turned around to find some wet wipes in my bag. And, in the 30 seconds it took to find those wipes, Rose had vanished.

In a chaotic swarm of 100,000 people, my daughter was nowhere to be seen.

I stood up and scanned the crowd, frantic. I was in the darkest game of Where's Wally. My legs were jelly. I ran in one direction. Couldn't see her. Ran the other way. No sign. Just thousands of bodies moving, marching, chanting.

My first thought was: 'My wife is going to kill me.'

Then I had two competing thoughts.

Thought one said: 'Something terrible is going to happen to her, someone might have kidnapped her, and I might never see her again.'

Thought two said: 'She will be OK, someone will hand her into the police. I will find her eventually. People are generally kind and caring (but my wife will still kill me).'

I started asking people if they'd seen her. I bumped into a mum I'd met once at a kid's group. She sprang into action and asked other people to help. Soon there was a mycelial network of mums, branching out across the march, all helping to look for Rose.

The next ten minutes were the slowest and most excruciating I have ever experienced. If you've ever lost a child, even for a minute, you'll know how I felt. Then, out of nowhere, a mum who I vaguely recognised from a kid's nature group came walking towards me, Rose in her arms. Rose looked shell-shocked. The mum had recognised Rose and her orange jumper with a jellyfish on it.

I've never felt such relief.

It still feels miraculous that through a network of mothers, in a throng of 100,000 people, Rose was rescued and handed back to me in only ten minutes.

It took me a long while to recover from those ten minutes.

No virtue signalling

These stories reveal something important about human nature. Alongside our capacities for self-centredness and narcissism described in the last chapter, and despite the horror stories we hear about child abductions, humans have an in-built potential for compassion, co-operation and, at times, total selflessness. Sometimes these virtues get explained away – we are only kind for selfish reasons, it's our selfish genes, or we're virtue signalling. But when a spontaneous network of mothers forms to bring a toddler back to her dad in the middle of a huge march, there is no virtue signalling. And when a father risks his life to save a child who's not his own from being crushed by a train, you'd be scraping the barrel to attribute any selfish motive.

There are countless stories of people sacrificing their lives to save others, young or old, kin or not. But there are also acts of compassion happening every day, gestures of care that you will rarely hear about in the news but that you can easily spot, if you look for them.

The science of compassion

The Dalai Lama describes compassion thus: 'Compassion is the wish that all sentient beings be free from suffering. Compassion is a necessity not a luxury. Without it, the human species cannot survive.' Compassion is a precious gift; it means we are able to feel the suffering of other beings – including animals, trees and even people we really don't like – and are motivated to prevent and alleviate that suffering. It's good for our bodies, our minds, our societies and our earth, too.

From a parent's point of view, what kind of world do you want your child to grow up in? A dog-eat-dog world, each man for himself, full of bullies and narcissists? Or a world where people are kinder to each other and to the planet?

This isn't some hippy ideal where we spend our time drinking yogi tea and having group hugs (although hugs can help!). Nor does it mean being soft, a pushover. There is 'fierce compassion', where you connect to the suffering of others and take a strong stand for what you believe is right.

The good news is that we are born with compassion. From the age of around eight months, if a baby sees someone hurt, they will make faces, gestures and sounds that show concern and empathy. From 14 months old, your toddler will help you if you've dropped something or you can't reach it. And a 2020 study from the University of Washington showed that 19-month-old toddlers will give away a tasty snack to a stranger in need without any encouragement, instruction or reinforcement, even when the toddler is hungry. This innate capacity for altruism distinguishes humans from other primates, who only share resources under restricted conditions. Monkeys don't tend to give away delicious food that they need for themselves.

Why are we born with this quality of compassion? Well, humans are a deeply social species. Our ancestors survived by coming together and taking care of each other. Charles Darwin said that sympathy was the strongest of all human instincts, and that, 'those communities, which included the greatest number of the most sympathetic members would flourish best.'

In the human body, compassion is linked to the activation of the vagus nerve, which runs from the bottom of our brain to the gut, through the heart. The vagus nerve is associated with a key hormone, oxytocin, also known as the 'love molecule' or the 'bonding hormone'. Oxytocin is in many ways a wonder of mammal biology – it is released when mothers are breastfeeding and when we receive a hug. If you spray oxytocin up a woman's nose, she will find babies more appealing.

You may have felt that warm heart-feeling of oxytocin from holding a baby, watching a sunset or listening to a beautiful piece of music. Mystics have long sensed that the heart is the place though which we connect to the world around us. Indian teacher Nisargadatta said, 'The mind creates the abyss, the heart crosses it.' In many cultures around the world, people place their hand on their heart when they greet you, which I find much warmer than a firm handshake.

I'd discovered many years ago that I could cultivate this warm-hearted feeling through certain meditations (more on this shortly). And so it struck me as profound, somehow, when I later discovered this science, that humans have this capacity for compassion firmly built in, and that thousands of years ago some wise beings had discovered simple techniques to help us access these better parts of our nature.

The three circles

So, how can we tap into our warm-hearted biology?

Paul Gilbert is a psychology professor who recognised the power of compassion and devised a form of therapy around it: compassion-focused therapy (CFT). He created a model that a lot of my clients have found helpful for understanding themselves and growing compassion. Each circle in this diagram represents one of your three basic motivational systems. You are always in one of them. But if you spend too much time in any one of them, your life is out of balance and difficulties can arise.

DRIVE SYSTEM
Function: achieve goals, consume, accomplish tasks, seek rewards in the future
Hormone: dopamine

SOOTHING SYSTEM
Function: slow down, rest and digest, care compassion, contentment
Hormone: oxytocin

THREAT SYSTEM
Fuction: self-protection, seeking safety
Hormone: adrenaline and cortisol

Our basic motivational systems

We are in the threat system (often shown as a red circle), fight or flight, when we are stressed or under threat. Compassion is in short supply here; studies have shown that when we are stressed we tend to focus much more on ourselves. We're in the drive system (usually shown as a blue circle) when we're seeking rewards in the future and here we are fuelled by dopamine. When our reward-seeking is triggered by fear or focused on personal achievements, this limits our capacity for compassion, too. Finally, the soothing system (usually green) is the caring 'tend and befriend' zone. This is where we feel safe and where we can access compassion.

In the twenty-first century, we are so focused on growing, building, acquiring and striving that we neglect the healing available to us in the soothing system. As Russell Brand says, 'Our culture has jump-leads on our consciousness.' We are sucked into the drive and threat systems by powerful forces – dopamine-fuelling environments, fear and outrage, growing polarisation and, crucially, when it comes to developing compassion, a tribalism that people in power exploit (we'll explore the roots of tribalism below).

When I used to teach mindfulness, my favourite story to win over the reluctant boys was of rugby player Jonny Wilkinson. He reached the pinnacle of any rugby career – kicking the winning goal in the Rugby World Cup final. But shortly afterwards, he fell into a depression, having spent so long in the competitive, reward-seeking drive system. The happy ending to the story is, of course, that he discovered meditation and compassion. This is what he said in an interview a few years ago: 'As a rugby player, it often felt like I was pushing myself to achieve goals that weren't always in line with who I actually am. I was trying to dominate the world but that didn't make me happy. Now it is very much my mission . . . to embrace all the positive aspects of humanity such as acceptance, compassion and a true connection with others.'

The dark side of love

Before we learn how to grow this most precious fruit of compassion, we first need to understand the dark side to our compassion biology. It turns out that oxytocin, the so-called love hormone, can actually fuel tribalism. In 2010, researchers from the University of Amsterdam discovered that giving oxytocin to people strengthens their bond with their in-group (good) but also increases aggression towards the out-group (not good), an effect known as 'tend and defend'.

However, researchers have since realised that this effect depends on the context. In these studies, when people are primed for scarcity – for example, when they're told a pot of money is limited – then oxytocin makes them turn tribal. But remove this element of scarcity and oxytocin promotes both care for the in-group and increased empathy towards the out-group. In one study by Shamay-Tsoory *et al* from 2013, Jewish Israelis given oxytocin were more likely to experience empathy for the pain experienced by Palestinian Arabs.

So why does this matter? Because there is artificial scarcity in the world – *'Flash sale: this limited edition book is available for a short time only, and there are only two left in stock!'* We will explore scarcity more in the next chapter. For now, just keep in mind how, in conditions of artificial scarcity, that warm-hearted feeling of compassion can turn into red-blooded hatred towards anyone not like us.

Compassion starts with you

When our children are stressed, anxious, overwhelmed or beating themselves up, our job is to help them shift into the soothing system. We do this naturally when we are ourselves in that system. But, let's be real – as grown-ups who care for children in this mad world, we can easily become stressed and exhausted and lose track of our own needs. And as writer Eleanor Browns puts it, 'You can't serve from an empty vessel.' If you want your children to grow compassion for themselves and others, first fill up your own cup. This is self-compassion – when we treat ourselves the same way we would treat a beloved friend. This may sound obvious. But how consistently do you do it? I am here to give you extra permission and encouragement.

Ultimately, we need to let go of the excess burden of guilt and self-blame that we modern parents carry, for the sake of our children's mental health. Buddha once said that you could search the whole world and not find anyone more deserving of your love and compassion than yourself. Let that sink in for a moment. A 2020 review of self-compassion for parents showed that it consistently reduces depression, anxiety and stress in parents. A recent study of over 900 Dutch families showed that parents with less self-blame had teenagers with fewer symptoms of depression and anxiety.

Are you ready to try some self-compassion now?

SOME TIPS TO GET INTO THE COMPASSION ZONE

These are many evidence-based ways to move yourself into a self-compassionate state.* Below are just a selection I tend to use for myself and in my practice. Only if you find

* For more, see self-compassion.org/ and www.compassionatemind. co.uk/resource/resources

---

these exercises personally helpful should you then use them with your children.

1. **Remember our common humanity** – simply remember that all human beings experience suffering, that we all have what Paul Gilbert calls 'tricky brains' – easily influenced by this mad world we live in. Can you see your struggles and failures as basic elements of what makes us human, rather than as personal failings that separate you from other people who you imagine are better than you are?

2. **Love your inner critic** – we all have an Inner Critic, the harsh, punitive voice that says we are not enough, not worthy of compassion. If you grew up in a very critical environment, it makes sense to beat yourself up before someone else does. In my experience, this sense of unworthiness is like a hedgehog's spikes trying to protect a soft, vulnerable part of you that has been hurt before. Whenever you notice this Inner Critic, send them some love, thank them for protecting you – and ask them to take a well-deserved holiday.

3. **Developing a compassionate inner voice** – imagine if, from the moment you woke up, you spoke to yourself the way your best friend or your most loyal supporter, or the most compassionate person you know (real or fictional) would. Your day, your life, your children and the world would be so much better, right? You can grow this compassionate voice within by remembering times when you felt loved or by imagining the most compassionate person you know guiding you, a loving voice inside your own mind.

4. Kindness breath – tune into your body and find that place inside that is tense or stressed. Now imagine that part is a younger version of you. Put a nurturing hand on that part of the body. Say (out loud or silently) 'There, there' or 'It's OK for you to be there' or 'I understand why you feel like this'. Now imagine that you are breathing in kindness to this part of you. You can say on the in-breath: 'breathing in kindness'.

Widening our circle of compassion

Albert Einstein famously said: 'Our task must be to free ourselves from this prison by widening our circle of compassion to embrace all living creatures and the whole of nature in its beauty.' Once we are tending and befriending ourselves, we can begin to practise with our children widening our circle of compassion to include other humans who aren't like us, who aren't in our in-group, who may live in a different country, have different colour skin, different beliefs. And as we, our children, and their children all depend on the natural world and the living things in it, we need to widen our compassion to include all creatures on this precious planet.

An excellent place to start is with the Buddhist *metta*, or loving-kindness meditation. This practice has been around for over 2,500 years and there is now growing evidence that it reduces anxiety, depression and other negative emotional states, decreases the experience of pain and increases positive emotions and compassion to self and others. One study even showed it can slow down ageing! You can do this variation alone or with children from around five years old.

SENDING KIND WISHES TO THE WORLD

You can spend five minutes or half an hour on this, depending on the time you have and the child's attention span. The idea is to do it together, rather than you teaching them.

1. Start by agreeing on the kind wishes you want to send out into the world. Most often, people say: *May they be safe, may they be healthy, may they be happy, may they find peace.* But please feel free to make up your own wishes. Just think with your child what you would most wish for other people in the world to experience, especially those who are struggling.

2. Ask the child to bring to mind a time when they felt safe and loved. This is to activate their internal feeling of compassion. It could be a simple moment like a hug with a grandparent or a nice day out with a kind friend. You can both try putting a hand on your heart and closing your eyes for a minute. As you do, imagine the love flowing within you like a warm light.

3. Now, apply the kind wishes to yourself. The usual form here is: *May I be safe, may I be healthy, may I be happy, may I find peace.* Say it to yourself or out loud. It can help to visualise the compassion as a warm light going around your body. Visualise and feel what it might be like to live with these kind wishes being true. Compassion often arises as a warm feeling across our chest, so tune into this part of your body.

4. Next, think of someone you really appreciate, someone who has been kind to you, someone you love. Apply the wishes to them: *May they be safe, may . . .* and so on. Your child might want to send wishes to a pet, a stuffed

animal or to a character in a movie they love. It can also be lovely to send kind wishes to each person in the family, in turn.

5. Now, apply the wishes to someone who is struggling with life, someone who may really need them.

6. Next, apply the wishes to someone you find difficult. You may have had a row with them, it could be an ex-friend or someone who has been unkind. If this feels hard, don't worry (and don't start with the most difficult person in your life!).

7. Finally, extend the wishes out to all beings in the world. *May all beings everywhere be safe* . . . You can include Mother Earth and a wish for the healing of damage that human beings have caused to her.

Compassion-in-action

Empathy and compassion are different. Compassion is empathy (feeling the suffering of another) plus the motivation to help. In fact, empathy on its own can do more harm than good. A person might believe that empathy alone will help someone who is suffering. And it might in some cases. But if I'm homeless, penniless or my house is on fire, I don't need your empathy, ta. And empathy can leave a person drowning in the feelings of others. We are now exposed to the suffering of every other being on the planet at the click of a button, leaving us at risk of what researchers call 'psychic numbing' or 'compassion collapse'.

Children need us to guide them through their own suffering, and through the suffering of the world, and we can't do that when we are ourselves overwhelmed. Of course, part of the solution is to spend less time watching the news and on social media. But it's also really important that we help our children practise compassion-in-action. At best, empathy provides the emotional fuel for compassion.

Below, I've suggested just some of the many ways to practise compassion-in-action. And, as with any behaviour, you'll only reinforce it in your child with repetition, repetition, repetition! You are teaching your child to keep their hearts open in the face of suffering and to respond to it from a place of empowerment, courage and compassion. What an incredible gift to give to them and to the world!

1. **Immerse them in stories of compassion.** Look for stories that include someone being compassionate. Include stories about the child's life, too; Rose loves the story of her being found by all those kind mums. Share them at mealtimes.

2. **Don't shy away from suffering.** Suffering can open our hearts and unite us because we know, at some point, we will all suffer. As activist and writer Joanna Macy says, 'The heart that breaks open contains the whole universe.' So, when suffering comes up, talk about it. It might be someone in the family who is having a hard time, a child at school who is being bullied, a homeless person you pass or even a pigeon that has been run over. Ask your child questions to help them reflect. If you are talking about someone being bullied, ask your child how seeing it made them feel. Ask them what they would have liked to have done to help, if it was possible. Having these conversations with your child will give them some confidence that they can let themselves

be moved by the suffering in the world and still be able to act.

3. **Choose a focus for compassion.** Ask your child to think of a group of people (or creatures) or a cause or issue that they most want to help. Is it homeless people, an endangered species, the rainforests? Once they've decided, find a story that you can read, watch or listen to together. Before you start the story, agree to share the feelings that come up in your body. Remember, you're learning together that it's OK to have feelings about other people's suffering. Now, transform these feelings into action. (There is more guidance on feelings in Chapter 11.) Together, think of one thing that you could do to support your issue. It doesn't need to be big, it could be making a donation, writing a letter or volunteering.

Redefining success

We all teach our kids to be kind and caring, right?

Well, not according to a big 2014 Harvard study called 'The Children We Mean to Raise: The Real Messages Adults Are Sending About Values'. This study reviewed the literature on parental transmission of values and then surveyed over 10,000 students, asking them about their own values and what values their parents promoted to them. While most parents and teachers say that developing caring children is a top priority for them, ranking it as more important than their children's achievements, this was not the experience of the young people interviewed in this study. Around 80 per cent said their parents and teachers cared more about them having individual success than about them caring for others. And in an analysis of day-to-day conversations, there was a much higher frequency of messages from parents to their kids promoting individual success than promoting caring for others. The authors of the report called this the 'rhetoric/reality gap'. Although parents thought 'caring' was important, they weren't actually living or relaying that value to their kids.

We want our children to grow up in a world where people take care of each other. But we may not be preparing our children to help build this world. It's not that we do this on purpose. We are usually not fully aware of the implicit values that drive our interactions with our kids. And we do not usually think critically about our definition of success, for ourselves and for our kids.

But look at it this way: who are your personal heroes or heroines? Usually, at least in Western culture, they are individuals whose stories of success tend to be of the lone wolf battling against the odds to win. How much do you know about the team behind your own heroes? The networks they depend on? We might hear an Oscar-winner thanking their mum but do you have any idea who their mum is and what they actually did for them?

Here is a little tip: when your child achieves something, whether it's a school exam or some sporting competition, ask them to think more widely about who or what helped them to achieve that goal. This will help them honour the natural and human networks that underpin everything we achieve.

I regularly work with parents who are questioning their definition of 'success'. Usually, it's because what we tend to think of as success – fame, money, status – has not brought them to the promised land of everlasting joy. Surprise, surprise. It can be hard for us to find new definitions of success, mainly because they don't appear so often in mainstream media. But the good news is this: you are 100 per cent free to define 'success' for yourself and your family in a way that feels authentic and meaningful to you. And given the big problems in the world and in our children's minds, I believe we urgently need to redefine 'success'. And it begins with getting super clear on our values.

I worked with a family where the parents were very high-powered, financially 'successful' people. But Parul, their 17-year-old daughter, was depressed. And nobody in the family was talking about how they felt or about her depression. Time at home was spent mostly in their own rooms, on their own devices. The goal they set in our first session was to feel closer to one another.

One way of thinking about depression is that it signals when we are not living in accordance with our values. So, as an early task, I gave the family a list of core values (you can find them in the Further Resources section at the end of the book) and I set them the challenge of agreeing on five for the family. I asked them to think when choosing their values about what kind of a world they wanted to live in. First, they picked ten each, then looked for those that were shared between them. These would become the north star for their family, the basis of their new definition of success.

When they returned the next week, they told me they'd found the exercise both surprisingly easy and clarifying. Together, they'd chosen kindness, creativity, gratitude, honesty, loyalty. They then agreed they'd hold each other accountable to these values. For example, they decided to discuss the weekly value over dinner. Honesty week was challenging, as Parul said she felt her parents worked too hard and didn't have enough time for the family. But the family had all chosen this value, so it kept them connected – a kind of emotional glue.

Over the next few weeks, the family really talked about what mattered most to them and it made them feel closer. And gradually, as they bonded around their shared values, the family's focus shifted outwards to what kind acts they could do in the world. Parul and her father began volunteering once a week at an animal shelter. Just getting clear on your definition of success and having a shared framework to implement it has a tangible impact.

Co-operation is our superpower

> *Everything relies on everything else in the cosmos in order to manifest – whether a star, a cloud, a flower, a tree, or you and me . . . If we look at a child, it's easy to see the child's mother and father, grandmother and grandfather, in her . . . If at times we cannot understand why the child is acting a certain way, it is helpful to remember that she is not a separate self-entity. She is a continuation. Her parents and ancestors are inside her . . . We do not exist independently. We inter-are.* – Thich Nhat Hanh

Right at the start of this book, I said that if there is one lesson we are learning in the twenty-first century it's that we are in this together. And, it turns out, it's quite easy to find examples of our togetherness if we look for examples of co-operation. Co-operation means working together towards a common goal. Like compassion, co-operation breaks us free from being too focused on ourselves. Co-operation is the antidote to a self-destructing, dog-eat-dog world. I relied on a network of mothers co-operating to help find my daughter in a crowd of 100,000 people.

You are a living, breathing example of co-operation. Right now, your lungs are breathing in air without you even thinking about it, diffusing the oxygen into your blood and releasing carbon dioxide back into the environment as a waste product. This carbon dioxide is being absorbed by plants and trees who then release oxygen back into the environment as a waste product. Meanwhile, there are approximately 1,200 different species of bacteria and fungi in your gut working symbiotically with the cells in your intestines to digest your last meal and to defend against pathogens.

In fact, co-operation is our human superpower. Where most social mammals only co-operate with their relatives, humans have found ways to get along with and work together with people who live in different countries, speak different languages and have different beliefs.

Psychologist Michael Tomasello and his team have done amazing work highlighting how human co-operation begins with shared attention. Unless we can share our attention, looking together towards the same goal, we can't co-operate. You may have noticed this in your own baby: from around nine months, most babies begin to point things out to you. When you look at what they are pointing at you are sharing your attention on the same goal. So don't underestimate the power of shared attention to lay the foundations of co-operation in your child. Whatever your baby, child or even teenager is into, find a way to join in, even just for ten minutes a week. According to one study, even violent video games, when played as a team rather than competitively, lead to more co-operative behaviour afterwards.

It also really helps to take turns to lead. I've worked with families where children initially really struggled to let someone else take the lead but with just a little persistence this habit of turn-taking is quite easy to build. If you are going for a walk, or planning an activity, take turns to be the leader.

Nature is a great teacher here, full of examples of co-operation you can point out, whether it's bees pollinating flowers, ants carrying food back to their colony or mycelial networks transporting nutrients to other plants and trees. A 2015 paper showed that just being in nature makes us less self-centred, more generous and more co-operative.

From the climate emergency to the child mental health crisis, the problems we face are complex and will only be solved from a place where we connect to our deepest level of compassion and co-operation. It is time to shift our way of seeing and being, to cease being self-centred competitors and the biggest predators on planet Earth, and instead become big-hearted super co-operators.

8

ROOT FOUR: SCARCITY

How we can learn to love the part of us that doesn't feel enough

I laugh when I hear a fish in the sea is thirsty
– Kabir

Are you struggling with something in your life? Do you worry about getting older? Crow's feet? Grey hair? Frizzy hair? Flat hair? Going bald?

Do you jump out of bed full of energy and raring to go or do you have to drag yourself from under the duvet, bleary-eyed and dreading another day of the same old shit?

Do you ever question if you are in the right place? The right body? The right job? The right life?

Have you thought about setting up your own business? Building your own platform? Turning your knowledge into profits?

Are your children not behaving the way you would like? Could they be happier, better behaved, more kind, less shy, more academic, more sporty, more confident?

Has your partner lost their sheen? Do you ever wish they were someone else? Is your sex life not the 24-hour rompathon you once dreamed of?

Do you ever wonder if there might be something wrong . . .
. . . with you?
. . . with your partner?
. . . with your child?
We can fix that.

The word advert means to turn (vert) to one side (ad). Every day, our attention is turned towards messages and images that make us feel we are not enough. When we fear we are not enough, we produce more and consume more. And a lot of the things we consume – that big bag of Minstrels, a new bathroom, daily news, the latest phone – we don't really need. This fear of 'not enough' spreads invisibly, a virus of the mind. The virus latches onto our underlying traumas and wounds – the parts of us that already feel broken – and replicates there.

I know I'm infected whenever I find myself working too hard, feeling resentful of other people, questioning my value as a parent, a therapist, a human being. In my clients, I've seen it come out in other ways: body dysmorphia, staying in a relationship that's toxic, working so hard they have a breakdown. And this pressure to constantly upgrade our phones, our selves, and even our children is increasing. Our children are drowning in messages telling them they are not enough: not smart enough, not calm enough, not funny enough, not slim enough, not beautiful enough, not 'influencer' enough.

How can we protect ourselves against this virus, reach herd immunity? Really, how can we remember that we are enough?

Ever felt you're a bad parent?

When Rose was 15 months old, we took her on holiday to India. As I wrote before, she was a terrible sleeper. What were we thinking?

A month in a foreign bed in a foreign land turned out to be exhausting. There were two days and nights that were particularly bad. Rose was unsettled, clingy, volatile, full power screaming through the night. By the third day, the three of us were wiped out. So we decided to take a rejuvenating walk along the beach and we bumped into a super cool, hippy Israeli couple with a baby. They had cool sunglasses, cool long hair, cool handmade leather bumbags, cool tattoos. But Laurey and I were more interested in latching onto them as parents, as real deal human beings, who would surely understand the sleepless hell we had been going through for the last 48 hours. We asked them how they were finding travelling with their baby.

'Yeah, travelling with the baby is just so easy, it's just so beautiful man,' they said. 'We just go with the flow and everything is beautiful. Our baby is just sleeping like a dream because we are just going with the flow man. It's beautiful.'

Go with the flow. Go with the flow. Go with the fucking flow. Not what we wanted to hear. This perfect family left us feeling out of flow, isolated and ashamed. Not that it was their fault. Life is the greatest teacher. I guess we should stop comparing ourselves to others. But some lessons are harder to swallow than others. *Gulp*

We continued our weary walk along the beach, and just a few minutes later, we sat down for a juice at a cafe and next to us were a family from Boulder, Colorado, with two kids. This family was friendly, a bit less 'cool', a bit more human. Desperately in need of reassurance, we again shared our two days and nights of sleepless hell. The mother listened carefully and said, 'That sounds like hell. I know how you must feel.' We instantly felt at home.

She continued to say that she knew how hard travelling with a family could be. She even told us about some of their struggles with their own kids. Theirs weren't to do with sleep but that didn't matter. What mattered was our shared moment of 'struggling-through' humanity. In this private, non-Instagrammable moment we felt less alone, we felt understood, we felt enough.

Parenting isn't perfection

They say that parenting is the hardest job you will ever do – and it turns out to be largely true. We have 24/7, whole-life responsibility for this creature that is incredibly complex, with its own unique DNA, temperament, soul. And, of course, we really want to get it right. Add to that, your child is guaranteed to bring up any unresolved trauma in your life. Remember, because they come from us, are made from us, resemble us, like a mirror they reflect back to us all the juicy, unresolved, unloved parts of our self.

This leaves us desperate for guidance, for someone to come and tell us what to do, to fix whatever problem it is we are experiencing. And it makes us particularly vulnerable to the virus of feeling we are not enough. That is why the parenting advice market is so successful and why it's growing. There are parenting coaches, parenting podcasts, parenting gurus, parenting TV programmes, parenting courses. There is a lot of great advice out there, but the sheer volume of advice and the size of the market speaks to our insecurity. Book titles promise perfect family lives, such as *Calm Parents, Happy Kids*; *The Happiest Baby on the Block*; *Peaceful Parent, Happy Siblings*; *The Danish Way of Parenting: What the Happiest People in the World Know About Raising Confident, Capable Kids*; *French Children Don't Throw Food*.

Of course we want to be peaceful. Of course we want our children to be happy. Of course we want our kids to not throw food. But like the Israeli couple on the beach, these titles promote an image of perfection that feeds vulture-like on the carcass of our unworthiness. And the truth is that, while machines respond predictably to formulas, a child is not a machine. A lot of parenting formulas either won't work for our child or will work for a while and then stop working. When this happens, I often see parents blaming themselves, feeling like they aren't enough.

This anxious, guilt-soaked parenting is not sustainable and it can lead to resentment or worse. Mothers who feel they need to be perfect parents and who care for their children intensively have higher anxiety levels, higher stress levels, lower levels of self-efficacy and are more likely to develop depression. And dads are increasingly joining the club, too. A 2015 Pew survey showed that most dads don't feel like they are doing a good enough job or spending enough time with their children, despite spending three times as much time with their kids as fathers did in 1965.

I say: enough is enough! Some advice is good. But my strong, overriding feeling is that we need to protect our minds and those of our children from the constant nagging, anxiety-inducing pressure that we could be better, that what is happening right now is not enough. Can you just for a moment let in the idea, the feeling that you are enough? You are doing your best.

Our deepest fear? Running out of loo roll

Before 2020, the only time I can ever remember worrying about not having loo roll was at the Burning Man festival circa 2007.

I'd fallen for a Mexican lady and we were roaming around the desert one night when suddenly I just had to go. I found a

toilet and realised, belatedly, there was no loo roll. I panicked. This was the coolest party on earth; I had a beautiful
girl waiting for me outside and I had no means of wiping my
bum. I managed to sneak out of the portaloo without her
noticing, ran up to several people and desperately asked if
anyone had any loo roll. This was not my proudest moment.
Finally, thank god, I found a kind-hearted soul with a few
spare sheets and I managed to sneak back in to the loo and
clean myself up without being caught out. Fortunately, the girl
was still waiting for me. I brushed off my self-consciousness
and we had a magical night together wandering the desert,
the memory of nearly being caught-short dissolving in a blur
of psychedelic beats and unicorn tricycles.

In 2020, when faced with the prospect of dying from a
virus spreading rapidly around the world, what was the first
thing we panicked about? Not vitamin C. Not chocolate. Not
tins of tomato soup. Bloody loo roll!

Why loo roll? We could go into the Freudian psychology
of this, how our worst fear is that we won't be able to wipe
our own bums so that all the stinky crap we've been hiding
from the world will be exposed. And I think there is some
truth in this. But the reason I'm sharing these loo-roll sagas
here is simply to demonstrate how irrationally we behave
when our primal fears are triggered.

Connected to our root fear that we are not enough is our
fear of not having enough. We have a deep, primal fear of
scarcity. This fear lurks, waiting for some external cue – a
virus or, more recently in the UK, a lack of lorry drivers – to
come out. We have a deep fear that the loo roll will run out
and everyone will see the dirty, smelly, unlovable parts of our
self. We have a deep fear the food will run out and we'll starve
to death. We have a deep fear the love will run out; we'll
never be good enough and will die alone. These primal fears

get hijacked by the world around us and cause us to act in ways that make us – and our children – suffer.

There is a simple test for knowing whether your decision to do, to be or to buy something is driven by scarcity. Ask yourself: 'Am I doing this out of fear or love?' You need to keep checking in with this question, not just for your own sake, or for the sake of your children, but for the sake of the planet. Because, as I'm sure you already know, overconsumption is a primary cause of the current climate crisis. When our scarcity mindset is triggered, when we are ruled by the fear of not enough, we buy stuff and we hoard stuff. Black Friday is just an extreme example of how our desires and our fears of missing out are manipulated to make us accumulate more. Next time you are about to click that 'buy now' button, take a moment to breathe, tune inwardly and ask yourself: 'Am I doing this out of fear or love?' If you want to go deeper with this practice, check out the exercise in the box below.

SAY HELLO TO YOUR SCARCITY MINDSET

Ask yourself the following questions, journal your answers, and notice any sign of fear arising in your body. When fear arises, just put a loving hand on the part of your body where you feel it. Let it be there.

- Where in your life is this scarcity mindset alive and kicking? Who or what doesn't feel enough? Your self, your child, your partner, your parenting, your house, your bank balance, your spirituality?

- Write down your fears about the area of your self or your life that you worry isn't enough. The more specific

---

you can be about your fears, the more you can have mastery over them. This is called 'fear-setting'.

- Take a moment to reflect and journal on how these fears of not enough are colouring your view of yourself, and of your world. How do these fears of not enough make you feel in your body? When driven by a scarcity mindset, what behaviours do you engage in that you know are not good for you, or your family, or the world?

- Now, let's find the root of this primal fear in your body. Instead of pathologising this part of us, let's bring it some compassion. Can you find the deepest root of 'not enough' somewhere in your body, that primal fear? If you can, bring your loving attention here, place a gentle hand on this part of you, and try saying to this primal fear: 'I see you. I hear you. I love you.'

- You can even enter into a dialogue with the fear. Ask this fear: what do you really need to feel safe? (I bet you'll find the answer isn't more loo roll.)

How scarcity takes hold in you

A virus needs a host. And that host is the place in your own psyche that has been disowned, pushed into a dark corner of the forest. For scarcity, this particular corner is where our envy and our unworthiness loiter. The not-enough virus spreads rapidly here. The next two sections are about shining a loving light into these dark corners of envy and unworthiness, to help us protect ourselves and our children from the virus of not-enough.

Envy

In the opening scene of *Borat*, the comedy about a journalist from Kazakhstan who travels to America in search of fame and fortune, Borat introduces his neighbour: 'He is my neighbour Nursultan Tuliagby. He is pain in my assholes. I get a window from a glass; he must get a window from a glass. I get a step; he must get a step. I get a clock radio; he cannot afford. Great success!'

This is funny because we all can relate. Envy is normal. We all want what other people have. Every parent knows the refrain 'it's not fair'.

I once took Rose to a soft play in London's Finsbury Park. This place had the best toys, hamsters you could feed, and a machine with two big, bright, red-and-green buttons that rocketed balls to the other side of the room. As Rose scanned the room, her eyes latched onto a green tractor in the corner. This was a supremely dull, coin-operated toy that rocked back and forth making dull, tractor noises. But . . . there was a boy on it, and so Rose wanted what he had. I had to repeatedly stop her from climbing onto the machine until the tractor finally stopped rocking and the boy dismounted. Now that Rose finally had a seat, she refused to get off, even when the tractor stopped its rocking motion, and even though the other children were clearly having loads of fun elsewhere.

We desire what others desire, even if it's not fun and even if it's actually bad for us and bad for our planet. Philosopher René Girard called this 'mimetic desire'. Has your child ever, like Rose, refused to hand over a toy they were bored with just because they've seen another child wants it? Let's be honest though. It's not just kids that want what other people have. What if everything you've ever wanted, even your whole life, is an unconscious ride on a green tractor?

The roots of envy run do run deep. In the Ten Commandments, the tenth commandment, the very last one, the one positioned to stick in your mind, is about envy: 'Thou shalt not covet thy neighbour's house, thou shalt not covet thy neighbour's wife, nor his servant, nor his handmaid, nor his ox, nor his ass, nor anything which belongeth unto thy neighbour.'

If only it was as simple as following a commandment!

Old descriptions talk about envy as a disease of the body that needs treating. In Ovid's *Metamorphoses*, envy has 'sallow cheeks', 'shrunk body', 'decayed teeth' and 'venom-coated tongue'. In the Middle Ages, people talked about envy as being contagious. The proverbial advice was not to get too close to the breath of the envious or to share bread with them. In 1676, physician John Harris wrote about envy, 'It burneth the heart, and wasteth the body, and is like the worm that breedeth in the timber and consumeth it.' It feels true, this sense that envy can eat you up from the inside, that it's contagious.

Envy can make us want to destroy the person who has the thing we want. Cain killed his brother Abel because he was so deeply envious that God preferred Abel's sacrifice. I'm not suggesting you want to murder the people you're envious of, but notice how you might talk or think about them. Gossip can be a way of 'murdering' someone's reputation. Even if you don't gossip, have you ever torn someone to pieces in the privacy of your own mind? This might make us feel better for a short while but in the long run we are left with the basic feeling that we are not enough.

There can be a positive side to envy. One theory is that envy evolved as a bodily signal, guiding us to make sure we have enough resources for ourselves. Imagine back in the old days: Alan the alpha caveman is stronger than you and has a bigger club, and he is getting most of the buffalo meat and most of the cavewomen. You feel a pain in your heart (envy) which directs you to find your own niche. You know you can't beat Alan in a fight but you realise that if you tie a buffalo bone in your hair, paint some ochre on your face and start chanting songs then people respect you. They see you as a healer, a shaman. Thanks to envy, now you have found your niche. You get better buffalo meat and a better choice of warm bodies to sleep with, and therefore you don't die freezing and alone when winter comes.

A kind of envy can also guide us to seek equality and justice. 'It's not fair!' is the energy behind many revolutions. Of course, when our child says 'It's not fair!' most of the time we might think they are being childish. But these are important parenting moments. You have a choice. You can tell them nothing is fair in this world. Or you can help them channel that sense of injustice beyond plastic toys to things that really matter. First, you need to validate and normalise their feelings (more on this in Fruit Five, 'Feeling'). You might say: 'I feel like the world isn't fair sometimes, too.' Only when there is a bit more calm can you broaden the perspective and discuss with them things in the world that aren't fair that you might both want to try to do something about.

BRING YOUR ENVY INTO THE LIGHT

If we don't directly address our envy it leaves us vulnerable to a culture that is constantly telling us we are not (good) enough. Just being honest about your envy will go some way to freshening envy's venomous breath. And bonus: when we shine our loving light onto our envy, it can help us get clear about what we really want. This exercise will hopefully take you beyond your envy of green tractors and other stuff to the qualities you really want more of in your life.

- Who is one person in your life that you secretly or not-so-secretly feel envious of? Bring them to mind. Notice any resistance to doing this, any thoughts telling you that you don't feel envious. Call BS on those thoughts.

- Once you have this person in mind, ask yourself: 'What is the one quality I see in that person that I secretly wish I could have?' (The quality could be anything from confidence to compassion.)

- Now, turn this one thing into a statement that begins: I want to develop more X . . . (where X is the quality you want to grow).

Now you are clear on what it is you want, ask yourself if you are willing to take the action needed to pursue that want. It doesn't matter if the answer is yes or no. Getting clear either way can keep our envy at bay.

Unworthiness

A client called Shayla, aged 20, came to see me because she was really struggling with OCD and suicidal thoughts, and it was putting her university course at risk. She lived in a house with other people and she would regularly go into a panic attack if the house was messy. And she had a particular problem with things that weren't straight. She could, for example, spend upwards of an hour arranging a row of shoes until they were perfectly lined up, making her late for college.

When Shayla was growing up, her dad had been very critical and her mum overbearing. I have found these qualities are common in the parents of children with OCD. One way of understanding OCD is that by controlling, ordering and straightening up the outside world, we might be able to mend our deepest sense of being broken, unworthy.

One session, Shayla came to see me and said, 'I want to get to the core of my trauma, find the place where I'm really broken.' So I guided her through a meditation. I asked her to tune into her body to see if she could connect with a sense of the wound she was carrying. She told me she had a wringing feeling in her stomach. I asked her if she could allow that feeling to be there, stay curious about it. As she allowed it to be there, she felt the energy move up into her head, to a part of her that was terrified of going too deep into the trauma.

I invited her to connect with and allow this terrified part to be there. I asked her what shape or character this part might take. She described a mangled piece of metal. I asked her to imagine this piece of metal had a voice. If it did, what would it say?

Shayla burst into tears as she connected with the vulnerability beneath this mangled piece of metal: 'It just wants to be straightened out.'

By giving a shape to Shayla's unworthiness, we were able to work with it. Not to straighten it out but to give this part the acceptance and love it never received.

Unworthiness is the feeling that we are broken, faulty, deficient in some way. We experience it when we don't feel of equal importance to someone else, don't live up to an imaginary family or social standard. Unworthiness can also arise when envy turns malignant, when being envious of what other people have turns and attacks our own sense of self. Unworthiness says: 'I will never be good enough to have what they have.'

Unworthiness might appear as a lack of confidence, imposter syndrome, not trying things in case they fail. At its root, it's feeling not worthy of being loved. The parts of you that feel unworthy of love are the parts that have been kicked out into the forest beyond the clearing. When unworthiness is playing, we scan our environment looking for evidence we are unlovable. And lord knows, we find it – someone doesn't respond to our message and we collapse; we speak quietly and quickly in conversations because we think no one is really listening; we don't leave a job we hate or go for that other job because surely there are better people out there; our child doesn't give us a hug one morning and we feel totally rejected.

Like the Victim we met in Chapter 2, the unworthy parts of us are often waiting to be rescued. They secretly hope that someone might sweep in and declare: 'No, you are more than enough!' Or we might convince ourselves that if only we achieved more, were more successful, had more followers, then surely we would feel more worthy, more loved, more enough. But when the hero doesn't come, or when we achieve things and still don't feel enough, unworthiness can turn into depression. In *The Burnout Society*, philosopher Byung-Chul Han says that 'Depression reflects a humanity waging war on itself. The complaint of the depressive individual, "Nothing is possible" can only occur in a society that thinks, "Nothing is impossible".'

We don't talk about this enough. We carry so much fear and shame around our broken-ness. We pathologise any parts of our self that don't fit with the achievement norms of our tribe. And, as a result, we end up lost in what psychologist Tara Brach calls the 'trance of unworthiness'. 'Failure could be around any corner, so it is hard to lay down our hypervigilance and relax. Whether we fear being exposed as defective either to ourselves or to others, we carry the sense that if they knew . . . they wouldn't love us.' But it is also simply human to feel unworthy. Unworthiness is a deep and recurring pattern in our ancient human drama. We just don't want it running the show.

So, to protect ourselves, we need to come to know and love the deepest part of us that feels in some way broken.

GOOEY OOEY WORMS

There is a song my dad used to sing to us when we were children, usually when we were upset about something. I'm not sure this would reach the gold standard of parenting in the twenty-first century but I actually think it kind of worked. The song goes like this:

> *Nobody loves me, everybody hates me. I'm going to the garden to eat worms.*
> *Long thin slimy ones, short fat fuzzy ones; Gooey gooey, gooey ooey worms.*

In psychotherapy, there is a technique called externalisation, where you create a character that represents that problem and you write about it, draw it, make a song about it. The reason I think the 'gooey ooey worms' song worked is because it externalised unworthiness, made light of it.

So let's do some externalising now. Take a moment to close your eyes and connect to your own sense of brokenness, any part of you that might feel deficient, unworthy, less than. It can help to bring to mind certain people or situations that might trigger your sense of unworthiness.

- Notice what sensations or feelings come up in your body. Allow them to be there. Can you imagine this energy of brokenness having a shape or a character? Take a moment to imagine some of the details of this character, perhaps the tone of its voice.

- Now, if it feels OK, you could ask that character to reveal its deepest wish. Maybe it has a song it wants to share, a sound or a movement. Perhaps you can connect to the energy of anger or protest within your sense of brokenness.

- If you were going to take your sense of brokenness to the streets, what would you write on your banner or sandwich board? I know what I would write: 'LEAVE ME AND MY CHILDREN ALONE. WE ARE ENOUGH.'

This exercise may leave you feeling a bit shaken and stirred. That's OK. These parts of us that feel broken are often buried quite deep. And like a frightened little animal, they can feel a bit shaky when exposed to the light. If you do feel wobbly, take a moment to feel both of your feet on the ground. It can help to imagine putting this tender part of you back inside your body, like putting a genie back in a bottle, where it can feel safe. Imagine that you are surrounded by a field of loving energy. This loving energy is holding you; it's holding all your glorious, beautiful brokenness.

Immunisation protocol

My Dear Friend,

When the world is telling you you aren't enough.

When you have lost touch with a sense of the sacred.

When your relationships have become a means to an end.

When the fear of missing out has sidled into even the most private moments (like checking your emails on the loo).

When you sacrifice friendships, family, love, joy in the belief that if you work just a little bit harder, then surely that next blog, project, film, business will finally bring you the success and recognition you deserve.

When you notice that sneaky little snake slithering inside your soul enticing you to do more, to have more, to be more. My dear friend, you have contracted the scarcity mind-virus.

This is your immunisation protocol:

Inject yourself with these words and let the soul cells circulate through your system dissolving any trace of the virus:

I am enough.

I am enough.

I am enough.

This is enough.

This is enough.

This is enough.

We are enough.

We are enough.

We are enough.

(N.B. This immunisation has no adverse reactions, no side effects. If you take this medicine regularly, if you really let it sink into your cells, your children will be grateful.)

9

FRUIT FOUR: ABUNDANCE

The art of remembering we are enough and we have enough

I like you just the way you are
– Fred Rogers

Fred Rogers was a shy, overweight, often sick child with asthma, scarlet fever, and 'every childhood disease imaginable'. He struggled to fit in, had no friends at school and he got bullied badly. His peers would chase him home from school threatening to beat him up while calling him Fat Freddy. Whenever Fred was alone he would cry to himself.

But then in high school things changed.

Jim Stumbaugh was a popular football player at the school who ended up in hospital after being injured in a game. Fred's mum arranged for Fred to bring Jim homework while he was in hospital and to tutor him. The two boys became friends for life and Jim helped Fred integrate at school. When Fred reflected on this experience, he wrote: 'That made all the difference in the world for me. What a difference one person can make in the life of another. It's almost as if he had said, "I like you just the way you are." '

From this experience – of being loved just for who he

was – Fred went on to become one of the most popular and loved American TV hosts. When his show *Mister Rogers' Neighbourhood* aired in 1968, it was the first programme to highlight children's social and emotional needs. Fred worked with child psychologists to craft scripts that went to the heart of issues that affect children, from divorce to racism to death. It ushered in a quiet psychological revolution for children and their carers. And the one core theme that ran throughout Fred's work? Unconditional love. He ended every programme by saying, 'You've made this day a special day, by just your being you. There's no person in the whole world like you and I like you just the way you are.'

Fred was not without his critics. In 2007, four years after Fred died, Fox News dedicated an entire section to criticising the impact of Mister Rogers, calling Fred 'an evil, evil man', who, in their view, had single-handedly 'ruined an entire generation', creating entitled snowflakes who grew up believing they were special. On a Yahoo Answers forum, a discussion page about him begins with this post: 'Mr Rogers spent years telling little creeps that he liked them just the way they were. He should have been telling them there was a lot of room for improvement . . .'

So, which is true? Do our children need to be loved 'just the way they are'? Or does this fluffy approach lead to entitled snowflakes with no chance of coping in this complex, uncertain world?

Does unconditional love work?

To answer this question, let's meet another Mr Rogers – Carl Rogers, the founder of Humanistic Psychology and a man considered one of the most eminent psychologists of the twentieth century.

Carl's career began in 1928 at the Rochester Society for the Prevention of Cruelty to Children in New York State, USA. Here he worked with children with a range of emotional and behavioural difficulties, from stealing to aggression, excessive thumb-sucking to school exclusion. This clinical experience led Carl to question whether traditional therapy – the therapist-knows-best approach – was the most effective. He had noticed through his work with these children that what he called a 'person-centred' approach seemed to be producing the best results. In this approach, the therapist trusts that 'it is the client who knows what hurts, what directions to go, what problems are crucial, what experiences have been deeply buried.'

Rogers went on to develop and refine his model. And at the heart of it, he put this essential quality: 'unconditional positive regard'. This is where the therapist offers a deep acceptance of the child, of their thoughts, their feelings and their behaviours. Rogers called it, 'a gullible caring, in which clients are accepted as they say they are, not with a lurking suspicion in the therapist's mind that they may, in fact, be otherwise. This attitude is not stupidity on the therapist's part; it is the kind of attitude that is most likely to lead to trust.'

Now, Carl Rogers was definitely not fluffy. He was rigorous and scientific in his approach, and he both led and inspired a huge body of research into therapy, research that has continued to this day.

We now have over half a century of study into what works and what doesn't in therapy. And there's one consistent conclusion: specific therapy techniques, such as CBT, mindfulness or art therapy, have almost zero bearing on outcomes. Bruce Wampold, who has done more research into what makes psychotherapy work than almost anyone else says: 'I would put the differences between various types of psychotherapy at very close to zero per cent.'

But there is one thing that has been shown to have a clear, consistent and significant impact: the relationship between the therapist and the client. And the one absolutely key quality in that relationship? Unconditional positive regard.

Loving a child just the way they are turns out to be one of the most critical ingredients for supporting children to heal and to grow. Unconditional positive regard isn't just for therapists. Parents, teachers – anyone can cultivate this attitude. In the words of Carl Rogers, you just need to 'lay aside your own views and values in order to enter another's world without prejudice.'

But is it really that easy to love a child just the way they are?

What happens when your child is challenging, stubborn, self-centred, attention-seeking, manipulative, cruel? If you don't feel like this about your children now, you will someday (and you might have felt like this three times since breakfast). Remember, children are perfectly designed to reveal the shadow parts of our self. When triggered, our love quickly becomes conditional, turning to frustration or hatred, even. So how can we stay connected to love when the kids are driving us mad?

GARETH: UNRELENTING LOVE

I've been blessed to work with many children who've helped me to expand my capacity for love. The therapeutic school I used to run was called The Treehouse – a nice, friendly name for a school teaching kids with complex trauma. These kids had been kicked out of every other school and we were their last chance saloon. If we couldn't look after them, they would end up either in prison or a psychiatric unit. At this school, we had a 'No Exclusions' policy. No matter how 'bad' a student was, we never permanently excluded them. This policy twisted our hearts towards unconditional positive regard, even at times when every fibre of my being wanted to punish and exclude.

One day, about two years into my tenure at the school, there was a big fight between two pupils. I was keyworker to one of them, Gareth. The whole school was watching and the other kids were going wild. I found myself needing to restrain Gareth who, at age 15, was already over six foot and weighed about 14 stone so was capable of doing serious damage. We had just learned a new humane restraining technique (I had my doubts about it) that was based on using 'caring Cs': putting your hands in a C shape around someone's wrists to prevent them from lashing out and causing more damage.

Unfortunately, after a long struggle to restrain Gareth, he managed to wriggle to the ground with me still desperately cupping his wrists in this goddamned caring C grip. From his new position he flung his legs over his head and, with boots flying like jackhammers, hit me square in the nose. My nose was bleeding heavily. Two other staff members dragged Gareth away.

In any 'normal' school, this behaviour would most likely lead to a full exclusion. But not here. The motto we had on our wall read: 'children recover with unrelenting love'.

I went to the bathroom to tidy myself up and take a few deep breaths. By the time I came downstairs, Gareth had calmed down. I decided to take him for a walk around the block to clear the air. Gareth was very apologetic. And I wasn't holding a grudge. Gareth and I had a good relationship. And I knew that Gareth's wild energy and flying boot was largely a trauma response. By the time we got back for lunch, we had made our peace. Gareth and I walked side by side into the dining hall where the other students were having lunch. They looked up at us in shock. A student had just bust a teacher's nose and half an hour later they were eating lunch together.

After this, something shifted in the energy of the school. Perhaps it took an incident like this to prove that us grown-ups were committed to 'unrelenting love'.

I am not saying that it is easy to have this level of restraint. There have been plenty of other times at work and at home when I have completely lost my cool. But I am sharing this story to highlight what is possible when we bind ourselves to a value of unrelenting love.

In case you're wondering what happened to Gareth, I am still in touch with him. We met for lunch recently and I was so pleased to hear he has a stable job, a stable girlfriend and is doing OK. I asked Gareth about his Treehouse days. He said, 'Yeah, it was safe, man. I don't know where I'd be now without that place.'

Testing our capacity for love

A lot of challenging child behaviour can be understood as the child unconsciously testing our capacity to love them. Imagine you need to walk across an icy lake to go home. First, you'd tap your foot on the ice as hard as you could to make sure it isn't going to break beneath your weight. Children also tap their feet to test whether we are solid enough to hold them.

When we find ourselves challenged by the children in our care, we have two basic choices: reject them or love them. Rejecting them might look like scolding them, shaming them, bribing them, threatening them, sending them to the naughty corner or sending them to boarding school. We each have our own ways of withdrawing love. And look, we are only human after all. Sometimes we need to close our hearts a bit, protect ourselves, retreat and take stock, especially if our children are particularly challenging. Please don't judge or blame or shame yourself for the times you have lost your shit (we all have), screamed obscenities (we all have) and generally wished you had a different, better child (we all have). But it's important to remember that our children are mirrors to our own shadow parts. We usually aren't reacting to the child in front of us. We are reacting to an image we project onto the child. As Anaïs Nin said, 'We don't see things as they are; we see them as we are.'

When our children are 'challenging' or 'naughty', the image we project onto them is coloured by our own unresolved shadow material. By closing our hearts, we lose the possibility of healing for ourselves. And we risk becoming vectors, spreading the cultural virus of 'not enough'. That doesn't mean we never correct our children's behaviour. Of course we need to do that (more on this below). But we want to do this from a place of love.

Do you know one of the single most effective way to heal psychological distress in our children? Stop trying to fix them. I know this might seem difficult to believe, naive or idealistic. But in my experience, it is true. There is a good deal of wisdom in that old adage 'what you resist, persists'. Meditation teacher Byron Katie wrote: 'I am a lover of what is, not because I'm a spiritual person, but because it hurts when I argue with reality.' This feels especially true when it comes to raising children. When we argue with the truth of our child as they are, we create suffering for both of us.

More than anything else, 'symptoms' need love. Both Mr Rogers were right.

LOVING WHAT IS MOST DIFFICULT TO ACCEPT IN OUR CHILDREN

This simple exercise can help you to enter your child's world without prejudice. (The same exercise can be used for a partner, a parent, a colleague, a boss, anyone!) It's adapted from an exercise in *Loving What Is* by Byron Katie.

Write down your answers to the following questions:

1. Bring to mind one aspect of your child that you find really hard to accept. What about them triggers the strongest reaction in you?

2. What story do you tell yourself about that hard-to-accept thing? Let out onto the page all the hidden judgements and resentments. For example, if your child refuses to listen to you, perhaps you tell yourself that they are 'irritating', 'stubborn', 'a little tyrant', 'just like their dad', or that they 'need to be fixed'? Perhaps the story you tell about this difficult-to-accept part is also a story about you: 'I'm a terrible parent' or 'Nobody listens to me.'

3. How do you want them to change? What is it that you want them to be/do differently?

4. When you think about the hard-to-accept thing, what feelings come up in your body? Can you allow those feelings to be there, just for a moment?

5. Imagine letting go of the story about the hard-to-accept thing.

   i. Who would **you** be without this story?

   ii. Who would **they** be without this story?

6. When you have answered these questions, see if for the next few days you can practise being with the hard-to-accept aspect of your child without the story. Notice what happens if instead of trying to fix them, scold them,

shame them, etc., you a) take a moment to allow the feelings in your body to be there, b) remind yourself you are enough and they are enough, c) let go of any judgement, d) love whatever is presenting in your child. If you can love the part of your child that is hard to accept, there is magic to be found here. Remember, we don't see our children as they are; we see them as we are.

The ultimate reward

Even if you do happen to be Jesus, with a heart as infinite as the sky, ultimately, we can't get away from rewards and consequences. Some parents think rewards and consequences are bad, full stop. And there's an implicit expectation we sometimes carry that children should be naturally motivated to do exactly what we want them to do, exactly when we ask them to do it. Ha!

The reality is children are autonomous creatures with their own needs and desires. And a significant chunk of their neurology is wired to seek rewards in the future and to avoid the pain of not getting that reward. I'm talking here about the drive system of motivation, one of the three basic motivational systems we mentioned in Chapter 7. It's powered by dopamine, the 'molecule of more' that triggers us to seek future rewards. Dopamine has been discovered in many life forms, even in jellyfish and coral. For life to evolve, it needs this mechanism for motivation, for reward and punishment, for pain and pleasure. Indeed, we need it just to exist. In an experiment in the 1950s, neuroscientists implanted electrodes into the brains of rats, blocking the release of dopamine. The rats stopped eating. Stopped having sex. Stopped doing anything. Within a few days, they died of thirst.

Interestingly, studies suggest that the ultimate reward for a human child is a close, loving relationship. It's been shown, for example, that dopamine levels in both a baby's and a mother's brain fluctuate depending on the presence of the other. Research also suggests that when human beings don't get this ultimate reward of connection, we are more likely to look for other rewards that can be more addictive. Especially in childhood, if we don't get the right social-emotional stimulation then our dopamine systems go haywire. For example, rats separated from their mothers in their early development, even just for an hour a day, are much more likely to self-administer cocaine. The addiction and trauma specialist Gabor Maté says that at the root of all addiction is a seeking for connection.

To provide that ultimate reward of loving presence for a child, we grown-ups need to be in the green tend and befriend circle we discussed earlier. Sadly, we are living in the same mad world as our children are, where we are addicted to digital technologies designed to capture our attention and have us constantly, slavishly seeking rewards in the future. We all carry a constant, nagging, anxious feeling that there's 'a lot of room for improvement'. This deep, embodied sense of not enough puts us into a state where we struggle to provide our children with the ultimate reward.

An antidote to this is to set a time, ideally a regular time, when you can commit to being fully present with your child. And in this time, you do not let anything distract you. So turn off your phone, or at the very least place it out of reach. And let your child decide what they want to do, within reason. Of course, this same basic technique has been repeated in other places in this book and across so many parenting methods and child psychology books. So perhaps it sounds obvious. But sometimes it's about returning to the simplest things, as we can totally underestimate the power of this connection time. In case you need any more motivation, this connection time will give you as much of a good feeling as it will your child. Because connection is also the ultimate reward for grown-ups.

Do we have to use carrots and sticks?

We want our children to be all sorts of things: well-behaved, kind, focused, tidy, ambitious, confident, creative. But most parents I speak to don't want to use too many threats, bribes or rewards. I think this intuition is, partly, correct. Too many material rewards can turn our children into reward junkies, who only co-operate if there's something in it for them. Ideally, we'd like the motivation to come from them (intrinsic motivation), rather than from carrots and sticks imposed by us (extrinsic motivation). And children do have their own intrinsic desires and motivations. I suspect you never had to use a reward chart to get your child to eat ice cream.

Unfortunately for parents, one of our children's intrinsic motivations is to test boundaries and break rules. The other day, Rose's slightly older cousin taught her the word 'vagina' and told her that she should definitely not say it out loud (thanks, Jack!). So that evening, after bath time, Rose stuck her head out of the window and, with the neighbours sitting in their garden having a nice, peaceful supper, Rose screamed out, a gleeful look on her face: 'VAGINA! VAGINA! VAGINA!' We don't need a neuroscientist to tell us the natural pleasure she was experiencing in testing the boundary, exploring new terrain, doing something she wasn't supposed to.

Children are wired to derive pleasure from seeking out new things and testing boundaries. And this becomes especially true, of course, in adolescence. With this in mind, we don't need to pathologise defiance. If anything, the more we accept our children as the autonomous beings they are – with their own needs, their own desires and their own intrinsic motivation to seek out novelty and to test boundaries – the more we can love them just the way they are. This does not mean you just let them do whatever they want. Consequences and limits are necessary to guide your children's behaviour. There are consequences in the real world, after all. It's just that we want to deliver these with as much patience and love as we can muster. Let's look now at how to use rewards and consequences with love.

REWARDS AND CONSEQUENCES WITH LOVE

Your children may be small and not have as much control over their emotions or behaviours (or bladders) but they deserve to be treated with respect, especially if you want them to respect you back. So use rewards and consequences wisely, sparingly and lovingly, so your children do still feel enough. It really helps if, when using rewards and consequences, you can yourself come from a place of enoughness. To cultivate an inner state of abundance, experiment with the following mantras before you use any carrots or sticks with your child:

I am respected.
I am loved.
I am enough.
I can be free of other people's judgements.
This child is enough.
This child doesn't need to do anything to earn my love.
This child is fundamentally good.
I love and accept this child as they are.
I trust my child to make mistakes and I believe in their ability to learn from them.

- **Bring out the child's inner motivation.** Is there a consequence of this behaviour that would really bother your child? Can you spell it out to them? One girl's parents told me they were struggling to get her to brush her teeth. When they really spelled out to her the consequences of having bad breath, she really absorbed this. Then the parents decided to stop nagging her for a week. After a few days, she started brushing.

- **Try natural consequences.** This is when we trust life to be the best teacher. In the example above, if the child doesn't brush their teeth for a week the natural consequence might be that they will have bad breath and their friends at school will make fun of them. A child refuses to wear a hat outside? They get cold.

- **Give the child a loving and non-judgemental space** where they can reflect without shame on the natural consequences. The teenagers I work with are very capable of reflecting wisely on the negative impacts of their smartphone use. Supporting our children to reflect gives them the ability to learn from and adapt to other life challenges.

- **Show your emotions.** Sometimes the most natural consequence is for a child to see how upset you are in the moment. We aren't designed to be peaceful and happy all the time. This is especially true if they are doing something that could get them hurt, like running across a busy road. In these moments, shouting at them, showing your anger and fear, really letting them feel the pain of what could have happened can be totally appropriate. Pain is a good teacher, a strong way to teach them vital, potentially life-saving lessons. This is not an argument for shouting instructions on autopilot or physical discipline. Rather, it is about being human, being real. You can stay connected to your feelings (more on this in the next chapters) and use this emotional energy to get your point across.

- **Reward positive behaviour** by praising the specific quality involved. If saying 'well done' is a Facebook 'like', praising the specific quality is taking the time to write a thoughtful comment. You might say, 'I noticed that you cleaned up the mess in your bedroom, even though you didn't really want to, and that shows me that you are a caring person who cares about other people's feelings.'

- **Material rewards can work too**, if they are used to help set up a new habit or behaviour. But once the behaviour is established, you need to replace this with verbal praise or with connection time, doing an activity with you that your child loves.

Each child will respond differently, so try different approaches. And children who carry a lot of trauma may need much more 'loving them as they are', because they can experience any consequence or limit as a threat. Most of all, the crucial message for the child is that they are loved, regardless. Your child needs to know there is behaviour you can't accept but that does not mean you don't love them.

Trusting in the abundance of life

So far, we have focused on growing our inner sense of 'enough' and that of our children. But isn't inner abundance just a distraction from real-life worries, from our efforts to make sure our children have food on the table, clothes to keep them warm, a roof over their heads? Like, what if the loo rolls actually do run out?

To answer this, we need to understand what 'enough' means when it comes to stuff. How do we know when we 'have' enough? It's a hard question to answer. As we explored previously, we have mimetic desire, wanting what others have. And what we want is conditioned by the world around us – so many green tractors dangled in front of us.

Take toys. Before the twentieth century, children had very few toys. They might have had a wooden car, a jigsaw, a teddy bear or a doll. Dolls made from clay, wood, ivory or rags have been discovered in children's graves dating back to ancient Roman times. Fast-forward to now and most children's TV programmes and games are multimedia merchandising empires, manipulating our children's desire for more stuff. Children who can barely walk are getting hooked on characters like Peppa Pig, who flow from the TV screen into an endless stream of plastic products.

It's hard to say no to your child and to return to a simpler sense of what is 'enough' when surrounded by ubiquitous advertising. As John Naish says in his book *Enough,* 'We are girdled by multimillion-pound industries that use an ever-growing array of overt and hidden persuaders to get us to want things, work for things and buy more of them. We don't tend to complain but if you were physically forced by powerful gangs to spend all your time and energy in the pursuit of things you didn't need, didn't want and ultimately didn't enjoy, you'd feel sorely misused.'

I suspect this isn't breaking news to you. But you may not fully appreciate the effect it's having on your child. Tim Kasser, a professor of psychology at Duke University, has done more research than most into the effects of materialism on well-being. As well as wanting expensive consumer goods, he found that people who are materialistic (which here means more focused on wealth, possessions, image and status) tend to be less caring, less concerned by environmental issues and more likely to be stressed and depressed. Conversely, people who are not as materialistic are more likely to be kind to others, community and family-minded, and live according to deeply held beliefs. In one study, the researchers found that the more a country was focused on materialism, the worse the wellbeing of the child.

For a child, it's a very small step from being made to feel like you *don't have* enough to feeling like *you aren't* enough. So how can we help our children feel a sense of having 'enough', of abundance?

Ideas for growing your child's sense of abundance

1. **Gratitude.** This is the single biggest thing you can do to protect your children from excessive materialism. Gratitude takes us from the drive system, the dopamine zone, to the soothing system. It has been shown to reduce stress, anxiety and depression in children, inoculate us against trauma, improve sleep and even to lower levels of inflammation in the body. Grateful parents raise grateful children who are more likely to have positive relationships with other people and with the environment. The best way I have found to develop a habit of gratitude is to choose a regular time of day in which to do this. Mealtimes are good; you can practise talking about all the things that had to happen for the food to arrive on this plate – the sun, the rain, the soil, the farmer, the lorry driver, the checkout lady. You can imagine thanking each one of

these elements. Or, you can simply take turns to each say one thing you feel grateful for today. If the kids find this a bit weird at first, don't force it, just model it. N.B. Gratitude works better when you can feel it – putting a hand on your heart can help activate your warm-hearted biology.

2. **Gandhi's ultimate question.** Before Gandhi died, he left a note that read: 'Recall the face of the poorest and the weakest person you may have seen and ask yourself if the step you contemplate is going to be of any use to them.' Next time you are thinking of buying something for yourself or for your children, ask yourself this question. It's the strongest antidote I know to materialism.

3. **Reflect on your relationship to stuff.** As we know, your kids will imitate what you do. 'Kids are going to learn what their relationship with products should be by looking at our relationship with products,' according to Marsha Richins, a professor of marketing who specialises in children. Helpful questions to ask yourself are: 'How and when am I influenced to want what others have?' 'Do I buy things to make me happy?' 'Do I sacrifice a lot (time, energy, fun) to get more material stuff in the future?' Have open conversations with your kids about this.

4. **Digital Sabbath:** As our desires get hijacked mostly via digital media, think about regular committed time away from devices. The most helpful way my family have found is to declare one day of the weekend as a digital Sabbath. The whole family turns off their devices for the day or sticks to a clear limit. For you, it may be no games, no social media, no Amazon, just urgent phone calls. I've supported families who've put

their devices in a box for the day. Before they take them out, they talk about how their day felt.

A World of Enough

Enough
Enough. These few words are enough.
If not these words, this breath.
If not this breath, this sitting here.
This opening to the life
we have refused
again and again
until now.
Until now.

— David Whyte

Indeed, if there is one mantra that I come back to time and again it is the one from Chapter 8: *I AM ENOUGH*. That's because it really works. Repeat the phrase quietly to yourself and allow the words to carry the nectar of enoughness to each cell in your body. As you breathe in, imagine breathing in the energy of enough. Breathe into the parts of you that may feel particularly in need of a reminder of this quality right now. You are enough.

I am enough is a force field that can protect you and your children from the vultures that would feed off our unworthiness. Can you find where the unworthiness is, in your body? Breathe this energy of *I am enough* into those parts. Imagine as you do that the feeling of unworthiness transforms into something beautiful and strong, a fiery light, a field of proud and resilient sunflowers. When you are with your children, bathe them in this energy, creating a protective shield around them.

Repeat the mantra when you are with your children but this time turn it into *YOU ARE ENOUGH.* Feel the energy of enoughness shining through your face and your body filling your children with this energy without you or they needing to 'do' anything.

Now imagine extending this energy to all beings everywhere. To all the children, to all the grown-ups – *We are enough.* Imagine what the world could be like if we all lived our daily lives from this deep sense of enoughness. I can feel my shoulders dropping, my breath slowing down, my feet touching the ground. What can you notice?

10

ROOT FIVE: ANAESTHESIA

How we cut ourselves off
from our feelings

*What is happiness? It's the moment before you
need more happiness*

– Don Draper, *Mad Men*

Once upon a time there was a girl called Anastasia who lived with her family in a little house in a very small clearing in the middle of a big, dark forest. Anastasia's family loved her and they thought the best thing was for her be happy all the time. Every time she walked into a room with a smile on her face, they would clap and cheer. But whenever Anastasia was sad or angry, her father would send her off into the forest, shouting: 'And don't you come back until you've found that smile!' Anastasia did not like being in the forest all by herself. It was scary out there. So, to get back into the house, and back into her parents' good books, she learned how to put on a happy face, even when she felt sad or angry inside. And thus, her family continued to clap and cheer. (Little did they notice how strained her smiles were.)

But Anastasia woke up on her thirteenth birthday and, no matter how hard she tried, she simply couldn't make herself smile. She couldn't even get out of bed. Her body had turned into the most stubborn of mules. Thirteen years of pretending to be happy had exhausted her.

As Anastasia lay corpse-like in her room, her mind was filled with sad and dark thoughts. Her dad came in with a big smile and some birthday cake and tried hard to make her smile. But all Anastasia could think about was chopping off her dad's head. She didn't like having this dark thought. But it kept coming back.

When her mum came in and saw Anastasia lying there looking unhappy, she said: 'Anastasia, you are being very ungrateful.' At this point, Anastasia simply couldn't hold it in any more. She screamed: 'I can't stand this fake happiness. You're all fake and I can't trust any of you. Please just let me have my feelings.'

This is when Anastasia decided to go back out into the forest to learn about all of her different emotions. She spoke to a tigress who explained how anger helped her to protect her cubs. She spoke to a koala bear who told her he felt really sad because his brothers were killed in a fire. And as she talked to these animals, Anastasia learned that her feelings were really important. She learned to take care of her emotions as if they were precious flowers inside her heart.

When she went back home, Anastasia told her family everything she had learned in the forest. Thanks to Anastasia's honesty and courage, her family learned that they too could stop pretending to be happy all the time. And as they opened up about their different feelings, the family noticed they had so much more energy and they began to trust each other more, too.

The end.

I'll be happy when . . .

I used to teach a class for grown-ups about the wisdom of emotions. As part of the class, I had an exercise called 'The Emotion Line-Up'. I'd open with a brief discussion about the different core emotions and then I'd ask the group to imagine a line going across the room – one end of this imaginary line was the place to stand if you felt an emotion was completely positive and the other if you felt it was completely negative.

Then I'd call out an emotion word and ask the group – without thinking too long about the answer – to stand in the place in the line where they instinctively would place that emotion. When I called out 'HAPPINESS', pretty much every person stood at the positive end of the line. 'SADNESS' got more of a mixed review; some people felt it could be a positive but most people were towards the negative end. But when I called out 'ANGER' or 'FEAR', almost everyone stood right at the negative end.

The truth is, even if we think we value all our emotions equally, our behaviours tell a different story. In modern life, we tend to pursue happiness and avoid or repress the 'negative' emotions. And if these emotions pop up unexpectedly in the presence of others, we might feel ashamed or be shamed. We conclude there must be something wrong with us, and so we discover so many clever ways to cover these emotions up.

Think about this: on an average day, how much time, attention, money or energy do you spend allowing yourself to experience your anger, fear or sadness? For most of us, I suspect the answer is: not much. When we feel these feelings, we're like Mr McGregor when he sees Peter Rabbit in his nice vegetable garden; we chase them out shouting, 'Stop thief!'

Now, how much time do you spend trying to be happy? This is a slightly tricker question. We don't always realise that it's happiness we are going after but the pursuit of happiness lies behind so many of our day-to-day actions. Look at the following list and see if, when you think about doing these things, you have a sub-clause in your mind that says 'I will be happy when . . .':

1. I go to the gym.
2. I put the children to bed.
3. I meditate.
4. I buy a new coat.
5. I finish that piece of work.
6. I go on holiday.

What are you chasing in your day-to-day life that you're telling yourself is going to make you happy? The pursuit of happiness is an invisible driver behind our consumerist culture. It's the hidden promise behind most advertising. If we buy this scented candle, this transformational workshop, this spa break, then we will find happiness.

One big problem with this pursuit of happiness is that feelings are slippery eels: the more you chase them, the more they slip away. As William Blake, in his poem 'Eternity', says, 'He who binds to himself a joy/Does the winged life destroy. He who kisses the joy as it flies/Lives in eternity's sunrise.'

Another problem with the overemphasis on happiness is that we – both kids and grown-ups – are not designed to be happy all the time. We are born with a set of emotional responses to the world. Children get scared. They get shy. They get angry. When they don't get what they want, their bottom lip drops. When they taste something that surprises or disgusts them, their nose and face scrunch up so their feelings are clear for all to see (as is the food spat onto the carpet). And, of course, children get happy, ecstatically so at times.

But our culture gives us a false and damaging ideal: that happiness is the only emotion worth having. It has not always been this way, as we will see later on in this chapter. But today, when we experience any emotion other than happiness, we tend to reach for something to numb or distract us from it, whether it's food, alcohol, shopping, social media, spiritual platitudes, productivity, or intense exercise. In a world where the most powerful companies in history are using the most powerful technologies ever invented to provide us with endless ways to distract from our feelings, this problem has now reached a whole new level. Psychotherapist Francis Weller has declared 'anaesthesia' to be one of the cardinal sins of our modern culture.

Take the new diagnosis of prolonged grief disorder, in the psychiatric manual for mental health, the *Diagnostic and Statistical Manual of Mental Disorders* fifth edition, known as the *DSM-V*. Now, someone who's still showing signs of grief just six months or more after the death of a loved one can be diagnosed and possibly even medicated. Contrast this with the ancient Jewish mourning tradition. When a parent dies, the mourner enters into a year-long, community-based framework for grief, where haircuts are prohibited, there are regular prayers, people visit your house to show support and the mourner is supported to make a deeper spiritual connection.

As we will see in the next chapter, our emotions give us vital information, telling us when the world around us isn't meeting our most basic needs. By escaping and numbing, we lose our capacity to learn from the rich emotional tapestry of life. We lose touch with our souls and their yearning for a deeper sense of belonging.

Hans Christian Andersen wrote in *The Little Mermaid*, 'But a mermaid has no tears and therefore she suffers so much more.' In a culture with little room for sadness and other non-happy feelings, it's no coincidence that the number of antidepressants prescribed in the UK doubled between 2008 and 2018, up to 70.9 million prescriptions a year. Although we may be trying to avoid suffering by sending our sad feelings out into the forest, these feelings don't simply vanish. They can't – because they are a fundamental part of who we are.

The downside of mental health awareness

As I write, it's Mental Health Awareness week in the UK. Every individual and organisation with a platform is using this opportunity to raise awareness and funds for their cause. I know this space well because I run a mental health charity.

What does it mean to be more 'aware' of mental health? If the outcome is getting people to think about and offer meaningful support to those who are struggling with their mental health, it is surely a good thing. But mental health awareness can also pathologise normal human experience. It can make people afraid that there might be something wrong with them, without giving them the right tools to analyse their own experience.

It's true that mental health is a spectrum. But there is a very clear difference between, say, chronic and debilitating depression and a prolonged episode of sadness. In her book *Losing Our Minds*, psychologist Lucy Foulkes makes the point very clearly: 'OCD, depression, bipolar disorder . . . these terms have been let loose into society, but without sufficient depth of information, they take on a life of their own . . . in the rush to destigmatise mental illness, all kinds of normal negative emotions and experiences are being labelled as mental disorders – or at the very least as problems that instantly need to be fixed.'

Now, I want to be very clear here: there is a small proportion of children and young people who have a serious mental health problem and who need professional help. But when mental health awareness collides with a culture that tells us happiness is the only allowed emotion, this creates a breeding ground for depression.

Unlike chicken pox or a broken leg, you can't see mental illness. This doesn't mean mental illness isn't real. It does mean that there is a greater level of subjectivity both in how we interpret our inner signals and how the world around us conditions us to interpret those signals.

Imagine you are a young person who hates school and your parents have just been through a messy separation. You feel sad, really sad. And then you read a typical mental health awareness statistic like '1 in 4 girls will have depression by the time they are 14'. You might worry: *Oh, maybe I have depression.* Then you carry this awareness with you like an oversensitive smoke alarm that goes off every time you have a thought or a feeling that isn't happy.

A good analogy here is how during the Covid pandemic, particularly at the start, we became highly attuned to any possible symptoms of the virus – the slightest cough made us panic. The psychological term for this is 'hypervigilance', which refers to the way that after a trauma, you constantly scan for signs – both outside you but also in your own head – that the traumatic event might be about to occur again. What you seek, you shall find. If you are hypervigilantly scanning your thoughts for signs there might be something wrong with you, signs that you might be depressed or anxious, then you can almost guarantee you will find evidence that you are.

The more we pathologise our 'negative' emotions like sadness or anger, the more fear we create around these feelings. We push them out into the dark forest, where these feelings turn into demons, monsters, wild animals that threaten to destroy the sanctity (sanity) of our clearing. If we do this for long enough, it can make us mentally ill.

BEFRIENDING THE HYPERVIGILANT ONE

If at any time you find yourself hyperaware or hyper-vigilant about signs of mental health problems in yourself or your children, this one's for you.

Let's begin by bringing some compassion to the hyper-vigilant part of you. Perhaps this part is scanning for signs of depression or other issues because of a family history of mental illness. Or perhaps you have been through a divorce, experienced a loss or have read some worrying statistics. Whatever the reason, it's important that you turn towards this hypervigilant part with tenderness. Underneath it lies a worry that you or your children are in some way deficient, broken. It might help to give this hypervigilant part a character or a shape, or to find where its energy sits in the body. Can you just allow it to be there for a moment? Can you thank it for trying to keep you safe? And if there are any sensations or emotions (sadness, anger, fear, etc.) that this hypervigilant part is seeking/finding, can you also gently turn towards these sensations as you find them in your body. Can you let these sensations be there, just for a moment? Place a loving hand on them. You will find more often than not that any 'negative' sensations or emotions will soften, dissolve or transmute into something else.

Happy-washing

Let's play: Who Am I? I have a yellow face, two black dots for eyes and a broad smile. You see my picture on your phone. In the 1990s, you might have taken a pill with my face on and danced all night long.

Yes, I'm Smiley Face – our symbol of happiness.

Where did this iconic face come from?

It's 1963, in Massachusetts. The State Mutual Life Assurance Company has just bought out another insurance firm and the merger has left staff feeling down. Someone in the company has a bright idea. They hire graphic designer Harvey Ball and ask him to come up with a morale booster for the team. They pay him $45 and he creates the design in ten minutes – a yellow face, two black dots for eyes and a broad smile. The insurance company prints hundreds of thousands of smiley face buttons and gives them to employees, to remind them that they must smile and appear happy when dealing with customers.

When did happiness become a must-have accessory for all, something we pin on our jackets to cover up poor working conditions or the only acceptable emotion in a world that is making our children mad?

According to historian Peter Stearns in his book *Happiness in World History*, before the eighteenth century, a 'melancholic demeanour' was in vogue and too much mirth was frowned upon. But then the Enlightenment happened, bringing new values and a great deal of optimism. In 1776, happiness was even enshrined as a core political value. The United States Declaration of Independence enshrined the unalienable rights of American citizens: life, liberty, and the pursuit of happiness. Around the same time, poet John Byrom declared, 'It was the best thing one could do to be always cheerful . . . and not suffer any sullenness.' Better dentistry meant people also became more willing to reveal their teeth in a smile. Think of the enigmatic expression of the *Mona Lisa*, painted around 1500. Painted 500 years later, she might have had a proper Tom Cruise-style grin.

While giving people the constitutional right to pursue their own happiness seems like a good thing, many historians agree that this arrival of 'happiness' in the American constitution covered up a deep and dark shadow: slavery. Those defending slavery would argue that slaves often had a 'down look' because they weren't capable of happiness. I know this sounds outrageous to us now, but these kind of justifications for slavery go back as far as the Ancient Greeks and Aristotle, who said that some groups of people were 'natural slaves' because they lacked *thymos* or 'spirit'.

To those defending slavery, the sadness of a slave was an indication of their faulty wiring, rather than a natural response to being enslaved. As historian Nicole Eustace explains, 'throughout history, beginning but not ending with Jefferson's Declaration, debates over happiness have been implicated in a wide variety of struggles over power.'*

The political use of happiness soon spread to childhood. The early twentieth century saw the first child-rearing manuals focused on the goal of happiness. One read: 'Happiness is as essential as food if a child is to develop into normal manhood or womanhood.' Now, happiness was becoming the single most important achievement for children and their parents. To have an unhappy child became a real problem. The happiness imperative continued throughout the Great Depression, when the Happy Birthday song became a standard family ritual. Around the same time, advertisers (a new profession then) were discovering that sales increased when products were associated with happiness. This is the backdrop to the formation of the Walt Disney company, whose motto was 'Make people happy'. And later, Ronald

* It's important to note that were several different (and contradictory) views held about non-white races, including slaves, in the eighteenth and nineteenth centuries. These included the beliefs that black people were less sensitive to pain; that they were unemotional; but also that they were over-emotional in a child-like way. There is also evidence of slaves being considered happy with their lot because they were observed behaving cheerfully (e.g. singing while working) – and also evidence that they behaved cheerfully because they were whipped if they didn't.

McDonald the 'Hamburger-Happy Clown' was created to spread smiles and happiness around the world along with fries, a burger and a fizzy drink – the Happy Meal.

Fast-forward to today and the UK has Richard Layard, known as a 'Happiness Tsar', who has used his powers to launch the United Nations' annual World Happiness Report, a league table of happy countries. The United Arab Emirates (UAE) are at the time of writing the twenty-fifth in the world, a fact they display proudly on their national website. But there is another table, the Human Freedom Index, that ranks countries' human rights. The UAE didn't fare so well in this one: 117th out of 162. Which isn't surprising in a state where women are legally obliged to look after the house and need a judge's permission to work, where homosexuality and other crimes are punishable by death.

I think we may need a new term: 'happy-washing', to describe how organisations and governments use happiness to cover up the real reasons why people might not be so happy. One study from 2018 showed that about 55 per cent of Brits feel regularly miserable at work, while nearly 40 per cent feel their jobs make no meaningful contribution to the world. But it's all fine because companies like Google and Amazon now have chief happiness officers. Instead of smiley face badges, they offer free food, free gyms, meditation pods. Happy-washing.

I recently spoke to a friend of mine, Nathan, who recruits teachers to special schools. He told me that it has been getting harder and harder to find teachers who want to teach because the conditions of teaching are so bad these days. So one of the solutions being implemented is to introduce a wellbeing programme for teachers. A few mindfulness lessons should help them get back on track. Happy-washing. We need to be aware of how happiness and wellbeing programmes might cover up deeper problems in our family, our work, or in our world.

The business of happy pills

I'm about to talk about antidepressants. You or your child may be on anti-depressant medication, and if you are finding them helpful then I am glad for you. What follows is just one perspective on the history, marketing and efficacy of these drugs. So please take what is helpful and leave what isn't.

In 1988, a new antidepressant was introduced by the drug company Eli Lilly. This drug was marketed as having few side effects, could make patients 'better than well' and was sold with the slogan 'happiness in a blister pack'. The company had named it Prozac. Billions of dollars have since been spent on marketing Prozac and drugs in the same family – known as SSRIs – and much of that spend goes on raising awareness of depression. For example, in the US, Eli Lilly gives a $4 million-a-year 'educational grant' to the National Mental Health Association's Campaign on Clinical Depression. Can you sense the dark side of mental health awareness now?

SSRIs soon became the leading kind of antidepressant. In the UK, from 1991 to 2018, the number of SSRI prescriptions went from 9 million a year to 70.9 million. Because of the huge commercial success of these happy pills, drug companies in the US developed child-friendly versions of antidepressant medication, such as a liquid form of Prozac (think Calpol for happy thoughts). And where the US led, we in the UK followed. Between 1992 and 2001, prescriptions of SSRIs for under-18s increased tenfold, despite the fact that none had a licence for use in children in the UK. These numbers continued to rise, particularly for the those aged 12 and under, where the number of prescriptions rose on average by 24 per cent between April 2015 and March 2018.

Then there was a bit of a PR disaster for companies who make antidepressants, such as GlaxoSmithKline. A 2002 BBC Panorama documentary revealed that one of the antidepressants most commonly prescribed to children and young people, Seroxat, was leading to increased suicidality among young people. And that these reports were being hidden by the drug companies. (A claim that was rejected by GlaxoSmithKline* in 2002, although they were later fined $3 billion in 2012 for bribing doctors to prescribe other unsuitable antidepressants to children.†) This caused a sad face for Big Pharma, as sales and use of antidepressant drugs dropped significantly. Fortunately for the drug companies, people have short memories (smiley face). Antidepressant use in children and adolescents increased significantly again between 2005 and 2012 in every Western country where this has been studied. The pharmaceutical industry now makes £12.5 billion each year from happy pills.

If you (like many of my clients) are questioning whether the antidepressant medication is working or making you worse, then you need to know this: according to the latest studies – there is little to no evidence to show that antidepressants are any better than a placebo for treating depression. And more recently evidence has emerged that more than half of people trying to stop taking antidepressants experience withdrawal, and half of those describe the withdrawal symptoms as severe. Even the newer SSRIs can increase risk of suicide (and homicide), with one study published in the British Medical Journal in 2016 showing that children and adolescents have a doubled risk of suicide when taking selective serotonin and serotonin-norepinephrine reuptake inhibitor drugs‡ to combat depression. This doesn't mean that if you or your child are taking these drugs that

* See http://news.bbc.co.uk/1/hi/programmes/panorama/6291947.stm and http://news.bbc.co.uk/1/hi/health/6308871.stm
† See https://www.theguardian.com/business/2012/jul/03/glaxosmithkline-fined-bribing-doctors-pharmaceuticals#:~:text=Despite%20knowing%20that%20three%20trials,antidepressant%20aimed%20only%20at%20adults
‡ Selective serotonin reuptake inhibitors (SSRIs) and Serotonin and norepinephrine reuptake inhibitors (SNRIs) are similar forms of antidepressant medication.

you should suddenly stop. But if you are questioning whether this medication is working or perhaps you are wondering if these pills may be making you or your child worse, it's really important you address this with your doctor. Be aware that – in my experience at least – some doctors may be biased in favour of the medication (we all have biases and blindspots) and may blame something other than the medication if you or your child are feeling worse. You need to be the ultimate judge of this.

Despite the billions spent on pills, depression is quickly becoming the biggest health problem in the world, according to the World Health Organization. Compare this to the huge advances made in other areas of medicine. As medical anthropologist James Davies notes in his book *Sedated:* 'If in the late 1970s a child had contracted this heart-breaking disease [leukemia], their chances of survival would have been around 20 per cent. But if a child contracts leukaemia today, their chances of survival are around 80 per cent.' This means outcomes have improved by over 300 per cent. Impressive rates of improvement can be found across almost every other area of medicine, apart from psychiatry, where 'not only have clinical outcomes broadly flatlined over the last thirty years, but according to some measures they have actually got worse.'

Based on figures like these, and on the experience of many people I have worked with, it seems that our way of thinking about and treating depression is not working.

MEET JOHN MCHAPPYPILL

I just read back over the last section and I feel angry. Do you? In the introduction, I mentioned my colleague child psychiatrist Sami Timimi, who more than anyone has spoken out about the 'McDonaldization' of child mental health. He captured the problem well with these words from in a recent article: 'medicalising mood creates great commercial opportunities'.

These are our children's minds. Their minds are precious. We have to protect them. And, as you know by now, the place to start is with our own minds. In the next chapter, you'll find ways to nurture and even celebrate the whole range of emotions in your children. For now, I'd like to guide us to a place where we can liberate our minds from the false god of happiness.

I would like you to take a moment to close your eyes and notice what's present in your body right now. Are there any feelings there other than happiness? Can you notice any fear, any sadness, any anger? Can you notice any resistance to those feelings, those sensations? Is there a subtle sense that they shouldn't be there?

If there is a part of you that says these feelings shouldn't be there, I want you to imagine that this gatekeeper part is the CEO of a huge pharmaceutical company. Let's call him John McHappypill. Imagine what this CEO looks like, what he is wearing. Imagine John McHappypill holding in his right hand a cheque for a billion dollars. You realise that the money is to be spent on convincing you that these feelings in your body shouldn't be there. Now imagine telling John McHappypill to FUCK OFF! Even better if you can say it out loud! Steal his cheque, kick him out of the room and lock the door.

Instead, picture spending that cheque on advertising to yourself that you are enough. Imagine being surrounded by an endless stream of unconditionally loving messages about your feelings and your innate beauty. Imagine that every time a sensation or feeling crops up that is anything other than 'happy', you turn towards that feeling with the deepest love and respect imaginable, that you honour the wisdom of your feelings. And that as you do, you find a deeper sense of meaning, a deeper sense of belonging, a deeper sense of peace.

Notice what is present now. Beneath the layers of conditioning, beneath the marketing and the ideology of happiness, there is just the sensation, just the feeling. It is neither good nor bad. It just is.

Of course, we have to practise doing this over and over again. And remember over and over again that our emotions are intelligent – they are giving us vital information about the world.

The roots of our anaesthesia

Do you remember the first time you saw your baby smile? And laugh? What a beautiful thing, to see a baby laugh. We love it when our children are happy.

What about when your baby or child is angry or sad or shy or nervous? How does that make you feel? The other day, Rose got really angry because I turned off her favourite tv show, *PJ Masks*. She hit me in the leg with a bamboo stick. I didn't like that.

I remember when we dropped Rose off at nursery for the first time. Ouch. She was crying, screaming, red in the face. 'Daddy, don't leeeave me!' she wailed as she gripped as hard as she could onto the door like a koala bear on steroids as the nursery teacher wrestled to bring her inside. I really didn't like that. It ripped my heart apart.

I love my daughter so deeply. As I said in the introduction, I want so much for her to feel safe in the world, to feel happy. So am I not following my own advice? Or is there something intrinsically desirable about being happy?

Really, there is nothing more compassionate than to wish that the people you love don't suffer. I feel that compassion for my daughter with a burning intensity. I will do anything to protect her from suffering. This is the deepest root of our anaesthesia – our aversion to suffering. The problem, as the Buddha rather brilliantly nailed it, comes when we refuse to acknowledge or accept that life is also suffering. We find the same fundamental problem with our modern pursuit of happiness: we think we and our children should be happy all the time and when we aren't happy, we think there is something wrong with us.

The ancients were generally more in tune with suffering, perhaps because it was more obviously present in their everyday lives. The Ancient Greek historian Herodotus wrote in the fifth century BCE, 'There is not a man in the world, either here or elsewhere, who is so happy that he does not wish – again and again – to be dead rather than alive.' Herodotus never did get that marketing role at Eli Lilly.

In his book, *Insane Medicine*, Sami Timimi captures brilliantly how progress in modern medicine has led to fantasies about eliminating suffering: 'Modern medicine has had some amazing successes in alleviating unnecessary suffering and reducing morbidity . . . But such progress awakens deeper, childish desires and fantasies that all suffering or unpleasant experiences have no value and are simply things we could and should eliminate from human experience.'

The most compassionate thing we can do for ourselves and for our children is to develop the courage and the capacity to turn towards the suffering that is inherent in life. Ironically, we are likely to discover a more sustainable type of happiness this way, as Thich Nhat Hanh says: 'If you know how to suffer, you suffer much, much less . . . The art of happiness and the art of suffering always go together.' We will explore this more in the following chapters. For now, here is a simple exercise for you which my clients find liberating.

Write down ten things in the world that really piss you off or make you feel sad. Here is my list:

1. Queuing for a mediocre ride in the pouring rain at Gulliver's World.

2. Companies that manipulate us into thinking we need to be more, have more, do more.

3. Children who grow up feeling like they are broken.

4. People who don't stop their cars, even though the traffic is moving slowly, to let the old lady or the mother and her child cross the busy road.

5. The proliferation of messaging services and social media platforms clogging up my time and my brain, leaving little time or patience for real human connection.

6. People who message 'we should meet up some time' followed by a full stop, and put no effort whatsoever into finding a time (admittedly I do that sometimes too).

7. The failure of our political leaders to have any integrity or even any vision beyond business as usual.

8. The fact that our time in this life is limited and we waste so much of it on things that really don't matter.

9. A vanishing sense of community as we all spend more time indoors, more time online.

10. The possible future my daughter faces.

Dear friend, whatever is on your list, I encourage you to trust the wisdom of your feelings. As we will discover in the next chapter, just because you feel sad or angry sometimes does not mean there is something wrong with you, your child or even your inner child.

It's OK for your (inner) child to be sad sometimes.

It's OK for your (inner) child to be angry sometimes.

It's OK for your (inner) child to be scared sometimes.

It's OK for your (inner) child to have a complete meltdown sometimes.

My hope is that we can all recover the emotional energy that has been stolen by those false prophets of happiness, that we can use that emotional energy to create a future that, without being a happily ever after, may at least be a bit more honest and meaningful.

11

FRUIT FIVE: FEELING

How we can learn to tune in to and learn from all our emotions

The crickets felt it was their duty to warn everybody that summertime cannot last for ever. Even on the most beautiful days in the whole year – the days when summer is changing into autumn – the crickets spread the rumour of sadness and change

– E B White, *Charlotte's Web*

I apologise in advance for the sad topic I'm about to introduce. It's suicide and it may feel uncomfortable, but please bear with me. Even if what follows feels extreme compared to your own life, it will help you and your child navigate the sometimes stormy world of emotions.

In the UK, about 7 per cent of children have attempted suicide by the age of 17. A question I'm commonly asked is whether an attempted suicide is really 'a cry for help'. The subtext of this question is: *If they really meant it, they would have done it.*

This is not an easy question to answer. How could anyone really know if the 15-year-old girl who takes 20 paracetamol tablets means to die or if she is asking for attention? She may not even know herself. And if a suicide attempt is ever a cry for help, then why did that person feel they couldn't just 'cry for help'?

To try and understand this, we'll take a closer look at what emotions are and how we relate to them in our children. Given the crisis in children's mental health and the rise in rates of suicide, we need to learn how to help them embrace all their emotions, so they don't feel so alone with them (like Anastasia) or feel the need to 'cry for help' in other, more extreme ways.

Children are no-holds-barred emotional creatures. They can't help but wear their little hearts on their sleeves. Babies 'cry for help' multiple times in a day. But no one would call a crying baby 'attention seeking'. Why is that? We don't think they have the ability to manipulate us or that they 'choose' their emotions to get their needs met. So at what point in a child's life do they start using their emotions as tools for manipulation? There isn't a clear-cut answer to this.

About 15 years ago, I worked in a psychiatric unit for teenagers. The unit was a place where young people with chronic, acute mental health problems would come for treatment. Skeletal girls who needed to be force-fed. Boys on 24/7 suicide watch. The unit had a big team of senior psychiatrists, psychologists, family therapists, and nurses. The psychiatrists were clearly at the top of the pecking order here, while I was a mere social worker. In one of my first clinical meetings, we discussed a young girl who was refusing to take her medication. Whenever the nurses would approach, this girl would throw herself onto the floor and scream hysterically. The senior nurse brought this issue into the meeting, saying, 'She is doing this on purpose.' The consultant psychiatrist gave a solemn, authoritative nod.

I came to realise this was a common refrain in these meetings – a senior staff member saying the child had 'chosen' problematic emotions or behaviours. I understood the rationale: they wanted to help these kids realise they have a choice. But for me, there was also a lot of judgement here, born, I suspect, out of frustration that the kids weren't playing ball.

In one such meeting, I decided to challenge this: 'It seems like you are saying they are in control, that they should know better?' I asked. 'How do you actually know they are doing this on purpose?' Silence filled the room.

I can't remember getting any answer. Really, there isn't an easy answer to this question, just as there isn't an easy answer to whether a teenage suicide attempt is just a cry for help. Even if the child is 'acting out', it can only be because they haven't learned a better way to express their emotions and get their needs met.

Growing out of emotions

While we generally don't think babies can be manipulative, at some point in a child's development our perspective shifts. When our toddler throws themselves wailing on the floor in the supermarket we might think they are doing it on purpose. We might feel anger or shame in our own bodies and shout at them: 'Stop crying!' or 'Drama queen!' or 'Crocodile tears!' When a teen posts on social media 'I hate my life' or 'I don't want to live any more', a part of us might quietly (or not so quietly) suspect they are being emotionally manipulative, attention-seeking.

We're not thinking or saying these things to be mean. A big part of our job as grown-ups is to socialise our children into the culture. So if a child is expressing emotions that don't fit with our cultural norms, it is totally understandable that a parent or teacher would want to correct that behaviour, to help the child fit in. But something about the way we deal with emotions is not working. Something is tipping our children's sadness or anger into depression, their fear into anxiety, their disgust into self-harm, their despair into suicide. I believe we need a different approach to emotions.

A key assumption in modern Western culture is that growing up means growing out of being emotional and growing into being more rational, more reasonable. In our model, grown-ups are not supposed to feel things so intensely and if they do, we may even diagnose them or give them medication. As psychotherapist Adam Phillips writes in his book *Going Sane*: 'Our earliest lives are lived in a state of sane madness – of intense feelings and fearfully acute sensations. We grow up to protect ourselves from these feelings; and then as adults we call this defence "sanity". Looked at this way, sanity begins to sound like a word we might use for all adult states of mind in which we are not children, in which we do not experience things intensely. We are poor indeed though if this is our only idea of sanity.' Can you begin to see how our model of growing up is also our model of becoming 'sane'?

But our assumptions about emotional development are not necessarily 'universal' or 'true', and in many ways they are problematic. We know, for example, from anthropological studies that the stages of development like 'the terrible twos' and even the grumpy, antisocial teenager do not seem to exist in certain other cultures.

We also know from scientific research that whether emotions are OK to express or not varies across culture and these variations often depend on power and status. In Japan, for example, adults with high social status tend to express anger more easily. In one incredible study, they tested biomarkers for inflammation in American and Japanese participants from different strata of society (they tested inflammation because anger has been shown to increase inflammation and was thought to do so universally, until this study). They found that the Japanese participants in positions of power expressed their anger often but, contrary to expectations, there was no increase in inflammation. Studies like these show that our cultural rules about who is allowed to express which emotions can affect even our physical health.

What family or cultural rules around emotional expression did you absorb as a child? Were you ever told to 'stop being so sensitive', or 'big girls don't cry' or, 'come on, be a big boy'? Can you begin to see how power and status might have played a role in your emotional development?

Ironically, as you now know, raising children is guaranteed to bring up a whole range of intense emotions in us 'grown-ups'. As Kate Figes and Jean Zimmerman write in *Life after Birth: What Even Your Friends Won't Tell You About Motherhood*: 'We revisit the raw emotions of our own childhood when we have a child. We feel intense love, undiluted hate and anger, as well as extreme anxiety and fear, and can swing from one extreme emotion to another.'

We are often trying to police, and ultimately banish, emotions in our kids that are simultaneously resurfacing in us. There is no judgement here. I feel intense emotions when Rose has a meltdown, especially if it's in a public place. And I sometimes notice in these moments that there is an angry part of me that is triggered by the meltdown and wants to punish that behaviour. But, it feels a bit unfair, don't you think, that we might want to control our kids' emotions so that we don't have to deal with ours? Of course we want to help our children regulate their emotional states so they can function in the world (we will explore this below). But for now, I'd like you just to question a little some of the hidden assumptions you might be carrying about emotional expression. And I'd like you to really pay loving attention to the whole range of emotions that arise inside you on a daily basis when you are with your child.

What do our emotions do for us?

There is an ongoing and (dare I say it) emotional debate between scientists on what an emotion actually is. One side says we all have the same emotions; they're universal and come from the inside, as in the Pixar movie *Inside Out*. The other side says they are socially constructed: the Utku Inuit of Canada, for example, don't have a concept that corresponds to anger.

In my work, the definition I find most helpful is that emotions are 'energy in motion'. Something in the world (a loss, a threat, a reward) triggers an energetic response in the body and this guides the creature (yes, animals have emotions too) towards a certain behaviour. We say we find a speech or a film or a piece of music *moving* when it triggers an emotion.

Emotions are 100 per cent natural. Certified organic. When animals feel emotions, they don't question them or try to suppress them. If a lioness sees a pack of hyenas approaching her cubs, she will reveal her fangs and give a blood-curdling growl. The lioness has not grown up learning it would be inappropriate, childish or attention-seeking to show her fangs. She doesn't need a therapist, a book or a technique to help her channel her anger.

Emotions give us vital information. To come back to the question I asked at the beginning of the chapter, we could say that emotions themselves are 'attention-seeking' – they are a sign from our bodies that something needs our attention. However, we humans have culture. We have layers of conditioning that shape the expression or repression of our emotions. And when we don't pay enough attention to emotions, they often find ever more dramatic ways to be heard, like psychosomatic illness or even suicide attempts.

As I said in the introduction, I believe that our children are like canaries in the coalmine because they haven't yet built up adult defences around their emotions. Their natural, emotional responses to the world contain valid and essential truths. Primatologist Frans de Waal studied emotions in humans and animals over many years and came to the conclusion that, 'Emotions often know better than we do what is good for us, even though not everyone is prepared to listen.'

Here is a question for you to ponder: what if the emotions that we try to coach our children out of are actually critical for the survival of our species?

UNDERSTANDING THE THREE LEAST WELCOME EMOTIONS

The following will give you a perspective on the deeper purpose of three emotions that we typically don't welcome.

1. **Fear** alerts us to a threat, either physical or psychological. Fear wants to protect us from harm. I find the most helpful way to tend to fear is to write down, very specifically, what you're afraid of. This is the 'fear-setting' exercise we mentioned earlier. It is often the deeper, buried fears that haunt us. But writing them down gives us a sense of acceptance and control.

2. **Anger** tells us that something precious – whether it's inside us or outside us – is being threatened and we need to take some action to protect it. Anger is often fear disguised. I have worked with a number of children with 'anger issues' who beneath their anger were so afraid, for example, that their parents were going to separate and abandon them. When we feel anger, we can ask: 'What is it that needs protecting here?' or 'What am I afraid of here?'

3. **Sadness** tells us that we are losing something we cherish. It reminds us of the capacity of our hearts for love. Sadness can be a signal that we need some space or some support to process a loss. It can also be a sign that something in the world around us – a job, a relationship, a way of living – is not meeting our deepest needs.

Emotions are catchy

As we saw in the previous chapter, in Western culture, happiness is the only emotion that it's really OK to pursue and to express. Everything else should be private. We take other emotions to the therapist or we take them out on our partner in the privacy of our own home. God forbid somebody else should see us being emotional. But really, emotions are not private, they are social. They reveal our basic interdependence. We are connected to and affected by the world around us.

When I think of emotions, I think of a mycelial network that binds us to the rest of the world – emotions are the fruits of that connection. If a child feels sadness or anger and there is no obvious trigger, they are likely to be experiencing feelings that other people in the family or in the school or in the world are feeling. It's the same for us grown-ups. When we notice feelings and don't have an obvious personal explanation for them (like, 'I had a shit night's sleep' or 'My child is being difficult'), then this doesn't mean you have faulty brain chemistry. It may be that your emotions are signalling to you something that is happening in the world around you.

But we don't like to accept that we're so susceptible to the emotions of others; it makes us feel we aren't in control. Next time you or your child experience an emotion, instead of judging it, it might help to tell yourself: 'I am a human with feelings. I am affected by the world.'

Emotions are contagious, just like laughter or a yawn. You'll have had encounters with someone angry that left you feeling angry and, vice versa, talked to a happy person who cheered you up. I see this a lot with parents. As parents, we can become completely fused with our children's emotions and it can add to our overwhelm.

I have worked with many young people who have really struggled to manage their emotions in response to viral news events – like the murder of George Floyd in the US, the murder of Sarah Everard in the UK and some of the shocking images and statistics around climate change. Thanks to the 24/7 news cycle, our bodies can with one click be flooded with emotional energy that isn't really ours. And through social media, we are constantly exposed to the emotions of billions of other people, spreading like wildfire. Fear, outrage, grief and even suicidal ideation travelling lightspeed across the planet and invading our souls.

Do we know any more what is our feeling and what belongs to someone else? It feels to me like the barrier between personal and collective emotions is dissolving. And we – and our children – are getting overwhelmed by these feelings. The off button is hard to find. The key is to make sure we create enough space to take care of our feelings.

Making a space for your feelings

Leon, aged 16, came to see me after his boyfriend, Jack, dumped him out of the blue. He'd already had some big losses in his earlier life, including his parents' divorce. So he was more susceptible to feeling these things more acutely.

The week after the dumping, Leon was scrolling through

Instagram and saw pictures of Jack with another boy from the same school. This hurt. Leon became self-destructive, constantly checking Jack's social media accounts to look for more proof of the new boyfriend. Social media can trigger our emotions and then, because it can be so addictive, leaves us with less space to process our emotions. Every time Leon found more proof, more pictures, more details of Jack's new relationship online, he felt worse. Leon's emotions became so overwhelming that he began to self-harm. What he really needed was space to process his feelings. Which is why he came to see me.

In this mad world, it is more important than ever that we create space to take care of our feelings. We don't want to wait until more worrying symptoms emerge and we need a therapist or medication. To create this space, we have to regularly withdraw from the outside world, because if we are continually 'catching' emotions, we have no chance of helping our children through theirs. Withdrawing from the world may mean time to yourself, away from devices. You might find meditation or journaling or a walk in nature helpful. I recently helped a client who was struggling with her emotions to make a 'feeling safe' playlist. She began to walk along the river at the end of a hard day listening to this playlist and it really helped her come back to her family with some space and peace around her feelings. Or making a space for feelings may mean connecting with a loved one who you feel comfortable sharing your feelings with.

Whatever you find works for you, the key is to set a clear intention. You are making a space for your feelings because you want to learn from them and because you want to be present enough to help your children navigate the emotional storms of twenty-first-century life.

Riding emotional storms

As a grown-up, once you have created enough space for your own feelings, your job is then to help your child navigate what can often be the stormy seas of their emotional world, to captain the ship.

I love what family therapist Susan Stiffelman says: 'What frustrated children need is not an explanation of why they can't get what they want, and they don't need someone who just gives in to their demands. What they need is the reassurance of knowing there's a grown-up in the room who can help them through their emotional storms by creating a safe space to let those big feelings move through.' Psychoanalyst Wilfred Bion called this 'containment'.

This is especially true of feelings that are uncomfortable for us, too. For example, we are increasingly seeing children with all sorts of feelings about the climate crisis. There are already big conferences and journal articles on child climate grief and child climate anxiety. We really need to listen to and validate their feelings about the climate crisis. We need to help them not get overwhelmed by these feelings.

So much mental health comes down to our capacity, individually and collectively, to be with feelings. Clients I have worked with who have thought about or attempted suicide have said it felt like the only way to stop feeling their intolerable, overwhelming feelings. What these clients needed was to feel that they were not alone in their feelings, to have a sense that their feelings were bearable.

Sometimes, of course, we don't have the time to tune into a child's feelings and that is perfectly fine, as long as whatever we use to get rid of those feelings (bribing, distracting, etc.) doesn't become an entrenched habit. In *The Book You Wish Your Parents Had Read*, Philippa Perry says that when we constantly distract our children from 'bad' feelings, they learn that 'whenever I have a bad feeling, the best solution is to distract myself.' Sound familiar? And distraction is never more than a click away in this age, where companies spend billions of dollars trying to hook our attention, at the same time as drowning us in content that can trigger all kinds of intense feelings.

We want to raise children who have the power and confidence to tune into their feelings, to learn from them and to resist those who will always try to distract us from them. Bearing uncomfortable feelings is going to be a vital twenty-first-century skill as things continue to heat up.

Below are the five key steps I have found that really help children (and grown-ups) to take care of feelings so that they feel safe and understood. These work for personal emotions but also if your child experiences any intense emotions about the climate crisis or any other big issue. Remember that emotions are fluid and the best way to work with them is also fluid. If you use a one-size-fits-all approach, your child will at some point realise you are speaking from a textbook. They need a human, not a robot.

1. Let them know it's OK for the feeling to be there

A mother who had recently divorced from her husband came to see me. Their ten-year-old daughter was distraught. 'What should I say?' she asked. 'I try to make it better but the feelings just won't go away.'

I replied, 'Stop trying to make the feelings go away. They are her natural energetic response to a real loss. They are energy in motion.'

I suggested she talk to her along these lines: 'This is really sad, isn't it? I know how much this hurts. I wish I could find a magic wand and make it all better.'

Paradoxically, sometimes saying we wish that the pain

could go away, without trying to make it go away, can really help things shift. When children have their feelings validated like this they feel understood, less alone.

It can be helpful to give your child a name for their emotion – if it's in an open and non-shaming way. For example, saying, 'This is really sad, I can see how sad you are. I feel sad too,' is non-shaming. Don't force the emotion on them. If you say, 'Look how angry you are,' and they say, 'I'M NOT ANGRY!' don't argue the point.

If you are stuck with the belief that your child shouldn't be having these feelings at their age or that they are being manipulative or attention-seeking, try imagining that the child, whatever age they are, has a baby inside that's having some big feelings. Then imagine your job is to soothe the baby, using a calming voice and approach, letting them know that their emotion has been understood and is not overwhelming.

Even if on some level your child is being 'manipulative', know that it's still just the best strategy they have, in that moment, to try to get your support. (The same is true of adults who play games to try to get seen and heard.) Gabor Maté said that when children don't have the language or the space to express their feelings in words, they demonstrate with behaviour, like charades: 'In a game of charades, where you're not allowed to speak, you have to act out to deliver your message. If you land in a country where nobody spoke your language, and you have to portray hunger, you have to act it out. Kids are acting out all the time. And our response is to control the behaviour. We respond to the form of the message, rather than the content of it. And then we wonder why it doesn't work.'

2. Ask: where can you feel the emotion?

While we want to help our child put their feelings into words, we don't want them to have only a conceptual relationship to feelings. Remember, concepts in the mind can separate us from our bodies. So if the child is receptive, you can help them explore the bodily energy beneath the words. In the 1960s, psychotherapist Eugene Gendlin named this the 'felt sense'. He studied thousands of therapy session notes and discovered that clients who got in touch with their 'felt sense' had much better outcomes. 'Every bad feeling is potential energy toward a more right way of being if you give it space to move,' he said.

When a child says 'I feel so lonely', the I in that sentence makes it feel overwhelming. But by locating it in their body, suddenly it becomes manageable. Ask them: 'Where in your body can you feel that sense of loneliness?' Once they have found it, ask them to let that feeling know it's OK for it to be there. Ask them to imagine the feeling as a scared animal that needs to be comforted. Often, just by giving the feeling permission to be there, you will notice a shift. You could then become curious, asking them to describe what this 'felt sense' feels like. Is it big or small? Does it have rough edges or smooth ones? Do any images come into their mind when they connect to that felt sense of loneliness? This is similar to using the language of parts. When my clients say 'I am angry' or 'I am anxious', I ask them to redescribe their experience, saying 'part of me is angry'. Then I invite them to see if they can find that part in their body and begin relating to it.

However, when a child is really distressed, they most likely won't be able to do this. In these moments, they need you to just stay with them as a steady, grounded presence – a captain of the ship – until the emotional storm passes. Sometimes just sitting by their side in silence is enough, as long as you have the time, obviously.

And sometimes, a child may have developed very strong defences around a feeling. We must respect their defences – they are there for a reason. The human mind is incredibly creative. We have evolved the most sophisticated psychological defences to protect us from emotional pain. Think of a psychological defence as having the same purpose as a physical defence. A hedgehog has spikes and can curl up into a ball to protect itself from predators. Humans have a whole range of psychological defences, including repression, avoidance, humour, rationalisation, fantasy and straight-up denial. These defences are incredibly intelligent. They protect us from psychological predators, from being flooded with emotions we can't tolerate. Respect your child's defences. Respect their hedgehog spikes.

3. Ask: what is this emotion trying to tell you?

If you encourage your child to speak to the emotion, they can find out what it is trying to tell them. Yes, this might sound a bit hippy. But really, it's the same as when you were learning what each of your baby's cries meant.

You can teach a child that their emotions contain important information, wisdom, and that your job together is to learn what it is. To do this, invite them to ask that felt sense of the feeling in the body 'What are you here to teach me?', or other words that suit you. It's OK not to 'get an answer', as such. Sometimes the response is subtle or will be understood later on. The curiosity itself is a big shift.

If this doesn't work, you can try drawing the emotion, turning it into a character and communicating with it that way. I once worked with a boy, Santiago, who had acute OCD. He found it difficult to tune into the felt sense in his body but he loved to draw. He developed a character for his OCD, that he called Zag. He drew Zag and we were able to talk to Zag, to understand why Zag was here and what he wanted. This led to a beautiful, detailed story involving cosmic travel but the simple conclusion was, 'Zag is really scared because his parents are arguing all the time and worried that they might leave Zag on a planet in space all by himself.'

4. Ask: is there an action you can take?

As emotions are energy in motion, sometimes we can use their wisdom to know how to act, which I call 'emotional empowerment'. This is what I did with Katie (see page 57), helping her turn her acute, hair-pulling anxiety into the power to express how she felt and what she wanted.

Can you think of a time when you felt moved by something you experienced, or read or heard, and then you took action? Sometimes children need help to break down the action. A single person can't fix the climate crisis but we can all figure out our role. How might you/your child transform their emotion into one small action that could help the bigger issue you/they are worried about? (More on this in Chapter 15.)

There is so much to be learned from our emotions. They are precious gifts. They can bring us closer together. They help us to navigate and make sense of the world. They tell us when the world isn't meeting our deepest needs. They can remind us of the things that are most precious to us, the things we want to protect, the things we love and the things we will one day lose. For the sake of our children and their future, it's vital that we honour these gifts.

12

ROOT SIX: CHAOS

How we can come to know and love the part of us that's addicted to stress

For a seed to achieve its greatest expression, it must come completely undone. The shell cracks, its insides come out and everything changes. To someone who doesn't understand growth, it would look like complete destruction

– Cynthia Occelli

At The Treehouse school, I became close with a Kurdish boy called Kadir. He was aged 15, about five foot nine, with a thick mop of shiny, dark hair, big, piercing blue-green eyes and a furrowed scar under his right eye.

The Iraqi refugee children I've met have all experienced so much trauma, and Kadir was no exception. At nine years old, he witnessed his parents being beaten almost to death right in front of his eyes. Kadir's body was in an almost constant state of fight or flight because it never knew when the next attack was going to come. His body could not allow itself to feel safe, even now he was 'safe' in London and his family were no longer in danger.

Then Kadir discovered Red Bull. Energy drinks, he found, could keep his body in the state of high alert that he was used to, a state that ironically felt safer to him than letting down his guard. It didn't take long for him to become addicted to energy drinks, or rather to the feeling they gave him. When I visited Kadir's house in Tottenham, north London, he was very proud to show me his bedroom where he had stacked around 40 cans in a pyramid. This was his monument to Red Bull, an altar to his sympathetic nervous system. I imagined a sign next to it: 'Lest we forget'.

One summer, we took the students on a sailing trip to the Solent. On these trips there would usually be drugs, fights, all sorts of shenanigans. But this trip was surprisingly positive and peaceful. It was only on the way home that the kids began to get tetchy. On reflection, I can see that having had such a positive experience, the reality of going home to their very challenging lives was bringing up a lot of feelings for the students.

It all went haywire at a service station on the M3. Kadir managed to buy a few cans of Red Bull and downed them. He became very agitated – and dangerous. It was only when we were about to leave that I realised Kadir was in a state. Everyone else was on the bus when Kadir turned up, eyes lit and mouth gurning. I stood in front of him and refused to let him on the bus until he had calmed down. In defiance, Kadir took out several packs of sugar he had just taken from the coffee shop, ripped them open and poured the sugar down his throat. Then he ran off.

I chased after him, just about reaching him as he was about to run into the first lane of the motorway. I dived on top of Kadir and managed to restrain him. As I held him, he was biting my hands trying to escape. I felt as if I'd trapped a wild, scared animal. Beneath the defiance, beneath the addictions to sugar and energy drinks, here was Kadir, an innocent, terrified child. The addictions were, ironically, his body's way of keeping him safe. But there, right on the edge of the M3, they could have killed him.

You might not identify with the trauma Kadir carried in his body. And you may not drink Red Bull. But really, we are all addicted to stress. Perhaps you get your adrenaline high from caffeine or hard exercising or high-paced Netflix shows? Or from hyper-productivity, filling your life so you are always on the edge of overwhelm? Or from living in chaos, putting out one fire after another?

There is a deep part of us that is compulsively drawn to stress, like flies to bright blue lights. The trouble is that while stress is biologically designed as a short-term response to a dangerous situation, our chronic, constant stress is burning us out. And whatever this chronic stress is doing to us, you can be sure it's doing the same to our children too.

Before we continue, let's take a moment together to slow down. Yes, there is a lot of stress in the world. But right now, I invite you to find a place in your body that feels safe. It could be anywhere – your forehead, your toes, anywhere. As you notice and breathe into this sense of safety, try saying silently to yourself the following mantra, which I will repeat throughout this chapter:
In this moment, I am safe.

Feeling alive

Even before the Covid pandemic started in 2020, people were more stressed than ever. In 2018, the largest ever study into the impact of stress revealed that 74 per cent of people in the UK had felt so stressed that year that they felt overwhelmed or unable to cope.

Stress left unchecked leads to burnout: feeling so exhausted that you can't function. Recent studies have shown that in the last few years teachers are more burned out, doctors and nurses are more burned out, academics are more burned out, therapists are more burned out, students are more burned out, millennials are more burned out, parents are more burned out, even the chilled-out Swedes are more burned out.

Have you like me been noticing a lot of stress around you or inside you lately? What the hell is going on? We know the usual suspects – the loss of any boundary between work and home life; our expectation that everything should arrive instantly, meaning we are losing our capacity to tolerate frustration; how hard it is to unplug.

But the truth is, stress isn't a modern phenomenon – it's a deep and recurring human pattern. In 1880, American physician Horatio C Wood wrote a book about his patients who were suffering from burnout, *Brain-Work and Overwork*. In it, he lamented: 'The number of overworked members of this community is something frightful . . . In the eager pursuit of wealth, fame, or other object, the maxims of wisdom are apt to be forgotten, and the warnings of the physician neglected; indeed, too often are the warnings of Nature herself overlooked, and the slight symptoms that presage the storm unnoticed.'

I love this last line, that we ignore the warnings from nature, the subtle symptoms that 'presage the storm'. The rise in chronic stress we are seeing in the twenty-first century is a warning from Nature telling us to rest.

In this moment, I am safe.

We do need a little stress. As described in Chapter 3, an appropriate challenge pushes us and our children to learn, to grow. But at some point, normal, episodic stress switches into chronic stress. Stress can become so normalised that we begin to crave it, like Kadir and his Red Bull. Why do we crave something that is simply not good for our health? The reasons for this are complex. But one factor is that stress helps us 'feel alive'. And why do we so yearn to remember that feeling of aliveness? We crave feeling alive because the opposite of feeling alive is . . . well. Remember in Chapter 4, when we looked at how we've become separated from our bodies and live mainly in our minds? Whilst children in the Congo strain their bodies mining the cobalt minerals that keep our smartphone batteries running, back in this world our disconnected brains keep the economy running. Well, our bodies will do anything to break free from this zombie living. And they do this by finding ways to excite our nervous systems. That might be *Game of Thrones*, CrossFit, an argument, an affair – anything to help us remember we are alive. Added to this, as we explored earlier, we all carry some level of unresolved trauma. And this trauma can leave our bodies needing to stay in high alert. If we don't take care of this trauma, it can turn our body's need to feel alive into a compulsion.

Sigmund Freud called this 'repetition compulsion'. He noticed how children, while playing, would re-enact painful situations. And that some of his patients who had experienced a trauma were compelled to repeat that trauma, even though it didn't seem to provide them with any relief. Freud noted that these patients simply could not learn from experience and instead behave as if 'pursued by a malignant fate or possessed by some "daemonic" power'. When we befriend this 'daemonic' power, we can find huge amounts of creative energy here. It's time to meet your inner chaos-creator.

SAY HELLO TO YOUR INNER CHAOS-CREATOR

It's time to get to know the part of you that's responsible for your compulsion to stress. It knows how to take a perfectly peaceful situation and turn it into madness, creating arguments, making a mess, taking on too much.

The idea of the chaos-creator comes from addiction therapy, specifically from 12 step programmes such as AA. The following exercise* will help you uncover where your chaos creator is at play so you can choose differently.

1. What are some things that you do to create chaos in your life? (Here are some examples):

   ☐ Being chronically late

   ☐ Overspending

   ☐ Agreeing to do/take on too much

   ☐ Constantly losing things

   ☐ Not saying no when you know you should

   ☐ Neglecting responsibilities or relationships

   ☐ Ignoring physical problems hoping they will go away or fix themselves

   ☐ Creating arguments out of thin air

   ☐ Taking on the burden of other people's problems

   ☐ Attempting to make something (or everything) perfect

2. Do you ever experience a feeling of familiarity, or 'sense of ease and comfort', when creating chaos?

3. Do you ever get uncomfortable or bored when things are running smoothly?

4. If you could imagine your inner chaos-creator as a character, what would it look like? The more exaggerated you can make it the better. Bonus points for drawing it. Double bonus for sharing the image with someone.

* These questions are adapted from *The Alcoholics Anonymous Idiot's Guide – for Chaos Creators.*

5. Can you identify one person in your family from whom you learned the art of chaos?

6. Take a moment to send forgiveness to that person for their own addiction to chaos. It wasn't their fault.

7. Take a moment to send forgiveness to yourself for your own addiction to chaos.

8. Acknowledge one positive outcome of your addiction to chaos. What have you achieved or what actual dangers has your inner chaos-creator helped you to avoid? For one of my clients, it allowed her to tap into a deep well of creative energy.

9. Can you imagine another way to access that positive outcome, one that doesn't require chronic activation of your nervous system?

What is stress, anyway?

My favourite definition of stress comes from the fifteenth century when the word was used to describe the pressure of two materials being pulled in opposite directions. Because at its most basic level, stress is when we are in one place but want to be somewhere else. For example, you're stuck in a traffic jam, or you discover your roof is leaking and the hassle and expense are unwanted, or you're feeling an emotion you don't want, such as fear before a job interview.

The stress response is designed to keep us safe and for this we can be grateful. Sometimes, we really do need to be somewhere other than where we are – say if we are being chased by a lion or a wildfire, or even the tax man. When we perceive a threat, the sympathetic nervous system activates instantly and automatically, sending warning signals from our brain down our spine to push us to act. In the case of a lion, that's running away. In the case of the taxman, it's paying our taxes. In animals, after the stress has passed, it switches off. But in humans, our stress response can stay switched on, so much so that it makes us ill, mentally and physically. What makes humans different?

We have already seen how our minds tell stories that can keep us stuck in cycles of stress and trauma. On top of this, our brains are prediction machines constantly scanning the environment for any signs that we might be safe – or not. This is what psychiatrist and trauma expert Stephen Porges calls 'neuroception'. It's as if there's a gang of fretting meerkats on tiptoes, jingle-jangling inside our nervous system. On top of this, our brains have evolved to focus more on danger and threats, known as the 'negativity bias'. This is true even at the level of our taste buds: we can notice sweetness when there is one part in 200 but we can detect bitter tastes (much more likely to indicate something is poisonous or not good for us) when there is just one part in two million. It seems likely our negativity bias has helped us to succeed as a species as we could anticipate and predict potential dangers and come up with ways to avoid or overcome them.

So, we constantly worry about past 'lions' and keeping possible 'lions' at bay. After an hour on a crowded train, for example, we can create scenarios of an invisible virus ruining our holiday plans, or infecting someone we love who then dies, or infecting our child so that a whole school bubble is sent home. Even when our child is safe and snuggly under their duvet, they can tell themself stress-making stories about how badly a test might go the next day.

In this moment, I am safe.

HOMAGE TO YOUR NERVOUS SYSTEM

Are you up for trying a little experiment, to see what happens when you give your frazzled nervous system some love? Because if some of your stress is mind-made, then you can unmake it.

So, let's slow down for a moment.

Put your left hand on your heart and your right hand on your belly (placing the hands on the body like this is a technique used in trauma treatment). As you place your hand on your heart, imaging you are activating your body's capacity for compassion. As you place your other hand on your belly, say hello to any fear or stress that is present (there is almost always some). If you feel OK to try this, you could then say to yourself: 'I am inviting any fear or stress in my body to just be here now.' Don't try to fix or change it. Just give it space.

Now, you're going to thank your nervous system for keeping you safe. You could say: 'Thank you for protecting me. Thank you for helping me remember what it is to feel alive.' Imagine the nerves are smiling back at you, a big collective, jingly-jangly smile all the way from your brain to your belly.

In this moment, I am safe.

Wildfires

In January 2020, photographer Brad Fleet posted a photo of a baby kangaroo burned to death against a barbed wire fence as it tried to escape the Australian bushfires. You can see the charred remains of the joey's arms wrapped around the fence and its head poking through a gap, clenched teeth standing out pale against the grey body and post-apocalyptic backdrop. When interviewed about taking the shot, Fleet said: 'It was overwhelmingly devastating . . . heart-breaking. The kangaroo was like a statue, frozen in time . . . I don't remember hearing any birds and you couldn't see any other life. At times, you could smell other animals that had been killed. It looked like it was a quick struggle but the reality is you don't know how long it was trying to cross the fence.'

The photo went viral. The comments on social media reveal the impact it had:

'Oh dear God this is the Apocalypse. It's so sad.😢'

'This picture paints 1000 very sad words.'

'Omg this is terribly sad 😢😢😢😢💔 This is a catastrophic event that effects the whole world. Wake up 🌍 and start paying attention we are destroying our only beautiful planet.'

That year – 2020 – was a year of wildfires. They spread through California, the Amazon and even the Arctic, a reminder of the fragility of life on our planet. The Wikipedia entry on Wildfires reads: 'Earth is an intrinsically flammable planet.'

Of the millions of images of these wildfires, why did this one go viral? The idea of a baby animal trying to escape danger hits us in the heart, evokes our fierce, maternal lioness instinct. Especially when that danger has been created by us. There is also something human-like about kangaroos, in particular the way they look after their young (we'll come back to this later).

And a picture can paint 1,000 words. It has so much more power than any statistic. This one image communicated the scale of the wildfire tragedy across the globe. An image triggers our strongest emotions – rage, grief, fear – and our stress response. In 2020, other images also sent shockwaves around the world. George Floyd with a knee on his neck. A man on a ventilator in Italy. As I mentioned in Chapter 11, a few clients

I worked with in 2020 really struggled to process the intense emotions these images provoked. As we all reeled from one shocking image to another, it felt as if we were reaching a tipping point, the fire of all fires.

In this moment, I am safe.

Our nervous systems are increasingly connected to the nervous systems of the eight billion people on our planet. This is the digital nervous system. The emotions that rage through the internet are often those that come from fight or flight – fear and outrage. And as our stress response is poked relentlessly, any trauma we might carry is made worse.

Remember that our brains are always scanning, assessing whether we're in danger or safe (neuroception). Well, the number one way we find out is via other people, especially their faces and voices. In evolutionary terms, this adaptation has protected us. If I see my tribe getting agitated, then my sympathetic nervous system will automatically be activated, too. As family therapist Bonnie Badenoch explains, in every moment, with every person, our nervous systems are asking the question *'Are you with me?'*

The problem now is that our neuroception is exposed to the threat signals of eight billion people via the digital nervous system. It's as if they're all shouting from the rooftops: 'IT'S NOT SAFE!' This happens in person, too: think about the stressed-out or shut-down faces you saw last time you walked down a street, or sat on a bus or a train.

I began this book with a question: What kind of safety can we provide our children in a world on the brink of collapse? What kind of safety can I provide Rose?

If our brains have evolved to focus primarily on threats, then can we ever feel safe? It's as if human beings are primed for apocalyptic perception.

We need to bring our catastrophising tendencies under control, lest we all go mad. This isn't to deny the reality of climate change or any other existential threat to our species. But the relentless sense of imminent threat is contributing to the mental health crisis among our children. For the sake of my daughter and her generation, I want to face the reality of existential threat. But burned out, I'm no good to my daughter at all.

In this moment, I am safe.

Why we all need more cuddles

In 1979, Edgar Rey was working in the Instituto Materno Infantil in Bogota. The hospital served the city's poorest, many of whom lived crammed in the *barrios* in the foothills of the surrounding mountains. It was the biggest neonatal unit in the whole of Colombia, delivering 30,000 babies a year. The doctors in the unit were facing an urgent challenge. There was a severe shortage of incubators, so that three babies would often share just one machine. Because of this over-crowding, serious infections were spreading through the patients. The death rate was spiralling, and more and more babies were being abandoned by impoverished mothers who, because they never even got to touch their babies, found it easier to just take off. The doctors faced an urgent challenge: how to protect these preterm babies, keep them warm, prevent them from contracting an infection, and give them a chance of life.

Looking for solutions, Dr Rey stumbled across a paper on the physiology of the kangaroo. The paper described how baby kangaroos are, like human babies, born very immature and bald (unlike human babies, they are as small as a peanut). They stay warm – and alive – by crawling into the mother's pouch. In here, their body temperature is regulated by skin-to-skin contact.

Inspired by nature's design, Dr Rey instructed the mothers of premature babies to carry them close to their skin, just like kangaroos. The results were astonishing. Infection and death rates dropped immediately and dramatically. And as more babies were signed off sooner from the hospital, overcrowding was reduced and the number of abandoned babies dropped. This was the birth of kangaroo care.

Human beings are not that different from kangaroos. The NHS now advises skin-to-skin contact for all newborns. We are designed to feel safe when we are in close contact with other people. As we saw in Chapter 4, touch helps us come into our bodies. We regulate each other's nervous systems through our touch, as well as through our tone of voice and our facial expressions. This is *co-regulation*. When we are stressed or traumatised, co-regulation is what we need.

The myth of self-regulation

You were probably taught to co-regulate, skin-to-skin, when your baby was born. And there's a growing number of people whose parenting is underpinned by co-regulation. You might know it as attachment parenting or hand-in-hand parenting. It might involve co-sleeping, for example, or just sitting next to your child during a meltdown rather than sending them to their room.

But in our lifetime, the dominant model underpinning how most children have been brought up in the West has been self-regulation. The idea here is that a child should learn to regulate their own nervous system; for example, we might use controlled crying to teach the child to self-soothe. Self-regulation underlies not only our parenting but our education system and even many of the child psychology models I've studied. You might recognise some of these parenting strategies based on the idea of self-regulation: crying it out, the naughty step, the naughty corner, or time out. (There is no judgement here, by the way – we all want the best for our children, we all have to balance duties and time with our children as best we can.)

In the model of self-regulation, if a child's emotions or behaviours don't match with the parent or teacher's expectations, and especially if the child doesn't listen to the parent or teacher, then the child is sent to a separate space where they can only come back into the fold when they have properly self-regulated. Out in the 'forest', children can and do find ways to self-regulate. They might distract themselves from the feelings. They might take their angry feelings and turn them into a fantasy of revenge. At best, they might do some kind of breathing or meditation to help calm their nervous system. From the outside, these strategies appear to work. The child comes back with their tail between their legs and life carries on.

Self-regulation is an important skill we all need to learn. As a parent and husband, sometimes I need to self-regulate to stop me taking my shit out on my loved ones. The problem is that in our individualist culture we put too much focus on self-regulation. And this leads to a harmful pattern in the child. They grow up learning 'when I am upset, when I have disappointed someone, when I have done something wrong, I must deal with the feelings on my own.' They then take this pattern into their other relationships.

I know this because this is my pattern. I tend to remove myself from conflict and regulate myself. The problem is that doing this can create an emotional chasm between me and the people I'm engaging with (or not engaging with). By cutting our connection with others, self-regulation leaves us feeling more exhausted (because it tends to require more energy) and more alone. In the same study on stress mentioned above, 37 per cent of adults who reported feeling stressed reported feeling lonely as a result. Could this be because of our reliance on self-regulation? Feeling stressed? Sort yourself out, Jimmy. What follows is an example of extreme self-regulation but these edge cases can reveal a lot about us folks in the clearing.

Johanna Haarer was a Nazi physician who wrote child-rearing books to help parents raise tough, obedient Nazis. *The German Mother and Her First Child* was published in 1934 and sold some 1.2 million copies. Haarer advised that children, especially babies, needed their will to be broken. 'The child is to be fed, bathed and dried off; apart from that left completely alone,' she wrote. There are images in this book showing mothers how to hold their children so there is as little skin-to-skin contact as possible. Modern-day researchers have theorised that these child-rearing practices have contributed to the particularly high levels of burnout, depression and emotional illnesses in Germany today.

That said, self-regulation can sometimes be the best option, especially when all the people around you are stressed, chaotic, dysregulated. Remember that children are constantly picking up cues from the world around them, constantly assessing if it is safe or not. When they are surrounded by teachers who are stressed to the point of burnout, is it a surprise that their sympathetic nervous systems are overactivated? In the words of neuroscientist Lisa Feldman Barrett: 'The best thing for your nervous system is another human and the worst thing for your nervous system is another human.'

Doesn't it seem cruel to send children off to self-regulate when they have most likely been triggered by the world (and the grown-ups) around them? Instead of saying to them 'the world is mad', self-regulation signals to our children that 'they are mad'.

In *The Continuum Concept*, author Jean Liedloff describes the psychological difference between a child raised with co-regulation and one raised with self-regulation: 'The feeling appropriate to an infant in arms is his feeling of rightness, or essential goodness . . . that he is right, good, and welcome.' We need this rightness, she says. 'A person without this sense often feels there is an empty space where he ought to be.'

I sure feel like this sometimes. But I don't want my daughter growing up inhabiting that empty space. I want her to feel in a deep and enduring way her essential goodness, that she is welcome this world. Don't we all want that?

So, can we all please take ourselves off the naughty step? If you aren't sure how to find co-regulation in your own life, can you think of one person with whom, when you talk to them, you feel totally at ease? If not, you could find a therapist or meditation teacher. For some, it's walking the dog in nature. Many people find group activities like singing, dancing, or even improv to be an effective tool for co-regulation.

Towards the end of 2020, on the bushfire-ravaged slopes of the Blue Mountains in New South Wales, thousands of beautiful rare pink flannel flowers bloomed. The seeds of these flowers lie dormant for years as they need the intense heat of a fire to break open and germinate, a process called 'pyriscence'. The Latin name for these flowers is *Actinotus forsythii* meaning 'bearing rays'. Their name fits their image, the carpet of colour lighting up a ravaged landscape.

Like these flowers, we need a certain level of stress to crack open the seeds of our potential. But if we are chronically stressed, if the fire continues to rage and we feel we have to deal with stress on our own, then this precious capacity to 'bear rays' can never bloom. Please don't forget: you are the safe space that your children's nervous systems depend on to find a way through the chaos of this world.

In this moment, I am safe.

13

FRUIT SIX: PEACE

Finding acceptance and stillness in the chaos of life

The question at the heart of this book is how can we help our children feel safe in a world that is in flames? Wildfires are spreading across our 'intrinsically flammable planet'. And they are also raging across our digital nervous system.

Deep down, we all want peace: inner peace and outer peace. We want our children to live in a world that is peaceful.

According to archaeologists, our long-ago ancestors very rarely went to war. I know this might be hard to believe; the story we've been told is that hunter-gatherers were primitive, brutish and had terrible table manners. But in *War, Peace, and Human Nature*, anthropologist and professor of peace and conflict studies Douglas Fry notes that from about 10,000 to 5,000 BCE there is virtually no evidence of war. There are also plenty of examples of hunter-gatherer societies in modern times that live peacefully, where war and murder are almost unknown, such as the Batek of Malaysia or the Hadza of Tanzania.

I believe our bodies retain this memory of peace. It tugs at us, whispers to us in soft tones like waves lapping at the shore of our frazzled minds, saying 'it doesn't have to be like this'.

In this chapter, you are going to discover a deeper kind of peace, for you and your children. For now, could you become an inner archaeologist, and look for a relic, a shard, a memory of peace? You will find it in a place in your body where you don't feel any stress or tension. Doing this is a great way to counteract the world that is making our children mad. As you read on, I invite you to stay open to the possibility of peace – both in yourself and in the world around you. You just need to be prepared that this peace might not always appear in the way you imagine, as we are about to discover.

Inner peace may not be what you think

There is almost nothing outside you that will help
in any kind of lasting way, unless you are waiting for
a donor organ – Anne Lamott

We all have different ideas of how to find inner peace – and they almost always rely on some kind of outer peace. Perhaps for you it's when your children are doing as they are told and playing beautifully, or quietly doing their homework. Or it might be the sound of rain against the window or interlacing with a warm body in bed. Or it could be a pint at the end of a hard week of work or sitting down in front of the *X Factor* with a packet of chocolate biscuits.

The problem is, our ideas of peace get in the way of us actually experiencing peace. Remember from the previous chapter that one definition of stress is wanting to be somewhere other than where you are. Most of our stress comes from jagged stories scratching away in our minds, stories we tell ourselves about what should and should not be happening. This is brilliant news, though, because it means that peace, true peace, has very little to do with the circumstances of your life and much more to do with your perspective. This isn't to say you shouldn't take action to change what's wrong but it does mean you can find peace in the middle of a child having a meltdown, a teenager refusing to go to school or a boss who's bullying you.

People have even found a kind of peace amid unimaginable suffering. Viktor Frankl was a Jewish psychiatrist who was rounded up by the Nazis from Vienna and sent to Auschwitz. He found himself in the unimaginable position of being the concentration camp shrink. How can you give meaningful advice to someone imprisoned in a death camp? Frankl came to realise there were, broadly speaking, two types of people in the camp: those who chose to find some meaning in the midst of suffering and those who didn't. Those who found meaning, Frankl observed, were more likely to survive. In his book *Man's Search For Meaning*, Frankl describes the moment he realised his own purpose within this awful situation: 'As soon as I had [. . .] made up my mind to stay with my patients, the unhappy feeling left me. I did not know what the following days would bring, but I had gained an inward peace that I had never experienced before.' He goes on to describe how he saw this principle repeated during his time in the camp: 'We who lived in concentration camps can remember the men who walked through the huts comforting others, giving away their last piece of bread. They may have been few in number, but they offer sufficient proof that everything can be taken from a man but one thing: the last of the human freedoms – to choose one's attitude in any given set of circumstances, to choose one's own way.'

Peace is a choice, a commitment. In stressful situations, you can practise saying, 'I choose peace.' It's not a magic wand. But it is a strength we can build over time.

WHAT'S YOUR IDEA OF PEACE?

This quick journaling exercise will help you unravel your limiting beliefs about inner peace so that you can choose peace more freely.

1. A time when I felt most at peace was . . .

2. The times when I feel the opposite of peace are . . .

3. The conditions I believe I need to experience peace are . . .

4. The things that help my child be peaceful are . . .

5. Without thinking about the answers, write as many responses as you can in one minute to the following statement: I will be peaceful when . . .

6. Without thinking about the answers, write as many responses as you can in one minute to the following statement: The world will be peaceful when . . .

7. Now, this is an important reflection: how might these beliefs (about the things you need to see happening in the external world to experience peace) actually be getting in the way of you or your children experiencing peace?

There is no such thing as safety

We've built our world on comfort, convenience and safety – brick walls, electric blankets, airbags, and Lemsip. But the pandemic and the climate crisis have shown us how easily these illusions can be shattered.

Terrorism is particularly effective in the West now, Yuval Harari says, because the modern state has got so good at excluding violence from within its borders that, 'A small coin in a big empty jar can make a lot of noise'. This principle is true of our personal fears, too. We try to create safety for ourselves and our children by pushing the things that don't make us feel safe out into the forest beyond the clearing. But as we know by now, these excluded parts don't disappear. They come back to haunt us in another form. They disturb our peace.

You might buy the Wizard Tracking Watch, a GPS device marketed to parents of younger kids. One review says: 'You want to know where they are and that they are safe at every moment.' But you end up tracking your child obsessively. Or you might fit one of those security doorbells that sends alerts to your phone. And then you can be relaxing on a paradise beach in St Lucia . . . and get a shot of adrenaline every time the post-man delivers a letter.

We all have our own 'security blankets' – the things we use or believe or do for a sense of comfort or safety. They are life choices as well as things, such as a 'secure' job, getting married, getting our children the best education we can, paying into a pension, believing in heaven or immortality and holding on to strong beliefs about 'how the world is'. There is nothing wrong with a comfort blankie, per se. But so many of the things we cling to for security lead us to make bad choices and so create suffering for ourselves and for our children. I have helped many people leave 'secure' jobs that they dreaded going to every day and 'secure' relationships that were making them miserable. I knew a man who worked very long hours to achieve financial security and rarely saw his family. He told himself he'd make up for it after retirement. But a week before his retirement date, he had a heart attack and died.

To be clear, of course we should take great care of our children and keep them safe. But our compulsive pursuit of safety creates constant anxiety and over-control in us and leads to our children becoming more anxious and fearful themselves. Alan Watts put it brilliantly in *The Wisdom of*

Insecurity: 'The desire for security and the feeling of insecurity are the same thing. To hold your breath is to lose your breath. A society based on the quest for security is nothing but a breath-retention contest in which everyone is as taut as a drum and as purple as a beet.'

I am sorry to say this but at some point life will reveal its essential insecurity to you and to your children with a trauma, a death, a natural disaster. Imagine yourself adrift at sea, clinging to a life raft that's falling apart piece by piece. Instead of holding on in the hope it will bring you to shore, it's much better to learn how to swim.

The first step is to accept that there is no such thing as safety, that life is insecure. A deeper peace can be found here. At first, when we try to let this idea sink in it can trigger some deeply uncomfortable places in us. Say to yourself, 'there is no such thing as safety'. Repeat the phrase a few times. What do you notice in your body? Put a hand on any discomfort that arises in your body and just let that discomfort know it's OK for it to be there.

If you can find a way to accept this basic fact of life, you and your children are less likely to drown when something shatters your life raft.

Know that conflict is normal!

Siblings argue on average 3.5 times an hour, parents argue with their kids six times a day and couples seven times a day. Conflict is normal. The more we accept that, the more we will find peace. When we don't, we tend to prolong conflicts, turning them into dramas that can last a lifetime.

It might help to think about it like this: each person in a family, a classroom, a team has their own needs. Inevitably, these needs will clash. Conflict is simply a way to negotiate those needs. There's a fantasy that if relationships are not all love and cuddles, there's something wrong with us or, more likely, something wrong with the other person. But it helps to let go of these idealised expectations. For example, studies show a mother is attuned to her baby, on average, only 30 per cent of the time. When she isn't, it can stress out the baby. But this isn't a problem as long as the mother repairs the bond, which she does through touch, eye contact, play and so on. This is known as rupture and repair.

And here is the really good news: it doesn't matter how many ruptures you have in a day. If you repair them, you're helping your child to learn that conflict is normal, bearable and repairable. Studies show that children who learn this from their primary relationships have better mental health. I've seen this knowledge help adults get on more peacefully with one another too. Of course, there are times when we need to get away from relationships that are too full of conflict, or violent, even. But for many family relationships, conflict gets aggravated and prolonged by our feeling that it is always wrong.

Take a moment to think about conflict. Do you avoid it at all costs? Or do you unconsciously seek it out? Do you trust in your body that conflicts can be repaired?

Please know that there is no right answer to these questions. We all carry a certain view of conflict from our childhood experiences. Please don't worry if you, like many people, don't feel grown-up conflicts are bearable and repairable. This might have been true in your life. The key is to check whether this is still true in your current relationships.

One tool that can help is to imagine this: inside the person you are in conflict with there is a younger version of themselves – an inner child. In my experience, most people trust that they can repair conflict with children, especially younger ones. So if a person flares up, gets angry or defensive, you could try imagining that this is just a younger version of them. This will help you to not take conflict so personally. As Don Miguel Ruiz says in *The Four Agreements*, 'There is a huge amount of freedom that comes to you when you take nothing personally.'

Transform triggers into Tiggers

At the moment, trigger is a bit of a buzzword. #triggered is trending on Instagram. And there are trigger warnings on blogs, videos, tweets and posts. Someone who finds something offensive might say, 'I find that really triggering.' What they mean is, something that happened has caused ('triggered') an emotional, stress or trauma response in them.

It's brilliant that more people are getting to know their triggers. But what we don't want is a world where our children are totally protected from triggers. This feeds into the helpless/ victim complex of Chapter 2. Remember, human beings are anti-fragile. The right kind of exposure to stress is necessary for us to grow. As Richard McNally, the director of clinical training in Harvard's department of psychology, says: 'Avoiding triggers is a symptom of PTSD, not a treatment for it.'

If we want to find a deeper kind of peace, we have to learn how to transform our triggers into Tiggers. You'll remember Tigger, the cheerful, outgoing tiger from *Winnie the Pooh*, who 'always seems bigger because of the way he bounces'. Instead of trying to get rid of, fix or change the trigger, choose to see it as an invitation to connect with your inner Tigger. (Of course, there is a big caveat here: if you have experienced a difficult or complex trauma, you may need professional help to work with your triggers.)

Transforming our triggers into Tiggers is especially important when it's our children who trigger us. My friend leadership guru Nick Jankel says our children are our zen masters: 'Welcome these fuzzy balls of crazy wisdom into your life and use their guidance to focus where you want to break through your challenges. They love you so much they will trigger all your patterns, in any way possible, so you can become whole.'

Often a large part of our emotional response is based on old or inherited traumas. For example, you might be triggered when your child does that thing that really reminds you of your ex and you react in the same way you reacted to your ex. And time and time again, I've seen a parent being triggered by their child at an age where the parent themselves has an old emotional wound that is stored as a memory in their body.

I worked with a family where the seven-year-old boy, Angus, had intense self-hatred, despite his parents being incredibly loving. Out of nowhere, he would say things like 'I wish I wasn't here,' and 'No family in the world would want me.' This self-hatred triggered a cascade of deep, emotional responses in his parents.

Because there was no obvious explanation for Angus' self-hatred, I decided to dig deeper into the family history. We discovered that Angus's great-grandfather had lost his wife to suicide and that this tragic loss left him in a state of total self-hatred. Angus's dad then told me that he would often comment on how much the boy reminded him of his grandfather.

You might think this sounds a bit mystical. But there is good science now confirming that ancestral or 'epigenetic' trauma (which we discussed back in Root Two, Chapter 4) can be inherited up to three generations down. In this case, having an explanation for Angus' self-hatred allowed both parents to see their son's symptoms in a more loving, peace-filled light, transforming this trigger into a tigger.

In *Healing Collective Trauma*, spiritual teacher Thomas Hübl says that by attending compassionately to ourselves and to each other when our nervous systems and trauma patterns are triggered, we can, together, 'bring the past into peace'. But we can only do so if we let go of our ideas about what peace 'should' look like and instead start practising what psychologist Tara Brach calls radical acceptance – 'the willingness to experience ourselves and our lives as it is'.

Importantly, radical acceptance does not mean we give up on our desire for justice in the world. We can choose peace and retain a strong sense of wanting to make a difference. In fact, when we come from a place of acceptance, the energy we put out into the world is much more likely to create peace. This is how inner peace can turn into outer peace. Peaceful relationships with ourselves and with our children add up to help make a peaceful world.

WHAT SCIENCE TELLS US ABOUT TURNING STRESS INTO PEACE FOR OUR KIDS

In his book *Why Zebras Don't Get Ulcers*, Robert Sapolsky highlights four factors that science tells us will help us turn stress into peace.

1. **Social support.** This is the single most important factor. A child who has just one positive relationship is far more likely to recover from a traumatic event.

2. **Predictability.** Children who have both routines and boundaries tend to feel as if the world is more manageable. Predictability also means that you give enough warning when a change is about to happen or something difficult is coming.

3. **Outlets for frustration.** For example, exercise, a punch bag or, dare I say it, video games (the co-operative, not competitive kind).

---

4. A sense of control. This comes from all the good stuff we discussed in Fruit One, 'Empowerment', giving a child a bit more trust, a bit more responsibility and choices as well as reflecting back their strengths.

Can we learn to forgive?

Forgiveness is the fragrance the violet sheds on the heel that has crushed it – Mark Twain

There can be no real peace without forgiveness. I believe our capacity for forgiveness is one of the most beautiful qualities in the human heart. If we could respond to challenging encounters with forgiveness instead of anger or blame then the world would be a more beautiful place.

Nelson Mandela was imprisoned for 27 years by the apartheid regime but when he was released he didn't seek revenge. Instead, he chose forgiveness, calling it a 'powerful weapon' because 'it liberates the soul, it removes fear'. Psychologist Edith Eger forgave the people who killed her parents in Auschwitz. She wrote: 'I don't have time to hate, because if I would hate, I would still be a hostage or a prisoner of the past.'

Forgiveness is happening every single day, right under your nose. Think of the teacher who forgives the student for acting out when they know that they have stuff going on at home. And think of you, when you forgave your child for getting paint/curry/felt tip on your favourite rug/sofa/coat (delete as applicable, voucher can be used more than once).

Evidence shows anger, bitterness and resentment have a negative impact on our physical health, affecting our immune system, our organ function and our metabolism. Fred Luskin, cofounder of the Stanford University Forgiveness Project, explains, 'When you don't forgive you release all the chemicals of the stress response. Each time you react, adrenaline, cortisol, and norepinephrine enter the body.' This is why spiritual teacher Wayne Dyer compared resentment to a snakebite. It's not the bite that kills you but the venom circulating around your bloodstream.

Can you remember a negative comment or a difficult interaction that affected your thoughts and feelings long after the incident? 'When it's a chronic grudge, you could think about it 20 times a day, and those chemicals limit creativity, they limit problem-solving. Cortisol and norepinephrine cause your brain to enter what we call 'the no-thinking zone', and over time, they lead you to feel helpless and like a victim,' says Dr Luskin. He goes on to advise, 'When you forgive, you wipe all of that clean.' Forgiveness is linked to less stress, better heart health, sleep and immune system functioning, and reduced anxiety, depression and PTSD symptoms. And, of course, when people are more forgiving, there is more peace in the world.

So how do we raise children who can forgive? Well, you won't be surprised to hear this but it starts with you. And you can't fake it. I have worked with a lot of clients who say they've forgiven people who hurt them but the truth of their bodies and behaviour belies this. This is cognitive forgiveness – our minds let go but our bodies carry the grudge. You might be polite, even friendly, to the person but inside, consciously or unconsciously, you're still burning with rage. The deeper level of forgiveness we can discover is known as 'emotional' or 'embodied' forgiveness.

Whenever I have run forgiveness workshops with parents, teachers and other grown-ups, it is always this deeper forgiveness that has the biggest impact. It is also good to remember that, in a culture where we beat ourselves up relentlessly, the person who usually needs the most forgiveness is . . . YOU!

RELEASING GRUDGES AND FINDING FORGIVENESS

Do this exercise on your own, with a friend or with your child.

1. Bring to mind someone who has caused you pain who you're holding a grudge against. N.B. Don't start with the most difficult person in your life.

2. Visualise a specific moment that this person hurt you. Notice what feelings come up in your body. Do you notice tension, anger, bitterness, sadness?

3. Whatever you notice in your body, see if you can really allow that feeling to be there. Place a hand on that part of your body where you feel it and let it know it's OK for it to be there. You might want to imagine that the part of you that is feeling hurt is a younger version of you. Poet David Whyte says, 'To forgive is to assume a larger identity than the person who was first hurt.'

4. Ask the part inside you that is hurt if it has something it wants to say, perhaps something it hasn't been able to say or hasn't felt heard in saying. Notice what happens in your body as you do this. Do you notice a softening, a lightness?

5. Now see if you can find a space to extend forgiveness to the person in whatever way feels right to you. Perhaps you can acknowledge even one good thing about that person. See if you can find a way to welcome them back into your heart. I really like meditation teacher Jack Kornfield's words: 'I now remember the many ways others have hurt or harmed me, wounded me, out of fear, pain, confusion and anger. I have carried this pain in my heart too long.

To the extent that I am ready, I offer them forgiveness. To those who have caused me harm, I offer my forgiveness, I forgive you.'

As you practise this meditation, you will find that other old hurts and resentments will come up. Welcome them all in the same way. Self-forgiveness is important too and you can also use this exact same exercise to forgive yourself – both when you have hurt others and for when you have hurt yourself.

How can we raise peaceful warriors?

On the 10 June 1963, 350 monks gathered at a temple in Saigon, Vietnam, and began to march in two columns, headed by a pale blue Austin Westminster sedan. They were protesting against a government that was discriminating against the Buddhist population and even burning down temples. When the procession arrived at a big crossroads, Buddhist monk Quảng Đức got out of the car followed by two more monks. One monk placed a cushion in the middle of the road; the other took a five-gallon can of petrol out of the car. Quảng Đức sat down on the cushion in the cross-legged lotus position. The marchers formed a circle around him as the second monk from the car poured the petrol over Quảng Đức's head. Quảng Đức began meditating, reciting a prayer and rotating his string of wooden prayer beads. He then lit a match and dropped it onto his robes. In an instant, his whole body was consumed by flames. While burning to death, he stayed perfectly still.

David Halberstam, an American journalist who was there at the time, wrote: 'He never moved a muscle, never uttered a sound, his outward composure in sharp contrast to the wailing people around him.' After ten minutes, Quảng Đức's body was fully immolated. He toppled onto his back, still in the lotus position. A black and white photo of 'the burning monk' appeared on the front pages of newspapers around the world. Quảng Đức's act of resistance woke people up to the plight of Buddhists in Vietnam, leading to the toppling of the corrupt government. To this day, it symbolises the power of peaceful resistance.

Quảng Đức was a peaceful warrior. But you don't need to have saffron robes, and I'd prefer it if you didn't set yourself on fire. A peaceful warrior is one who doesn't avoid conflict but instead works to transform fiery energy into peace.

In our uncertain world, with wildfires spreading, with technology creating fear, outrage and polarisation, where we will increasingly be exposed to uncomfortable truths, our children will need to be peaceful warriors. We want our children to grow up feeling like they can engage with the big problems in the world and stand up for what they believe is right without being overwhelmed by 'triggers', without expecting the world to bend around them just so they can feel safe. Because the world – increasingly – won't work like that.

There are now many brilliant books, courses and apps that teach children to find peace through meditation. But if we only teach them the 'peace' part without the 'warrior' part, they will become grown-ups whose response to the flood of information and worries in the world is to distract, to dissociate, to retreat into their preferred blankie. And yes, meditation used incorrectly can be the biggest blankie of all.

Finding a way to be with uncomfortable truths, as I described in the introduction, is much more likely to lead to peace than sitting in a quiet room with some incense burning, eyes closed, meditating. Using the same principle we've used throughout the book, your job is to help your child ask as many questions as they need to about whatever uncomfortable truth is bothering them. Don't sugar-coat the answers; do trust that they can handle uncertainty, as long as you are consistent. Together, find the uncomfortable feeling in the body and bring compassion to this feeling.

Viktor Frankl wrote, 'What is to give light must endure burning.' This is our duty as grown-ups now, to help our children develop the capacity to endure burning, feeling the flames of this mad world without being overwhelmed by them, so they can send ripples of peace wherever they go.

14

ROOT SEVEN: HOPELESSNESS

Finding deeper meaning through our darkest feelings

Where does one go from a world of insanity?
Somewhere on the other side of despair

– T S Eliot

The first time Ainsley came to my clinic, I remember noticing how delicate he looked for a 13-year-old boy. He was slight and the skin on his face was like porcelain. He spoke in a soft, gentle voice, as though he didn't want to disturb the world around him.

Ainsley had been referred to me after he was kicked out of school for not engaging in class and refusing to do any work. When his mum dropped him off for his first session, she said: 'He's such a good boy. I don't understand how he could have gone from being a top student to being thrown out of school.'

Ainsley told me he'd spent many long nights over the past year researching the climate crisis online. He'd discovered articles and videos from scientists and other trustworthy sources, discussing the likelihood of natural disasters, starvation, war and societal collapse. The more Ainsley learned, the more hopeless he felt. His growing awareness of the climate crisis felt like a painful contrast to his experience at school. There, he said, 'Everyone is just carrying on as though there's no issue.' When Ainsley looked at the teachers, all he could think was that they were 'being fake, with big fake smiles, acting as though everything was OK' while Ainsley could see the world was in a hopeless mess. So, not feeling able to share his despair, Ainsley retreated into himself. He began to ask himself some big questions, such as: 'What's the point of doing anything when the grown-ups aren't taking this seriously?' He fell into a deep pit of nihilism. He stopped caring or doing schoolwork. Eventually, he was excluded.

Even for the wise and emotionally attuned therapist I sometimes think I am, I found my first conversations with Ainsley confronting. A huge part of me wanted to give him hope, to give him some clean solutions to his problem, to tell him, 'It will all be OK'. I suggested he channel his despair into joining a movement, Extinction Rebellion or the Youth Climate Protests. My ideas were instantly rebuffed as palliative care. 'It's too late,' he said. 'I've read the science. Nothing we do now can make any difference.'

I felt stuck. My usual tools weren't working. Ainsley had pushed me to the edge of my experience.

After a few jarring sessions where each of my attempts to give him hope fell flat, I realised I had to do something different. I had to let go, completely let go, of my desire to make Ainsley feel better. I had to let myself accept that Ainsley's perspective contained an uncomfortable truth: that his future felt hopeless. And that my daughter's future might feel hopeless too.

This is not an easy space for any of us to inhabit. It certainly isn't for me. I have been described as relentlessly optimistic. (Perhaps you have to be to do the kind of work I do?) But, once I'd attuned to Ainsley's nihilism, once I'd let his despair become a possible truth in my heart, things began to shift. We became equals, collaborators, existentialists. Now we were both sat atop the mountain, looking together at a forsaken horizon.

This horizon reflected back to us a deeper question: *how can we choose to live when we know it's all going to end?* (Aka 'What's the point?')

Welcome to the darkest root

No tree, it is said, can grow to heaven unless its roots reach down to hell – Carl Jung

This chapter is the seventh and last root, our final descent to the deepest and darkest corner of the forest: hopelessness. I'm not going to lie. It's going to be uncomfortable. We need to talk in a bit more depth about some things that feel really hard to talk about, such as death, suicide and the possible-and-difficult-to-imagine future. I believe it's our duty to talk about them because they are part of our children's lived reality. If we can't, our children will find answers somewhere else. Maybe the wrong kinds of answers.

Right now, I want to bow down to your big heart, your courage. Yes you, the soul-behind-the-eyes reading these words. You, who has already faced some uncomfortable truths – about the madness of this world and the dark roots of this madness within us all. You who is seeking truth about the future your children, our children face.

I've been wondering what kind of spoonful of sugar might help the dark medicine of this chapter go down. I thought about weaving in some spiritual wisdom or talking about post-traumatic growth or advising 'what doesn't kill you makes you stronger'. But all of this felt like sugar-coating. I found some jokes about death. They didn't feel right either. It turns out that jokes about death aren't that funny (unless properly executed). In the end, I decided to trust that you can handle the bitter tastes contained in this deepest, darkest part of the forest. Like a tumbler of single malt whisky after a hard day, sometimes bitter tastes resonate with the darker roots within. It's vital we find a way to bring our attention to the most difficult-to-accept parts of ourselves and of the world without getting overwhelmed, scrolling down or rushing back to the supposed safety of the clearing. Our children need us to develop this capacity. 'One can only face in others what one can face in oneself,' wrote African-American writer and activist James Baldwin. 'On this confrontation depends the measure of our wisdom and compassion. This energy is all that one finds in the rubble of vanished civilizations, and the only hope for ours.'

To support this confrontation with the darker parts of our self, I offer you a mantra that my teacher Ram Dass taught me: *'I am loving awareness.'*

When we bring the light of loving awareness into the darkest corners of the forest, they don't feel so scary. I encourage you to stay connected to this energy of loving awareness as we now explore hopelessness.

Trust in the darkness

The truth is, there is a place inside me, and a place inside you, that sometimes just wants to give up. There is a place that sometimes asks, 'what's the point?' There is a place that may sometimes even want to die.

Even writing that last sentence feels like I'm trespassing on forbidden grounds. But isn't it a part of the human condition, to be faced with so much suffering that sometimes death feels like the only way to find peace? Most people I speak to, clients but also friends, have had some kind of suicidal thought at some point.

If there is a final taboo in our culture, then surely this is it. If someone has suicidal thoughts, we say they must have a mental illness, there must be something wrong with the chemistry in their brain. We respond to suicide as though that thought, that choice, can never be reasonable. Unless of course you have a terminal illness and live in Switzerland.

But what if our human species has a terminal illness? What if we are unconsciously committing a kind of collective suicide? This was Ainsley's diagnosis. Was he being unreasonable?

I'm not advocating for suicide. I've spent countless hours and deep reserves of emotional energy guiding people to choose life. And 99 per cent of the time it has worked. If there is one single factor that helps people through this depth of despair, it has to be the simple act of providing a safe space where it's OK to talk about and give compassion to the darkest parts of our self and of this world.

There is a dangerous myth that says if we talk about suicide we make it more real, more likely to happen. The research actually shows the opposite to be true (and confirms my clinical experience) – that when a grown-up provides a safe space for a child to talk about their self-harm and suicidal thoughts, it can reduce that child's distress and suicidal thinking.

Over the last few years, suicide rates of young people have steadily increased in some parts of the world. The National Center for Health Statistics in the US released data in 2018 showing that, between 1999 and 2017, for 10-to-24-year-olds, the rate of suicide per 100,000 increased from 3.5 to 7.5 in females and from 18.7 to 26 in males. I'm sure you have come across similar statistics. It's hard to fathom how our beautiful, precious children can feel this much darkness. But we have to find a way to face this uncomfortable truth. Like the well-meaning teachers in Ainsley's school, if we carry on as if everything is totally OK, business as usual, then we lose their trust. And in this post-truth world, our children increasingly don't know who to trust.

Having one person to trust is necessary for our children's mental health. Trust is required to say YES to life. Trust grows in the fertile soil of honest, authentic relationship. But when we avoid uncomfortable truths, and our children pick up on us doing this, trust erodes.

If we grown-ups can shine a little light in the darkness, we might find a solid answer to Ainsley's question: *How can we choose to live when we know it's all going to end?*

The only purpose is love

In 1967, Timothy Leary spoke at the Human Be-In, a crowd of 30,000 tripping hippies in Golden Gate Park, San Francisco. His speech was the first public mention of the now famous counterculture mantra: *turn on, tune in, drop out.*

During the 1960s, young people had become increasingly aware through the new mass media about social issues, the Civil Rights movement, anti-war protests, sexual freedom and free speech campaigns. The Human Be-In was the crystallisation of this but also the beginning of the end for psychedelics. By this time, there had been years of scientific research into the healing potential of LSD and psilocybin (the active ingredient in magic mushrooms). But as ever more people took these powerful drugs – disregarding any advice on tripping safely, losing their minds, flying out of windows and piling up in A&E departments – a moral panic grew. Eventually, most psychedelics became classified as illegal in many countries around the world. They went underground.

Fast-forward to today and psychedelics have returned to

the mainstream with a blast. There is growing evidence that certain psychedelics given in the right clinical setting are solving even the most trenchant of mental health issues. And so billions of dollars are now being poured into research and start-up companies, as psychedelics are touted as a mass market miracle cure for many psychological issues, from PTSD to depression.

This psychedelic renaissance was jump-started by a 2006 study in the *Journal of Psychopharmacology*. It found that after just two or three psilocybin sessions, terminal cancer patients reported significant positive mood changes. A third of the patients said their experience was as spiritually significant as the birth of a first child or the death of a parent. Further research has since shown similar and remarkable results. In the biggest study, at John Hopkins and New York University, two thirds of subjects reported their anxiety and depression had pretty much disappeared after a single dose of psilocybin. A follow-up five years later showed many of the positive effects lasted.

When I worked in a hospice, I saw and felt the acute existential dread that often comes with a terminal diagnosis. So when I came across this research I was curious as to what psychedelics can teach us. I was keen to learn how they help people who are staring down the barrel answer the kind of question Ainsley and I were faced with.

The first modern person to think about using a psychedelic drug to support the dying process was British philosopher Aldous Huxley. On the day he died, 22 November 1963, he asked his wife Laura Huxley to inject him with LSD. In a video interview, Laura Huxley describes how 'a beautiful expression' appeared on his face and his agitation disappeared for the hours until his final breath.

Since the re-emergence of psychedelics into the therapy world, we now have many other similar reports helping us understand how these compounds are guiding people through their despair. In his book *How to Change Your Mind*, author Michael Pollan describes 54-year-old former TV executive Patrick Mettes' therapist-guided psilocybin session, shortly after he learned that his cancer of the bile ducts was incurable:

Mettes lies on a couch, eye shades on, a curated playlist on his headphones of Brian Eno, Philip Glass and Ravi Shankar. He's been given a mantra for the session 'Trust and let go'. When he encounters anything threatening, he is told to speak directly to that thing and to ask questions like 'What are you doing in my mind?' or 'What can I learn from you?'

The therapist tells Mettes that he should 'actively look for the darkest corner in the basement and shine your light there.' A couple of hours into the trip, the therapist notices that Mettes is breathing heavily and crying. Then he begins convulsing and says the following: 'Birth and death is a lot of work. Birth and death is a lot of work.' A few moments later, Mettes reaches out to hold the hand of one of the assistants. His convulsing has relaxed and he says: 'Oh God, it all makes sense now, so simple and beautiful.' Shortly after, Mettes writes the following reflection in his notebook: 'From here on, love was the only consideration. It was and is the only purpose. Love.'

Happily ever after?

Everyone goes through dark times. The week before Rose was born, I lost my best friend to suicide. I've been on a maternity ward, surrounded by the crying of newborn babies, holding Laurey's hand as she delivered a baby – a girl – who we knew we had already lost in the womb.

If there is one consistent thread between those dark times,

it is this: they force me to ask myself that primordial human question, 'What's the point?' And each time, I eventually find the same place Patrick Mettes discovered during his psilocybin trip, the place where the only point that makes any sense to me is love.

However, had I tried to impart this wisdom on Ainsley, told him 'it's all about the lurrve, baby', he would have certainly lost trust in me. This primordial human question can never be satisfactorily answered by anyone other than oneself. Anyone who finds themself in a dark night of the soul, for whatever reason, has to discover their own truth. The best we can do – for ourselves and for our children – is to create the conditions in which an authentic answer to that question might emerge. We need to be willing to meet them in their despair, without getting lost in or overwhelmed by it.

Discover your most cherished value

If you ever find yourself worried about death or an apocalyptic future, if you ever find yourself asking 'what's the point?', please know that this despair can guide you to discover your most cherished value. For Patrick Mettes and for me it is love. Yours might be something completely different.

What value do you most cherish?

Is there a small action you could take towards that value? It helps to ask yourself this question: What would love have me do now? (Or replace 'love' with the value of your choice.)

What makes doing this so hard? Part of the answer can be found in our belief in progress, that the future will bring something better than the present. This so-called 'myth of progress' is baked into our politics, our economics, our science, our minds. We believe in a happy ending, whether it's a heaven full of virgins, the Second Coming of Christ or that last scene in *Dirty Dancing* when Patrick Swayze lifts

Jennifer Grey in his arms to the song '(I've Had) The Time of My Life'.

Once upon a time, when life was harder and death was more present, people weren't so fixated on happily-ever-after. In Hans Christian Andersen's original version of *The Little Mermaid*, first published in 1837, the mermaid can only join her beloved handsome prince on land if she drinks a poison that will make her feel as if she's walking on knives. A romantic, she chooses this sado-masochistic option only to find that her prince marries another woman. This leaves the Little Mermaid so despairing that she throws herself into the sea, where her body dissolves into foam. Similarly, the Middle Eastern fairy-tale collection *One Thousand and One Nights* ends with a darker twist than we're used to these days: 'They lived happily until there came to them the One who Destroys all Happiness', i.e. death.

Now, even in the most apocalyptic films of today, the characters we are made to care about almost always survive. American film critic Roger Ebert wrote this about Roland Emmerich's *The Day After Tomorrow*: 'Los Angeles is levelled by multiple tornadoes, New York is buried under ice and snow, the United Kingdom is flash-frozen, and much of the Northern Hemisphere is wiped out for good measure. Thank god that Jack, Sam, Laura, Jason and Dr Lucy Hall survive, along with Dr Hall's little cancer patient.' This idea is so deeply embedded in our culture and our minds that we convince ourselves that, even if everyone else is going to burn in the apocalypse, at least the ones we care about will survive. It's this same mythology that has led Silicon Valley billionaires to pump billions of dollars into their immortality projects with a stated aim 'to solve death'. The company motto could easily be 'happily ever after'.

Our modern belief in progress is based on the idea that through scientific innovation, economic growth and political progress, our lives can only get better. And, well, if the earth becomes uninhabitable, then at least we can cryo-preserve our bodies or colonise Mars. But the difficult-to-accept truth is this: while progress has made our lives more comfortable in so many ways, it also has a shadow side. As Christopher Ryan says in his book *Civilized to Death*: 'What we fail to recognise when in thrall to the Myth of Progress is that everything better is purchased at the price of something worse.' That something worse gathers in the dark forest. It includes Ainsley's nihilism, our child mental health crisis and the climate catastrophe.

Happily-ever-after leaves no space for us to explore our despair or hopelessness, no space for suicidal thoughts, for anger, heartbreak, for asking 'what's the point?' Yet at times we must face these things. When we know that our children are feeling ever increasing levels of depression and suicidal despair, we need to seriously question the myth of progress.

Deep adaptation

Jem Bendell is known as the chief doomsayer of the environment movement. Bendell, a professor of sustainability leadership, self-published a paper in July 2018 called 'Deep Adaptation'. This was the same month I began to see those pastel-coloured skulls on Extinction Rebellion posters around London. Bendell's paper went viral. At time of writing, it's been downloaded almost a million times. It's based on a deep review of the climate science that Bendell conducted in 2017 (the same time that Ainsley was doing his own research). Bendell's main conclusion is that 'Climate-induced societal collapse is now inevitable in the near term.' In around a decade.

It doesn't get any cheerier, sorry. Bendell writes, 'We might pray for time. But the evidence before us suggests that we are set for disruptive and probably uncontrollable levels of climate change, bringing starvation, destruction, migration, disease and war. When we contemplate this possibility of 'societal collapse', it can seem abstract . . . to be describing a situation to feel sorry about as we witness scenes on TV or online. But when I say starvation, destruction, migration, disease and war, I mean in your own life. With the power down, soon you wouldn't have water coming out of your tap. You will depend on your neighbours for food and some warmth. You will become malnourished. You won't know whether to stay or go. You will fear being violently killed before starving to death.'

How bleak is that? One commentator wrote, 'It's so depressing it sends people to therapy.' Good for my business, at least – thanks Jem.

But Bendell doesn't just leave us with the gloom and doom. He offers a framework for facing the uncomfortable truth that he calls 'deep adaptation'. Deep adaptation means letting go of our 'upbeat' allegiance to 'development' and 'progress' and adapting to changing circumstances 'so as to survive with valued norms and behaviours.' The way I understand it is that we need to turn with compassion towards the possible reality that the future is as bleak as Bendell predicts. When I have shared this model with clients who are really worried about the climate crisis, it has really helped them. In our happily-ever-after world, the part of us that feels despair is starving for some validation.

But before you switch on *Mary Poppins* for some light relief, please allow me a moment to elaborate, beginning with my favourite Zen nugget of wisdom: *Death is certain. Timing uncertain. So, what is important now?*

Fact: none of us know how long we will live for. Sergey Brin doesn't know. Jeff Bezos doesn't know. Even Jem Bendell doesn't know. We do know for sure that one day we are going to die. And we also can say with a fair degree of certainty that one day the modern Western civilisation will collapse, as every civilisation has before it.

When it does collapse, perhaps a new more peaceful civilisation will emerge in its place? It's also possible, perhaps probable, that human beings will one day become extinct. Do we really think that we are so special that we can continue to outwit the cosmos? But, while understanding this reality is one thing, allowing it in emotionally is another. This isn't easy to do and it's not a place anybody wants to inhabit for long. But as Irvin Yalom says in his book *Staring at the Sun*: 'The way to value life, the way to feel compassion for others, the way to love anything with greatest depth is to be aware that these experiences are destined to be lost.'

How to make friends with our despair

Despair . . . is the only cure for illusion. Without despair we cannot transfer our allegiance to reality – it's a kind of mourning period for our fantasies – Philip Slater

It is more than possible to have transformational experiences without psychedelics. The protocol is the same. We need to actively look for the darkest corner in the forest and shine our light there. So let's look into despair, aka hopelessness. What does despair mean to you? These are some of my thoughts.

Despair is the temporary breakdown of trust, of meaning, of faith.

Despair is the realisation that most of our ambitions have been built like a house of cards.

Despair is what Ainsley felt when he began reading about

the climate crisis and saw the grown-ups pretending every-thing was OK.

Despair is, the words of Joanna Macy, 'The loss of the assumption that the species will inevitably pull through.'

Despair demands radical change.

And despair is the only place we will find an authentic answer to the essential question: *What's the point?*

To give despair a home is to listen to its darkest wisdom. It's not easy to listen to this wisdom because despair is usually telling us that some deep change, a death and rebirth, needs to occur. And this isn't possible if we continue business as usual. Plus, there is a huge taboo against despair in our happily-ever-after world. Despair is often seen as a profound failure of character. So we tend to ignore it and it turns into a deeper darkness.

In *Healing Through the Dark Emotions,* psychotherapist Miriam Greenspan says, 'When we hate ourselves for the "weakness" of despair, for the experience of helplessness that is so much a part of it, and when we panic in response to it, these reactions sink us into the condition we call depression.'

So how can we listen to despair in a way that won't over-whelm us or our children?

HOW TO LISTEN TO DESPAIR

First, let's get clear about our intention. Mine is that I want the children I support, including my own daughter, to feel like their darker feelings are safe, that they don't need to feel so afraid of these places. What is yours?

Now we can ask ourselves a question that will take us one level deeper. This is a question I work with in clinic a lot: *What is most difficult for me to accept in this moment?*

Take a moment to let this question land in you. Pay loving attention to what comes up. Treat whatever arises like a scared, vulnerable child. Allow the feelings to be there. Like Mettes, ask the feelings, *What can I learn from you?* The feelings won't kill us. They might even save us.

This morning, as soon as I asked myself this question, a surge of sadness rose up through my belly into my chest, filling my eyes with tears. Just as Mettes did in his psychedelic trip, I asked the sadness, 'What can I learn from you?' Images came to me like lightning bolts: of my best friend Dan and the last phone call we had just three days before he killed himself. I feel I could have said something or done something that might have saved his life. Of course, the stock response to this is 'there's nothing you could have done'. But this is what people say to give comfort. The uncomfortable truth is that I don't know if I could have done something to save him.

I continued to ask the question: *What is most difficult for me to accept in this moment?* Other images come to mind, of children I have worked with who experience such despair about this life that they don't want to carry on. It's really difficult for me to accept that these beautiful, precious, vulnerable beings with (almost) infinite potential could experience such despair.

I asked again, this time letting the question sink deeper into my soul: *What is most difficult for me to accept in this moment?* This time a faint sense of dread rises up in my gut. This dread speaks of the possible future my daughter is facing. It is really difficult for me to accept that I have brought my precious daughter into a potentially uninhabitable planet.

My answers won't be the same as yours. But I wonder if they provoked some response in your mind or your heart?

I wonder if any of your spiky defences have popped up to protect you from the difficult truth? Can you sense or acknowledge that feeling of despair or the deep sadness beneath your defences?

If that question hasn't landed with you, you could try finishing these sentences from Joanna Macy and Chris Johnstone in their book *Active Hope*:

When I imagine the world we will leave our children it looks like . . .

One of my worst fears about the future is . . .

And if you can find a friend with whom to share what comes up for you, it can really help. Author and Buddhist activist Margaret Wheatley wrote: 'Many large-scale efforts – some of which have won the Nobel Peace Prize – began with the simple but courageous act of friends talking to one another about their fears and dreams.'

I am aware this chapter hasn't got any cheerier. Like me, you may be yearning for a happily-ever-after. The good news is that when we make a space for our darker feelings, there is great joy, great love and a deeper sense of beauty lying on the other side. American poet Naomi Shihab Nye articulates that dance between darkness and light in her poem 'Kindness':

Before you know what kindness really is
you must lose things,
feel the future dissolve in a moment
like salt in a weakened broth.

I'd love to leave you with a heroic punchline, something about how tending to this deepest, darkest root will make you more friends, bring you loadsa money, make you happier, live longer, save the world, etc. But in my experience, that would take away from the value of the process itself.

I could tell you that Ainsley discovered some meaning, that he went to a new school, made peace with the darkness in the world and in himself. And this is true. But it's also true that I don't know what the rest of his life will be like. Will he continue to feel connected to his purpose? Will he join a climate movement? Will he become the next Jem Bendell? Greta Thunberg? Or will he turn on, tune in and drop out? I have no idea.

The most satisfying conclusion I can offer here is really quite a simple one. If we bring loving awareness to our most difficult feelings, these feelings stop feeling so scary. And if they are less scary for us, then they will be less scary for our children. And we will very likely find that these darker places have something vital – possibly even life-affirming – to teach us.

I am loving awareness.

15

FRUIT SEVEN: HOPE

How we can imagine and co-create a more beautiful tomorrow

Oft hope is born, when all is forlorn

– Legolas, *Lord of the Rings*

Just the other day, I overheard Rose having a chat with her mum.

'Mummy, does everybody die?'

'Yes sweetheart, everyone dies one day.'

'Does that mean you and Daddy will die one day?'

'Yes, but I hope it won't be for a really, really long time.'

Rose started to cry. Then I saw a thought flash through her mind. Her face lit up, as she told her mum:

'One day, I'm going to grow a baby in my own tummy.'

Right at the start of this book, I described coming across an article by a father questioning the morality of bringing children into the world. That hit me hard, a gut punch. You may have heard of the 'birthstriker' movement. The 'birthstrikers' are people who've decided not to have children because of the climate crisis. But this does not help the children who are already alive on this planet, including your children and mine. We need to find an authentic hope with and for our children.

Rose found her hope by imagining having her own children. You might think she was being naive. But to see children as carriers of hope is in fact a deep and recurring pattern. Children bring into the world certain qualities that, as we will see, are full of hope.

The birth of hope

In the ancient Hindu scripture, the *Markandeya Purana,* there's a story about the end of the universe. There's a huge flood, a cosmic deluge that is wiping out humankind, and this is being witnessed by a sage called Markandeya (Manu for short): 'Black clouds obstructed the sun and hurled lightning in every direction. Unrelenting rains lashed the ground. The seven rivers began to swell and the four oceans started to overflow. Waves as high as mountains drowned the earth. This was *pralaya* [apocalypse], the final dissolution of the world, before its regeneration.'

As he watches these apocalyptic scenes, Markandeya spots a baby floating on the torrents, riding a banyan leaf. The baby looks as if he doesn't have a care in the world, kicking back on his leaf, sucking on his toe. Manu is deeply affected by this sight: 'The infant's heavenly smile negated the brutality of the *pralaya.* The baby looks at him, and in that moment the baby's compassionate glance reassured Manu that life would go on, convincing him that the world never ends, but only changes.'

Suddenly, Manu gets sucked inside the baby's body. Here, he discovers there is a whole world – skies, seas, earth, gods, demons, humans, animals and plants. As the old world is dying, this child carries inside the potential of a new one.

Manu eventually realises that this child is an incarnation of the divine Baby Krishna.

You can see the parallels to today. Our old world is falling apart. We are living through the end of an old way of being. You may find this hard to believe. You may, like me, have an inner voice that's saying, 'Things will carry on just as they always have, business as usual.' But the reality is, and always has been, that infinite growth isn't possible on a finite planet. We have reached the endgame of our way of being. This is a good thing for our planet, and good for our children too, because this way of being was making them mad.

In this ancient myth, the seed of hope breaks through right at the endpoint, rock bottom. And in this moment, Baby Krishna's compassionate glance 'convinces' Manu that 'the world never ends, it only changes'. As we will see below, there is something about children that tells us about the possibility, if not the necessity, of renewal.

Children are the future

The child as saviour of the world is a recurring myth across human history. Moses, Jesus, Horus, Harry Potter, Gus in the Netflix series *Sweet Tooth*.

Carl Jung recognised this. Having spent countless hours studying the archetype of the Child as it appeared in myths and in the dreams of his patients, he concluded, 'the child is potential future' representing 'the strongest, the most ineluctable urge in every being, namely the urge to realize itself'.

Just like Baby Krishna, our children contain the potential of a new world, a better tomorrow. They carry the seeds of precious human qualities – including all the fruits we have already explored and three other special qualities we will explore below. Yes, they can be selfish, cruel, narcissistic and tyrannical; they can drive us to distraction with their constant demands. But no matter how dark their dark side, our children carry the possibility of transcendence, the spirit of hope.

I believe there is something sacred about our children. Children tend to be more open to change. Their brains and nervous systems have had less time to be conditioned by the world. And they have a smaller collection of spiky defences. Often, all they need is one trusted adult, someone who can listen to them, respect them, empower them, and bring out their potential. That's why I have chosen to work with children (and those who care for them) for pretty much my whole working life. I have worked with children who are discarded by most as damaged goods. I choose to do this because I have hope. I believe that people can change, no matter how damaged they are. In fact, one of the most transcendent aspects of being a parent is the knowledge that we can give our children something we didn't have, help them become better, more peaceful, more loving, more empowered than we are.

This spirit of hope continues from childhood into adolescence, albeit with a more fiery energy. Greta Thunberg is a great example of a teenager who has become a symbol of hope. At first, she refused to go to school because she felt hopeless about the future. But then she discovered enough hope to take a stand.

Despite the stereotype of a teenager spending hours in a dark room, listening to trap music, playing shoot-em-ups and hating on the world, adolescence is in fact a developmental stage full of hope. As adolescents, we are biologically primed for taking risks, for separating away from the culture of our parents, for deciding what new world we want to birth into being. Young people are at the heart of most revolutions, from Tiananmen Square to the Arab Spring. They believe a better world is possible and worth fighting for. When I was a teenager, I felt disappointed and angry with the lack of authenticity I could see in the grown-up world. I rebelled against its hollowness, although my rebellion was channelled mainly through low-level disobedience and the Wu-Tang Clan. If you have teenage children, as much as they may wind you up, I encourage you to see the seeds of hope in their fiery rebellion. This energy sometimes just needs time to find an authentic outlet.

There is, however, a shadow side of our hopeful projections onto children. Does it feel right that we need a 15-year-old girl from Sweden to wake us up to the real damage we are doing to the world?

The child as saviour can easily become the problem child, drowning under the weight of our expectations. In clinic, I've seen a lot of children whose parents thought they were prodigies and put them into extreme sports training or academic hot-housing. That is, until the child developed symptoms like anxiety or suicidal ideation that were really just a desperate plea to be relieved of this burden. Children are not empty buckets for our unfulfilled dreams.

But I don't want us to get side-tracked by this shadow side. The main point to remember here is that as long as we can see and remember the (almost) infinite potential our children bring into this world, we can find hope. In this sense, hope is the mother of all the fruits. Every single day, I see grown-ups – parents, teachers, doctors, nurses, therapists – helping children to realise their potential, even in this mad, uncertain world. This gives me hope. You give me hope.

Heavenly qualities

The great British Romantic poet William Wordsworth was just seven years old when his beloved mother died from pneumonia. His dad couldn't cope with the grief and so he sent William and his four siblings to live with their grandparents. There were points during this period where William felt suicide was the only way to escape his pain. Then, when William was 13 years old, his father died too. Admittedly, so far this doesn't sound like a great story for a chapter on hope. But it's the background to one of Wordsworth's most famous poems 'Ode: Intimations of Immortality from Recollections of Early Childhood', about some of the most precious qualities that children bring into this world.

> *Heaven lies about us in our infancy!*
> *Shades of the prison-house begin to close*
> *Upon the growing Boy,*
> *But he beholds the light, and whence it flows,*
> *He sees it in his joy;*
> *The Youth, who daily farther from the east*
> *Must travel, still is Nature's priest,*
> *And by the vision splendid*
> *Is on his way attended;*
> *At length the Man perceives it die away,*
> *And fade into the light of common day.*

Wordsworth believed that we lose these qualities as we grow up, but that children can help us to find them again.

There are two qualities in particular that children bring into this world that are so deeply innate that they need very little help to grow. In fact, something needs to go badly wrong for them to be switched off. These qualities contain the sweetest nectar of hope. And just spending time with children can help these qualities come alive in us grown-ups again. These two qualities are playfulness and wonder.

How to grow playfulness

There is a photograph taken in London in 1940, the peak of the Blitz, of a group of children aged somewhere between four and eight playing on a seesaw. What's remarkable about it is that the children are wearing huge gas masks covering their whole heads. They make Covid face masks look pitiful in comparison. And the children are playing as though they don't have a care in the world. You can find similar images from other war-torn times and places: Sarajevo, Afghanistan, Gaza, Syria. In an account of children in concentration camps during the Holocaust, historian George Eisen describes how 'play burst forth spontaneously and uncontrollably'. He concludes play must be instinctual, 'an urge that springs from the soul of the children themselves'.

There is something magical about play. It's an indestructible energy that rises up from even the most apocalyptic of ruins. Play is the magic creative power behind all of life – in Hinduism it's called *lila*. You could call it 'evolution', or 'life-force'; you could just call it 'Ralph'. This energy is inside all of us – yes, including you. And it's constantly seeking to experiment with new forms, if you can just let it be.

I have seen this in my work. When children are given a protected space to play, healing happens. Playful energy can shift someone out of the darkest of spaces. Baby Krishna sucking on his toe has this energy, reminding Manu that 'the world never ends, but only changes'. Play is the way we learn best; in play mode our fight-flight-freeze systems are turned off. Our body and brain have capacity to experiment, to digest new information and to grow. Play is, in the words of animal behaviour expert Marek Spinka, 'training for the unexpected'. In play, meaning becomes fluid – a piece of cardboard can become a sword or a flower; an argument can turn into deep-bellied, tear-jerking laughter; a crisis can turn into an opportunity for renewal. When we play, as Graham Music says, 'reality is suspended' and we see potential in everything. In the twenty-first century, with our future feeling so uncertain, where we so desperately need to cultivate more hope, play is essential.

So what gets in the way of play? Well, you might have guessed it, but it's us – the grown-ups. It's when we are too rigid and serious. It's when we build up so much guilt, obligation and stress as we get older. The children I work with often come from homes where their playfulness has been rejected and becomes distorted. Sometimes this is because of trauma. Or due to driven parents who schedule much of their child's free time, worried the child will fall behind their peers if they don't.

Children need unscheduled, unstructured playtime to follow whatever they are curious about with little-to-no intervention from you. The more of this unstructured play, the better. It's been shown to lead to increased empathy and creativity, and to reduced stress, anxiety and depression.

If you are in play with them, it's really important to get on their level – i.e. if they are younger, get on the floor with them. Let them take the lead and as much as possible let go of any stress you might be carrying so that you can effortlessly drop into the play with them. In fact, just as children release tension and find healing during play, you can too.

If you struggle to reconnect with your own playful spirit, don't be hard on yourself. The simplest way to recover playfulness is to just stop taking everything so seriously, if you can. There will always be things to worry about, big and small, but often the best way to solve problems both in our own minds and in the world is to tap into our playful energy. Give your inner child permission to play, without the beady-eyed supervision of your serious, angsty inner adult. It can help to speak to this adult and tell them to relax, that they can have a break.

When we feel stuck, just allowing a glimmer of playful energy can open us up to a world of possibility. It doesn't have to be a radical shift; it can just be a subtle lightening or opening up. It can help me to think of an image or a person who's playful or fun. Who comes to mind for you?

I have these beautiful lines, written by Aldous Huxley, on the wall of my office:

> *It's dark because you are trying too hard.*
> *Lightly child, lightly. Learn to do everything lightly.*
> *Yes, feel lightly even though you're feeling deeply.*
> *Just lightly let things happen and lightly cope with*
> * them.*
> *So throw away your baggage and go forward.*
> *There are quicksands all about you, sucking at your*
> * feet,*
> *trying to suck you down into fear and self-pity and*
> * despair.*
> *That's why you must walk so lightly.*
> *Lightly my darling,*
> *on tiptoes and no luggage,*
> *not even a sponge bag,*
> *completely unencumbered.*

Awakening wonder

If you've ever taken a walk with a toddler, you've seen their capacity for wonder in action. They stop to look, touch, smell and wonder at all those things the adult you has stopped paying attention to – insects, flowers, grass, cracks in the pavement. Rose was once so entranced by a lamp post on a street in Hackney that she began to lick it, with zeal.

Wonder is a radical act in a world lost in speed, efficiency and productivity. Rachel Carson, the activist who launched the modern environmental movement in the 1960s, believed there was something deep and hopeful about wonder, that it wasn't just a sentimental ideal: 'Those who dwell, as scientists or laymen, among the beauties and mysteries of the earth are never alone or weary of life.' Carson wrote about precious days exploring nature with her nephew Roger. She noticed that children had instant access to a world of delight in the small and inconspicuous.

Interestingly, the wonder-full mind of a child is very similar to being on psychedelics. Yes, you heard me, your child is basically tripping. Alison Gopnik, a leading US child development psychologist and researcher, says, 'The experience of babies and young children is more like dreaming or tripping than like our usual grown-up consciousness.' They are 'immersed in the almost unbearably bright and exciting novelty of walls, shadows, voices, vividly aware of everything without being focused on any one thing in particular.'

So, if wonder carries hope, how can we grown-ups get it back?

One thing psychedelics do in the brain is to shut down the default mode network (DMN). The DMN's role is to keep order in your brain so things don't descend into anarchy. It's strongly linked to the self, leading some researchers to call it the 'me network'. I imagine it to be like a tight grip around the brain, keeping the conflicting parts of our mind together.

While having a relatively stable sense of self is essential to a stable life, many mental health problems like anxiety and depression can stem from being too absorbed in the self. And if that grip around our brain is too tight, or if we experience profound loss or trauma, we lose our sense of wonder. So, do we all need to run to the hills and start munching on magic mushrooms? No. The good news is we can access wonder in many other (legal) ways. One is to realise the wonder-full truth of that old maxim – seek and ye shall find. On the next mundane trip you take, say to the supermarket or a bus ride, set an intention to look for something different, unusual, surprising or beautiful.

The other way to let go of our bag of worries and to access wonder is to let our child share with us their natural fascination for the world, the beauty and magic in the everyday. It is an amazing world after all, isn't it? Flowers growing through the cracks of the pavement. People's faces are amazing – ancient scriptures containing the most incredible stories of their ancestors. Your body is a miracle too. How does this community of trillions of cells dance, make music, make love, write words?

Together, grown-ups and children can keep each other's sense of wonder alive, as Carson noticed: 'If a child is to keep alive his inborn sense of wonder, he needs the companionship of at least one adult who can share it, rediscovering with him the joy, excitement and mystery of the world we live in.'

Let your child open your eyes, your mind and your heart to the possibility of wonder that surrounds you. Franz Kafka said, 'Anyone who keeps the ability to see beauty never grows old.' Perhaps wonder is the secret to immortality, after all?

Learning hope

When Martin Seligman and his team did the learned helplessness experiments described in Chapter 2, giving electric shocks to those poor little dogs and conducting other tests on humans, watching how easily these creatures gave up hope, there was just one thing they couldn't explain . . .

. . . some of the human subjects did not give up.

Puzzled by this anomaly, Seligman and his team set out to figure what was different about these hopeful people. And after conducting a lot of research, they discovered one factor that predicted hope more than any other – 'explanatory style'. In the words of Martin Seligman, 'While you can't control your experiences, you can control your explanations.' Put simply, these people saw difficulties as temporary, local and specific. They didn't blame themselves or conclude life was going to be difficult forever. They believed they had agency and so were able to think creatively and flexibly about how to solve the problems they were faced with. Their attitude became known as 'learned hopefulness'. The key word here is 'learned', which means we can learn these tools for ourselves and teach them to our children.

If we expect that the world is going to end and there is nothing we can do about it, then guess what is going to happen? We give up, like the dogs after the electric shocks. However, if we acknowledge there is suffering in the world but believe our actions matter, then what? We have hope and are more likely to take positive action.

This leads nicely on to another insight from the field of learned hopefulness, which is about the power of small actions. If we only value big, dramatic, world-changing actions, then we will likely feel overwhelmed and hopeless. It's a big ask – to 'change the world'. But if we shift our focus to small actions, to the things we know we can do and that will make a difference, no matter how small, we water the seeds of hope. Rebecca Solnit wrote that hope is, 'The belief that what we do matters even though how and when it may matter, who and what it may impact, are not things we can know beforehand . . . history is full of people whose influence was most powerful after they were gone.'

When a single human chooses to be kind, when a parent chooses to heal their trauma, when a child stands up against a bully – these individual acts send ripples in every direction. Mother Teresa wisely said we can't all do great things, like save the planet, but we can all do small things with great love. When feeling overwhelmed by the world, never underestimate the power of small actions.

I get inspired by the power of small actions every morning as I walk past our local lollipop man. No matter whether it's chucking buckets of rain or a bright shiny day, no matter whether there is one sulky teenager crossing the road or a gaggle of little ones, the lollipop man is there, always smiling. I can see he's doing his job with great care. He's helping children get across a busy road. I'm grateful for people like him in the world.

BRING YOUR VISION TO LIFE

This exercise comes from the learned hopefulness research. It's about tapping into the power of positive imagination. Cosmologist Carl Sagan said, 'The visions we offer our children shape the future. It matters what those visions are. Often, they become self-fulfilling prophecies. Dreams are maps.' Those who imagine a positive outcome are more likely to keep going than those who don't. All you need is five minutes, a pen, some paper and quite possibly a cup of tea. You can do this exercise with your children or alone.

1. Write down up to five problems in your life or in the world that leave you or your child feeling overwhelmed, helpless or despairing. Next to each problem, write down one small helpful action that you can do in the next few days. Ignore the voice in your head that says it doesn't matter or it's too late. If the four horsemen are already here, give them some carrots.

2. Write down your vision for a more beautiful world. It can help to close your eyes and meditate on this for a minute. Invite this vision in, be open to experiencing it as a feeling, an image, an idea. Open your mind and heart and body and let go of judgement.

3. Write down at least five elements of this beautiful world that you and/or the children in your care would really like to see more of. As above, for each element, write one small action that you can do in the next few days that could help this element of a more beautiful world to grow.

The key to this exercise is to embrace how small the step can be. It could be just spending five minutes researching the topic. Or chatting to one friend. Or committing to a hug every morning at breakfast.

Keep on taking those tiny steps, tiny actions. Made over and over again, they can be surprisingly, maybe even life-changingly, powerful. All you need to do is take one tiny step today . . . and then another . . .

In search of authentic hope

Hope is the feeling that the feeling you have isn't permanent – Mignon McLaughlin

Our children carry hope into this world with their (almost) infinite potential and their heavenly qualities. And we can learn to be more hopeful, too. But there is a danger of being too optimistic. We don't want to get lost licking lamp posts while our house is burning down. We need to find authentic hope.

When our children feel despair, they need us to show them authentic hope. In the research into suicide prevention, hope is often found as a protective factor. People who are suicidal are often desperately wanting some hope. But, as I found with Ainsley and many other clients, that hope has to be authentic. 'Happily-ever-after' does not work here. But what does authentic hope look like?

This is how it looks for me:

Authentic hope has let go of 'happily-ever-after'.

Authentic hope is humble. It doesn't pretend to have all the answers. It can say 'I don't know'.

Authentic hope embraces uncertainty about the future our children face.

Authentic hope finds a reason to keep going, even if we know it's all going to end one day.

Authentic hope honours the power of our small everyday actions. It is the inner knowing that what we do matters, even though we can't always see how far those ripples go.

Authentic hope actively looks for the good in people, including in ourselves. It nurtures that essential goodness, that inner light, without denying the darkness.

Authentic hope knows that a more beautiful world is possible. It realises that to get to that world, we must choose to imagine it, feel it, live and breathe it right now.

But more than anything else, authentic hope isn't someone else's beliefs. Authentic hope can only work if it is true for you. So, what gives you hope? What keeps you going when life sometimes feels so hard? Find your own authentic hope. The seed is inside you, just waiting for a little light.

CONCLUSION

Hello you.

I want to begin this ending by checking in with you.

I'm aware this book may have taken you on quite a journey, emotionally and otherwise. And I'm curious. What are you noticing in your body as you come to these last few words? There is no right or wrong answer here. Whether you have read every word and religiously done every exercise, or whether you have skim-read and done no exercises, it's OK. If you don't feel in this moment a sense of perfect peace or infinite compassion, you haven't failed. Whatever you notice in your body right now, whatever thoughts might be stirring in your mind, remember to just let them be as they are.

I'd like to direct these parting words to a place inside of you that can't be touched by this mad world. In this place, you carry a deep and abiding sense that you are enough. In this place, you carry a feeling of being at home. If you can find a place in your body that feels like home, put a hand there. Take a moment to breathe into that sense, that feeling of home.

It's vital that we keep coming back to this place, this feeling of home. Because no matter where we are living, no matter what is going on in the world out there, for our children we are 'home'.

And the truth is, it's hard to feel at home when the worries of the world stream 24/7 through our four walls into our nervous systems. It's hard to feel at home when our natural home here on earth no longer feels secure.

So now we come back to the question I posed at the start

of this book: how can we help our children feel safe when the future feels increasingly uncertain?

Well, we have discovered that there are two kinds of safety. One is the kind where we numb difficult feelings, avoid uncomfortable truths, wrap our children in cotton wool and hope for the best. It turns out that this kind of safety doesn't actually feel very safe. And, when we train our children to be 'resilient' and 'well-adjusted', we teach them not to listen to their bodies or their feelings. In other words, we teach them not to feel at home in their bodies. And when our children's bodies respond to the world around them (which they will), when they signal to us through their symptoms that there is something not right in the bigger picture (which they will), then we will not be able to hear these cries. Instead, we will try to get rid of them, distract from them, fix them. This is how our children end up feeling broken. This is also how they end up losing trust in the world around them.

The other kind of safety comes, paradoxically, when we are willing to be honest about the difficult realities in the world. This kind of safety comes when we trust in our capacity to handle uncomfortable truths. This kind of safety comes when we fight back against the story that we are broken, when we listen to our bodies and the wisdom of our feelings, even the darker ones, when we allow ourselves to 'hear within us the sounds of the earth crying', as Thich Nhat Hanh once said. This kind of safety comes when we can explore, together, the dark forest beyond the clearing. You see, the forest is our home. It's home to all the unwanted, unloved parts of our selves. And there is a place inside of you that is a vast as the forest. In this place, there is no judgement, only love. When you tune into this place, you can provide a loving home to all those parts that have been exiled.

This is how we can help our children feel safe. This kind of safety doesn't bring any guarantees for the future. It is not a happily-ever-after. There will continue to be scary things out there. The world is going to continue to heat up. But no matter what is going on in the world, please never forget that you are your children's home.

I'm not saying it's easy to stay connected to this place. We need courage, discipline, commitment and community to keep bringing all the exiled parts of our self back to that place inside that feels like home. But it is only from this place that we can authentically begin to answer Ainsley's question, the question that sits (often unanswered) inside all of our hearts: *How can we choose to live when we know it's all going to end?* The answer I always come back to, the only answer that ever feels solid to me is love. Love is the point.

The world is making our children mad because it is short-circuiting our capacity for love. And so the way to help our children is by reclaiming love. As we learn to love the parts of our selves that really don't get much love, especially the parts we or the world find hard to accept, we can offer this same gift to our children, and they to the world.

The late anthropologist and activist David Graeber once said, 'The ultimate, hidden truth of the world is that it is something that we make and could just as easily make differently.' What could the world look like if we raised a generation of children with a deep sense of being loved?

Here's what I imagine, my vision for the year 2050. This is what the deepest part of my heart wishes for my daughter Rose Gaia, for your children and future generations.

We will appreciate way more what we already have, rather than constantly seeking more. The juggernaut of consumerism will grind to a halt because the feelings of lack and scarcity that drive it will have largely dissolved. As we realise that we don't need so much stuff, we stop working so hard. And when we stop working so hard, we will remember how much joy is possible in this precious life. As we slow down, we are able to build relationships that are more stable and more loving. We will spend way less time being addicted to productivity on the hunt for some imagined future reward. Instead, we will spend more time together, enjoying the ultimate reward of connection.

We will no longer follow the idea of success as defined by material things or how many followers we have on social media. We will feel a different kind of success, based on a life lived in accordance with our deepest, most cherished values.

We will remember the deep intelligence of our bodies and how this intelligence is just one beautiful expression of the intelligence of Mother Earth. We will remember to trust the intelligence of our emotions, of our symptoms, and we will continually support each other to transform these emotions into something beautiful.

Anxiety, depression, eating disorders, body dysmorphia, self-harm, suicide will all decrease, simply because children grow up with a deep sense of their own enoughness. In short, our children will stop hurting themselves and start loving themselves.

We will have broken free from the lonely illusion of separation. We won't even have a speck of doubt in our bones that we are all interconnected – feet to earth, heart to heart. And from this felt sense of interdependence, there will arise the most natural desire to take care of each other and Mother Earth.

And our children will grow up with a deep trust in their own capacity to handle suffering. They won't be afraid to ask difficult questions. They will have the courage to lead where necessary. Most importantly, they will know deep in their bones that they are enough.

We will find authentic hope in 2050 as we watch our children and maybe even our grandchildren play, as we join with them looking for the beauty in the everyday. And maybe we'll lick a few lamp posts together on the way.

The End.

BUILDING A HOME TOGETHER: A GUIDE TO FINDING THE OTHERS

Reading can be a lonely experience, as can parenting. And some of the ideas and exercises in this book are much better shared, especially some of the more challenging ones. So below is a suggestion for how you can find the others and build a home together.

Find one person who you think might be interested in exploring the ideas in this book together with you. It might be your partner. It might be a family member or a friend. Send them a note about the book and ask if they would be up for connecting around it. If they are, then great! Ask them if they know anyone else who might want to join. Once you have your group (and your group can be as small as two), if you send me an email to hello@louisweinstock.com with the subject line 'In This Together', I will send you for free the meditations I have recorded to accompany this book. This isn't a marketing ploy. I genuinely believe in the power of community and want to support this in whatever way I can.

Your group can organise as a very informal book club, sending messages about the book, perhaps having a call every now and then. Or you can structure it a bit more like a course. There are 14 roots and fruits in this book so if you'd like to, you can organise with your group a period of 14 weeks where you agree to read and practise one of the roots/fruits each week, and share feedback, insights, etc. The advantage of this approach is that you will get a lot more out of the experience and you can support each other to embed these essential practices into your life. Your kids will be grateful!

FURTHER RESOURCES

For further resources related to the themes in this book, including guided meditations, go to my website: louiswein-stock.com

Root One: Victimhood / Fruit One: Empowerment

- Official website for the Karpman Drama Triangle: www.karpmandramatriangle.com/
- Official website for Lea Waters, author of *The Strengths Switch*: www.leawaters.com/
- Free Range Kids and Let Grow – websites from Lenore Skenazy, dubbed 'America's Worst Mom' when she let her nine-year-old ride the subway on her own. Resources on how to give children more autonomy: letgrow.org/ www.freerangekids.com

Root Two: Virtual reality / Fruit Two: Bodies in nature

- *Beacon House* – has beautiful resources for parents and some child-friendly ones too on how to work with trauma in children: beaconhouse.org.uk/?section=welcome-to-beacon-house

- *Trauma Is Really Strange* – a really lovely, visual guide to trauma by somatic therapist Steve Haines, suitable for young people. This website also contains information on trauma release techniques that work with the body: bodycollege.net/trauma/

- *A More Beautiful Life* – Podcast with interviews about recognising, appreciating and integrating earliest life experiences: prenatal-and-perinatal-healing-online-learning. teachable.com/p/a-more-beautiful-life-podcast

- *Mark Wolwynn* – One of the leaders in the field of ancestral or inherited trauma. His website has lots of free content and resources: markwolynn.com

- *On Being* – Podcast interview with Rachel Yehuda, one of the most important scientists in the field of inherited trauma: onbeing.org/programs/rachel-yehuda-how-trauma-and-resilience-cross-generations-nov2017/

Root Three: Narcissism / Fruit Three: Compassion and co-operation

- *Free Online* Narcissism Test: openpsychometrics.org/tests/NPI/

- *Dr Craig Malkin* – Expert on healthy narcissism. Website with free resources: www.drcraigmalkin.com/

- *Marmalade Trust* – Charity with a focus on loneliness and some helpful resources on their website: www.marmaladetrust.org/loneliness

- *Compassionate Mind* – Paul Gilbert's website with loads of free resources on developing compassion: www.compassionatemind.co.uk
- *Self-Compassion* – Kristen Neff's website. She is the leading light in self-compassion. Some really good free resources here: self-compassion.org/
- *List of Core Values (see page 137):*

abundance	accountability	achievement	authenticity	adventure	autonomy
balance	beauty	commitment	compassion	co-operation	courage
creativity	curiosity	determination	emotional wisdom	empowerment	excellence
fairness	faith	family	financial	friendships	fun
future generations	health	honesty	hope	independence	influence
inner harmony	integrity	initiative	justice	kindness	leadership
learning	love	loyalty	making a difference	openness	peace
personal growth	play	respect	responsibility	risk-taking	self-discipline
self-expression	service	spirituality	stability	trust	wisdom

Root Four: Scarcity / Fruit Four: Abundance

- *Fear-setting* – a detailed breakdown of how to do fear-setting: www.teamstrength.com/wp-content/uploads/2018/03/Fear-Setting-with-Tim-Ferriss.pdf

Root Five: Anaesthesia / Fruit Five: Feelings

- *Centre For The History Of The Emotions* – brilliant resources to explore the history of our feelings from Professor Thomas Dixon and his team at Queen Mary University of London: projects.history.qmul.ac.uk/emotions/author/thomasdixon/
- *Atlas Of Emotions* – gorgeous interactive website from Paul Ekman exploring emotions: atlasofemotions.org/#triggers/
- *Lisa Feldman Barrett* – neuroscientist who believes our emotions are socially constructed. Loads of talks and podcasts on her website: lisafeldmanbarrett.com/multimedia/
- *Susan Stiffelman* – family therapist and parenting coach with great, free resources on navigating emotions in family life: susanstiffelman.com/
- *Focusing* – if you are interested in exploring the rich world of focusing, this website for the International Focusing Institute is a good place to start. You can find a focusing partner which can be a great source of free, mutual support: previous.focusing.org/index.html

Root Six: Chaos / Fruit Six: Peace

- *The Alcoholics Anonymous Idiot's Guide – for Chaos Creators*: www.bbaintheuk.weebly.com/uploads/6/5/1/4/65144095/idiots-guide-for-relationships_chaos_creators.pdf

- *The Polyvagal Institute* – learn more about Stephen Porges, neuroception and his theory and science of connection:
  www.polyvagalinstitute.org/
- *The Forgiveness Project* – amazing project with loads of inspiring stories and resources about forgiveness:
  www.theforgivenessproject.com/

Root Seven: Hopelessness / Fruit Seven: Hope

- *Deep Adaptation Website* – for intrepid explorers who want to learn more about how to face the reality of the climate crisis without losing hope:
  www.deepadaptation.info
- *Tiu De Haan on The Possibility of Wonder* – a friend who is brilliant at and specialises in helping adults access states of wonder. Here you can find a range of courses and offerings to help you access wonder:
  www.tiudehaan.com/thepossibilityofwonder
- *Dan Tomasulo on Learned Hopefulness* – loads of great resources and content here on cultivating learned hopefulness:
  www.dantomasulo.com/learnedhopefulness

REFERENCES

Introduction

J Krishnamurti, *What Are You Doing with Your Life?*, Rider, 2018

Discovering the roots

P Patalay and E Fitzsimons, 'Psychological distress, self-harm and attempted suicide in UK 17-year olds: prevalence and sociodemographic' *British Journal of Psychiatry*, Vol 219, Iss 2, August 2021

C G Jung, *Collected Works of C G Jung, Volume 5: Symbols of Transformation*, Princeton University Press, 1977

S Timimi, 'The McDonaldization of childhood: children's mental health in neo-liberal market cultures', *Transcultural Psychiatry*, Vol 47, Iss 5, November 2010

L Donnelly, 'Number of children taking antidepressants hits all-time peak during pandemic', *Telegraph*, 24 June 2021 www.telegraph.co.uk/news/2021/06/23/number-children-taking-antidepressants-hits-all-time-peak-pandemic/

P Conrad and M R Bergey, 'The impending globalization of ADHD: Notes on the expansion and growth of a medicalized disorder', *Social Science & Medicine*, Vol 122, December 2014

A Duckworth, *Grit: The Power of Passion and Perseverance*, Vermilion, 2019

Alexander Den Heijer, www.alexanderdenheijer.com/quotes

Root One: Victimhood

S F Maier and M E P Seligman, 'Learned Helplessness: Theory and Evidence', *Journal of Experimental Psychology: General*, Vol 105, No 1, 1976 ppc.sas.upenn.edu/sites/default/files/lhtheoryevidence.pdf

R M Sapolsky, *Why Zebras Don't Get Ulcers*, St. Martins Press, 2004

Q Liu et al, 'Changes in the global burden of depression from 1990 to 2017: Findings from the Global Burden of Disease Study', *Journal of Psychiatric Research*, Vol 126, July 2020

J Jowitt, 'What is depression and why is it rising?' *Guardian*, 4 June 2018 www.theguardian.com/news/2018/jun/04/what-is-depression-and-why-is-it-rising

D F Lancy, 'Playing with Knives: The Socialization of Self-Initiated Learners', *Child Development*, Vol 83, Iss 3, May 2016

F J Infurna et al, 'Childhood trauma and personal mastery: their influence on emotional reactivity to everyday events in a community sample of middle-aged adults', *PLoS One*, Vol 7, Iss 10, April 2015

T Harris, www.nytimes.com/2019/12/05/opinion/digital-technology-brain.html

Fruit One: Empowerment

L Dillner, 'How did a baby survive an air crash that killed over 100 people?', *Guardian*, 15 July 2003 www.theguardian.com/lifeandstyle/2003/jul/15/healthandwellbeing.health1

D F Lancy, 'Playing With Knives: The Socialization of Self-Initiated Learners' Child Development, Vol 83, Iss 3, May 2016

'Estimated Number of Injuries and Reported Deaths Associated with Inflatable Amusements 2003–13', USA Product Safety Commission, February 2015 www.cpsc.gov/s3fs-public/Inflatable_Amusements_Deaths_and_Injuries_2015.pdf

J Samenow, 'U.K. bounce house death highlights danger of inflatable structures and wind', *Washington Post*, 28 March 2016 www.washingtonpost.com/news/capital-weather-gang/wp/2016/03/28/uk-bounce-house-death-casts-light-on-dangers-of-inflatable-structures-and-wind/

'MP calls for bouncy castle ban after child's death', Sky News, 2 July 2018 news.sky.com/story/child-killed-after-thrown-from-bouncy-castle-in-norfolk-11422856

R Whetstone, 'BEACH HORROR Mum's screams as daughter, 3, was thrown 20ft into air and killed when inflatable exploded', *Sun*, 5 July 2018 www.thesun.co.uk/news/6669257/bouncy-castle-accident-explosion-tragedy-witnesses-mp-calls-ban/

Grieves Solicitors, 'Bouncy Castle Accident Claims & Compensation', www.grieves-solicitors.co.uk/injury-claims/child-accident-claims/bouncy-castle-accident-claims

E Thelwell, 'How common are child abductions in the UK?', BBC News, 29 September 2016 www.bbc.co.uk/news/uk-37504781

H H Schiffrin, 'Helping or Hovering? The Effects of Helicopter Parenting on College Students' Well-Being', *Journal of Child and Family Studies*, Vol 23, 2014

S Marsh, 'About 7% of UK children have attempted suicide by age of 17 – study', *Guardian*, 21 February 2021 www.theguardian.com/society/2021/feb/21/uk-17-year-olds-mental-health-crisis

R Merryfield, 'Kids more likely to be struck by lightning than die of coronavirus, figures suggest', *Mirror*, 10 June 2020 www.mirror.co.uk/news/uk-news/kids-more-likely-struck-lightning-22166411

Local Government Inform, 'Children aged 0-15 killed or seriously injured in road traffic accidents in England' lginform.local.gov.uk/reports/lga standard?mod-metric=305&mod-area=E92000001&mod-group=All Regions_England&mod-type=namedComparisonGroup

S Weale, 'UK children not allowed to play outside until two years older than parents' generation', *Guardian*, 20 April 2021 www.theguardian.com/society/2021/apr/20/gradual-lockdown-of-uk-children-as-age-for-solo-outdoor-play-rises

School House Magazine, 'What Age Can Children Walk to School Alone?', www.schoolhousemagazine.co.uk/q-and-a/age-children-walk-to-school-alone/

Root Two: Virtual Reality

Vision Direct, 'How much time do we spend looking at screens?', vision direct.co.uk, 30 June 2020 www.visiondirect.co.uk/blog/research-reveals-screen-time-habits/

G Music, *Nurturing Natures*, Routledge, 2016

D A Tahhan, 'Two Plus One Still Equals Two: Inclusion and Exclusion in the Japanese Family', dijtokyo.org/doc/Js19_Tahhan.pdf

D A Tahhan, 'Blurring the Boundaries between Bodies: Skinship and Bodily Intimacy in Japan', *Japanese Studies*, Vol 30, Iss 2, September 2010

D Narvaez et al, 'The importance of early life touch for psychosocial and moral development', *Psicologia: Reflexão e Crítica*, Vol 32, 2019

A Bigelow et al, 'Effect of mother/infant skin-to-skin contact on postpartum depressive symptoms and maternal physiological stress', *Journal of Obstetric, Gynecologic and Neonatal Nursing*, Vol 41, Iss 3, May–June 2014

E Elsworthy, 'Average Adult Will Spend 34 Years of Their Life Looking at Screens, Poll Claims', *Independent*, 11 May 2020 www.independent.co.uk/life-style/fashion/news/screen-time-average-lifetime-years-phone-laptop-tv-a9508751.html

K Rodgers, 'US teens use screens more than seven hours a day on average – and that's not including school work', *CNN*, 29 October 2019 edition.

cnn.com/2019/10/29/health/common-sense-kids-media-use-report-wellness/index.html

D Carrington, 'Three-quarters of UK children spend less time outdoors than prison inmates – survey', *Guardian*, 25 March 2016 www.the guardian.com/environment/2016/mar/25/three-quarters-of-uk-children-spend-less-time-outdoors-than-prison-inmates-survey

A Rzhetsky et al, 'Environmental and State-Level Regulatory Factors Affect the Incidence of Autism and Intellectual Disability', *PLoS*, Vol 10, Iss 3, 2014

L J Rudy, 'Why Autism Diagnoses Have Soared', Very Well Health, 2 February 2021 www.verywellhealth.com/is-there-a-real-increase-in-the-incidence-of-autism-260133

G A Bonanno, 'Loss, Trauma, and Human Resilience: Have We Underestimated the Human Capacity to Thrive After Extremely Aversive Events?', *American Psychologist*, Vol 59, Iss 1, 2004

L Foulkes, *Losing Our Minds: What Mental Illness Really Is – and What It Isn't*, Bodley Head, 2021

B Yang et al, 'Child Abuse and Epigenetic Mechanisms of Disease Risk', *American Journal of Preventative Medicine*, Vol 44, Iss 2, 2013

A S Dick et al, 'Neural vulnerability and hurricane-related media are associated with post-traumatic stress in youth', *Nature Human Behaviour*, Vol 5, 2021 www.nature.com/articles/s41562-021-01216-3

P Fonagy, 'When adversity turns into trauma Understanding the long term effects of adverse childhood experience' www.healthylondon.org/wp-content/uploads/2019/07/Peter-Fonagy-When-adversity-turns-into-trauma.pdf

Scientific American, 'Measuring the Daily Destruction of the World's Rainforests', *Scientific American*, 19 November 2009 www.scientific american.com/article/earth-talks-daily-destruction/

SciNews, 'Scientists categorize Earth as a "toxic planet"', Phys.org, 7 February 2017, phys.org/news/2017-02-scientists-categorize-earth-toxic-planet.html

S Anitei, 'The Rate of Extinction: 3 Species per Hour', Softpedia News, 23 March 2007 news.softpedia.com/news/The-Rate-of-Extinction-3-Species-per-Hour-55411.shtml

A Willers, 'Calico Immortality', Andre's Why, 22 October 2013 andreswhy.blogspot.com/2013/10/calico-immortality.html

A Gabbatt, 'Is Silicon Valley's quest for immortality a fate worse than death?' *Guardian*, 23 February 2019 www.theguardian.com/technology/2019/feb/22/silicon-valley-immortality-blood-infusion-gene-therapy

Fruit Two: Bodies in Nature

PACEY, 'Children as young as 3 unhappy with their bodies', Professional Association for Childcare and Early Years, 31 August 2016 www.pacey.org.uk/news-and-views/news/archive/2016-news/august-2016/children-as-young-as-3-unhappy-with-their-bodies/

G Owen, 'Botox is to be banned for under-18s amid growing concern at "Love Island surge" in teens seeking cosmetic enhancements', *Daily Mail*, 4 September 2021 www.dailymail.co.uk/news/article-9958209/amp/Botox-banned-18s-amid-surge-teens-seeking-cosmetic-enhancements.html

S Kale, 'Gym, eat, repeat: the shocking rise of muscle dysmorphia', *Guardian*, 17 July 2019 www.theguardian.com/lifeandstyle/2019/jul/17/gym-eat-repeat-the-shocking-rise-of-muscle-dysmorphia

TFBI, 'New research compares forest bathing and mindfulness', The Forest Bathing Institute, tfb.institute/scientific-research/

A F Taylor and F E Kuo, 'Children with attention deficits concentrate better after walk in the park', *Journal of Attention Discord*, Vol 12, Iss 5, March 2009

N Weinstein et al, 'Seeing Community for the Trees: The Links among Contact with Natural Environments, Community Cohesion, and Crime', *BioScience*, Vol 65, Iss 12, December 2015 academic.oup.com/bioscience/article/65/12/1141/223866

M P White et al, 'Spending at least 120 minutes a week in nature is associated with good health and wellbeing', *Scientific Reports*, Vol 9, 2019 www.nature.com/articles/s41598-019-44097-3/

J L Oschman, 'The effects of grounding (earthing) on inflammation, the immune response, wound healing, and prevention and treatment of chronic inflammatory and autoimmune diseases', *Journal of Inflammation Research*, Vol 8, 2015

Public Health England, 'Improving access to greenspace: A new review for 2020' assets.publishing.service.gov.uk/government/uploads/system/uploads/attachment_data/file/904439/Improving_access_to_greenspace_2020_review.pdf

'Monitor of Engagement with the Natural Environment pilot study: visits to the natural environment by children', Gov.UK www.gov.uk/government/statistics/monitor-of-engagement-with-the-natural-environment-pilot-study-visits-to-the-natural-environment-by-children

J Lent, *The Web of Meaning*, Profile, 2021

'A Haudenosaunee "Thanksgiving" Prayer', www.firstpeople.us/html/A-Haudenosaunee-Thanksgiving-Prayer.html

Root Three: Narcissism

L M Twenge, 'The Evidence for Generation Me and Against Generation We', *Emerging Adulthood*, Vol 1, Iss 1, 2013

C Pollard, 'Narcissism: From Kohut to CAT', *Reformulation*, 1997 www.acat.me.uk/reformulation.php?issue_id=36&article_id=376

'Narcissistic Personality Inventory' openpsychometrics.org/tests/NPI/

Research Digest, 'Cross-cultural studies of toddler self-awareness have been using an unfair test', The British Psychology Society, 5 February 2016 digest.bps.org.uk/2016/02/05/cross-cultural-studies-of-toddler-self-awareness-have-been-using-an-unfair-test/

D F Lancy, *Raising Children: Surprising Insights from Other Cultures*, Cambridge University Press, 2017

A Epstein and Quartz, 'Pop Stars Actually Do Die Too Young', *The Atlantic*, 2014, www.theatlantic.com/entertainment/archive/2014/10/pop-stars-really-are-doomed/382067/

J Holt-Lunstad et al, 'Social relationships and mortality risk: a meta-analytic review', *PLoS medicine*, Vol 7, Iss 7, 2010

Fruit Three: Compassion and co-operation

https://www.tribpub.com/gdpr/nydailynews.com/

M E Liddle, 'Baby Empathy: Infant Distress and Peer Prosocial Responses', *Infant Mental Health Journal*, Vol 36, Iss 4, 2015

F Warneken and M Tomasello, 'The Roots of Human Altruism', *British Journal of Psychology*, Vol 100, Iss 3, August 2009

'Jonny Wilkinson: 5 things I can't live without', *Daily Express*, 20 August 2018 www.express.co.uk/life-style/life/1005698/5-things-cant-live-without-jonny-wilkinson-rugby-union-tv-pundit

C Darwin, *The Descent of Man, and Selection in Relation to Sex*, Penguin Books, 1871/2004

S Pappas and A Harvey, 'Oxytocin: Facts about the "cuddle hormone"', LiveScience, 27 October 2021 www.livescience.com/42198-what-is-oxytocin.html

K W De Dreu Carsten et al, 'The Neuropeptide Oxytocin Regulates Parochial Altruism in Intergroup Conflict Among Humans', *Science*, 11 June 2010

www.express.co.uk/life-style/life/1005698/5-things-cant-live-without-jonny-wilkinson-rugby-union-tv-pundit

S G Shamay-Tsoory et al, 'Giving peace a chance: Oxytocin increases empathy to pain in the context of the Israeli–Palestinian conflict', *Psychoneuroendocrinology*, Vol 38, Iss 12, December 2013 uploads-ssl.webflow.com/59faaf5b01b9500001e95457/5bc562a6514198361ddac3da_Shamay-Tsoory%2C%20Simone%20G.%2C%20et%20al%202013.pdf

N Geurtzen et al, 'Association Between Mindful Parenting and Adolescents' Internalizing Problems: Non-judgmental Acceptance of Parenting as Core Element', *Journal of Child and Family Studies*, Vol 24, 2015

E Seppälä, '18 Science-Backed Reasons to Try Loving-Kindness Meditation', *Psychology Today*, 15 September 2014 www.psychologytoday.

com/us/blog/feeling-it/201409/18-science-backed-reasons-try-loving-kindness-meditation

MCCP, 'The Children We Mean to Raise: The Real Messages Adults Are Sending About Values', Making Caring Common Project, July 2014 www.eva.mpg.de/documents/Cambridge/Tomasello_Understanding_BehBrainSci_2005_1555292.pdf mcc.gse.harvard.edu/reports/children-mean-raise

D R Ewoldsen et al, 'Effect of playing violent video games cooperatively or competitively on subsequent cooperative behavior', *Cyberpsychology, Behavior, and Social Networking*, Vol 15, Iss 5, May 2012

J M Zelenski et al, 'Cooperation is in our nature: Nature exposure may promote cooperative and environmentally sustainable behavior', *Journal of Environmental Psychology*, Vol 42, June 2015 www.sciencedirect.com/science/article/pii/S0272494415000195

Root Four: Scarcity

F Sirois et al, 'Self-compassion improves parental well-being in response to challenging parenting events', *Journal of Psychology*, 2018 eprints. whiterose.ac.uk/135429/1/Sirois%20Emerson%20Bogels%20JoP%20accepted.pdf

A Henderson et al, 'The Price Mothers Pay, Even When They Are Not Buying It: Mental Health Consequences of Idealized Motherhood', *Sex Roles*, Vol 74, 2015

G Livingstone and K Parker, '8 facts about American dads', Pew Research Center, 12 June 2019, www.pewresearch.org/fact-tank/2019/06/12/fathers-day-facts/

L Minou, 'Envy's pathology: Historical contexts [version 2], Wellcome Open Research, 2017 wellcomeopenresearch.org/articles/2-3

R H Smith, *Envy: Theory and Research*, OUP USA, 2008

T Brach, 'Awakening From the Trance of Unworthiness', *Inquiring Mind*, Vol 17, Iss 2, Spring 2001 www.tarabrach.com/articles-interviews/inquiring-trance/

Fruit Four: Abundance

D Austin, 'The True Story Behind Mr. Rogers' Empathy', *Reader's Digest Canada*, www.readersdigest.ca/culture/true-story-mr-rogers/

'Mr. Rogers is a evil Man [sic]' www.youtube.com/watch?v=29lmR_357rA&feature=emb_logo

J Zaslow, 'Blame It on Mr. Rogers: Why Young Adults Feel So Entitled', *Wall Street Journal*, 5 July 2007 www.wsj.com/articles/SB118358476840657463

H Kirschenbaum, *The Life and Work of Carl Rogers*, PCCS Books, 2007 www.bacp.co.uk/media/9667/bacp-what-works-counselling-psychotherapy-relationships-gpacp004-sep20.pdf

G Arnold, 'Bruce Wampold on What Actually Makes Us Good Therapists', psychothereapy.net www.psychotherapy.net/interview/bruce-wampold-psychotherapy-effectiveness

B Katie, *Loving What Is: Four Questions That Can Change Your Life*, Rider, 2002

D Z Lieberman and M E Long, *The Molecule of More: How a Single Chemical in Your Brain Drives Love, Sex, and Creativity – and Will Determine the Fate of the Human Race*, BenBella Books, 2018

A Routtenberg, 'The Reward System of the Brain', *Scientific American*, Vol 239, Iss 5, 1978

S Atzil et al, 'Dopamine in the medial amygdala network mediates human bonding', *PNAS*, Vol 114, Iss 9, February 2017

G Maté, 'Addiction: Childhood Trauma, Stress and the Biology of Addiction', *Journal of Restorative Medicine*, Vol 1, 2012 restorativemedicine.org/wp-content/uploads/2012/09/Stress-and-the-Biology-of-Addiction.pdf

'Punishing a child is effective if done correctly', Science Daily, 6 August 2015, www.sciencedaily.com/releases/2015/08/150806144419.htm

T Kasser et al, 'Changes in materialism, changes in psychological well-being: Evidence from three longitudinal studies and an intervention experiment', *Motivation and Emotion*, Vol 38, 2014 selfdeterminationtheory.org/SDT/documents/2014_Kasser_et_al_materialism.pdf

H Dittmar and M Hurst, 'The Impact of a Materialistic Value Orientation on Well-Being', 2019 sro.sussex.ac.uk/id/eprint/85211/3/DITTMAR_Book_Chapter_JUL_2019_author_copy.pdf natelambert.info/images/stories/pdf/2009jpp.pdf

J Pinsker, 'Why Kids Want Things', *The Atlantic*, 30 August 2018 www.theatlantic.com/family/archive/2018/08/kids-materialism/568987/

Root Five: Anaesthesia

G Iacobucci, 'NHS prescribed record number of antidepressants last year', *BMJ*, Vol 364, 29 March 2019

L Foulkes, *Losing Our Minds: What Mental Illness Really Is – and What It Isn't*, Bodley Head, 2021

E Taggart, 'Who Invented the Smiley Face? Discover the Not-So-Smiley History of the Graphic Yellow Icon', My Modern Net, 18 August 2020 mymodernmet.com/smiley-face/

J Lewis, *The Pursuit of Happiness: Family and Values in Jefferson's Virginia*, Cambridge University Press, 1983

REFERENCES

P N Stearns, 'The History of Happiness', *Harvard Business Review*, January–February 2012, hbr.org/2012/01/the-history-of-happiness

'Post Traumatic Slave Syndrome' www.bethehealing.com/post-traumatic-slave-syndrome

National Mental Health Development Unit, 'Count Me In in 2010', Care Quality Commission, April 2011 www.cqc.org.uk/sites/default/files/documents/count_me_in_2010_final_tagged.pdf

C Taylor, 'Review of the Youth Justice System in England and Wales', Ministry of Justice, December 2016 assets.publishing.service.gov.uk/government/uploads/system/uploads/attachment_data/file/577103/youth-justice-review-final-report.pdf

P N Stearns, 'Happy Children: A Modern Emotional Commitment', *Frontiers in Psychology*, 6 September 2019 www.frontiersin.org/articles/10.3389/fpsyg.2019.02025/full

The World Happiness Report 2020, worldhappiness.report/ed/2020/

'Happiness', The United Arab Emirates' Government portal u.ae/en/about-the-uae/the-uae-government/government-of-future/happiness/

'The Human Freedom Index 2020', Fraser Institute, 17 December 2020, www.fraserinstitute.org/studies/human-freedom-index-2020

A Moore, 'Eternal Sunshine', *Observer*, 13 May 2007 www.theguardian.com/society/2007/may/13/socialcare.medicineandhealth

W Dahlgreen, '37% of British Workers Think Their Jobs Are Meaningless', YouGov, 2013 yougov.co.uk/topics/lifestyle/articles-reports/2015/08/12/british-jobs-meaningless/

J Davies, *Sedated: How Modern Capitalism Created our Mental Health Crisis*, Atlantic Books, 2021

S Timimi, 'Chapter 5: The Manufacture of Childhood Depression (Part 2)', Mad in the UK, 15 December 2020 www.madintheuk.com/2020/12/chapter-5-the-manufacture-of-childhood-depression-part-2/

S Boseley, 'Antidepressant withdrawal symptoms severe, says new report', *Guardian*, 2 October 2018 www.theguardian.com/society/2018/oct/02/antidepressant-withdrawal-symptoms-severe-says-new-report

J Wise, 'Antidepressants may double risk of suicide and aggression in children, study finds', *BMJ, Vol 352*, 28 January 2016

J Davies, *Cracked: Why Psychiatry is Doing More Harm Than Good*, Icon Books, 2013

A Cockburn and F Gardner, 'Prozac and the Marketing of Depression', *Depression in Primary Care: Vol 2 – Treatment of Major Depression* beyondthc.com/prozac-and-the-marketing-of-depression/

M L Murray et al, 'A drug utilisation study of antidepressants in children and adolescents using the General Practice Research Database', *Archives of Disease in Childhood*, Vol 89, Iss 12, 2004 adc.bmj.com/content/89/12/1098

O Newlan, 'Antidepressant prescriptions for children on the rise', BBC News, 24 July 2018 www.bbc.com/news/health-44821886.amp

'The secrets of seroxat', BBC News, news.bbc.co.uk/1/hi/programmes/panorama/2310197.stm

I Kirsch, 'Antidepressants and the Placebo Effect', *Zeitschrift für Psychologie*, Vol 222, Iss 3, 2014

J Davies and J Read, 'A systematic review into the incidence, severity and duration of antidepressant withdrawal effects: Are guidelines evidence-based?', *Addictive Behaviors*, Vol 97, 2019

NHS, 'Side effects – Selective serotonin reuptake inhibitors (SSRIs)' www.nhs.uk/mental-health/talking-therapies-medicine-treatments/medicines-and-psychiatry/ssri-antidepressants/side-effects/

World Federation for Mental Health, 'Depression: A Global Crisis', World Health Organization, 10 October 2012 www.who.int/mental_health/management/depression/wfmh_paper_depression_wmhd_2012.pdf

J Bilsen, 'Suicide and Youth: Risk Factors', *Frontiers in Psychiatry*, Vol 9, 2018

Fruit Five: Feeling

S Marsh, 'About 7% of UK children have attempted suicide by age of 17 – study', *Guardian*, 21 February 2021 www.theguardian.com/society/2021/feb/21/uk-17-year-olds-mental-health-crisis

A Phillips, *Going Sane*, Penguin, 2005

C Mosier and B Rogoff, 'Privileged treatment of toddlers: Cultural aspects of individual choice and responsibility', *Developmental Psychology*, Vol 39, 2003

A Schlegel and H Barry III, *Adolescence: An anthropological inquiry*, Free Press, 1991

S Kitayama et al, 'Expression of Anger and Ill Health in Two Cultures: An Examination of Inflammation and Cardiovascular Risk', *Psychological Science*, Vol 26, Iss 2, February 2015 pubmed.ncbi.nlm.nih.gov/25564521/

P Ekman and D Keltner, 'Are Facial Expressions Universal?', *Greater Good Magazine*, 12 March 2014 greatergood.berkeley.edu/article/item/are_facial_expressions_universal

L Feldman Barrett, *How Emotions Are Made: The Secret Life of the Brain*, Macmillan, 2017

P Ekman and D Keltner, 'Darwin's Claim of Universals in Facial Expression Not Challenged: A response to Lisa Feldman-Barrett's recent contribution', Paul Ekman Group, March 2014 www.paulekman.com/tag/lisa-feldman-barrett/

F de Waal, *Mama's Last Hug: Animal Emotions and What They Teach Us about Ourselves*, W. W. Norton, 2019

E T Gendlin, *Focusing: How to Gain Direct Access to Your Body's Knowledge*, Rider, 1978; 2003

Root Six: Chaos

D Campbell, 'Three in four Britons felt overwhelmed by stress, survey reveals', *Guardian*, 14 May 2018 www.theguardian.com/society/2018/may/14/three-in-four-britons-felt-overwhelmed-by-stress-survey-reveals

D Ferguson, 'Record levels of stress "put teachers at breaking point"', *Guardian*, 10 November 2019, www.theguardian.com/education/2019/nov/10/stressed-teachers-at-breaking-point-says-report

'Burnout', Mental Health UK, mentalhealth-uk.org/burnout/

C Corker and D B O'Connor, 'Burnout in psychological therapists: A cross-sectional study investigating the role of supervisory relationship quality', *Clinical Psychologist*, 2020 eprints.whiterose.ac.uk/156870/3/VERSION%20FOR%20ARCHIVING.pdf

E Berger, '"I can't do this any more": US faces nurse shortage from burnout', *Guardian*, 19 November 2021, www.theguardian.com/us-news/2021/nov/19/us-faces-nurse-shortage-burnout-covid

V Gewin, 'Pandemic burnout is rampant in academia', *Nature*, 15 March 2021 www.nature.com/articles/d41586-021-00663-2

C H Griffith, 'The Learning Environment and Medical Student Burnout', JAMA Network, 9 August 2021 jamanetwork.com/journals/jamanetworkopen/article-abstract/2782838

A H Petersen, 'How Millennials Became The Burnout Generation', Buzzfeed, 5 January 2019 www.buzzfeednews.com/article/annehelenpetersen/millennials-burnout-generation-debt-work

M Savage, 'Burnout is rising in the land of work-life balance', BBC, 26 July 2019 www.bbc.com/worklife/article/20190719-why-is-burnout-rising-in-the-land-of-work-life-balance

(Harris and Ross, 1987) in G Music, *Nurturing Natures* (p. 236). Taylor and Francis, Kindle Edition

J Goldstein, 'Australian Photographer Reveals "Heartbreaking" Story Behind Viral Image of Kangaroo Killed in Fires', Yahoo News, 9 January 2020 nz.news.yahoo.com/australian-photographer-reveals-heartbreaking-story-023509408.html

@Bradfleet www.instagram.com/bradfleet/?hl=en

B Badenoch, *The Heart of Trauma: Healing the Embodied Brain in the Context of Relationships*, W. W. Norton & Company, 2018

L Corner, 'Kangaroo care: the radical skin-to-skin approach to saving premature babies', *Guardian*, 3 March 2017 www.theguardian.com/

global-development-professionals-network/2017/mar/03/kangaroo-care-the-radical-skin-to-skin-approach-to-saving-premature-babies

'Mental health statistics: stress', Mental Heath Foundation, www.mentalhealth.org.uk/statistics/mental-health-statistics-stress

A Kratzer, 'Harsh Nazi Parenting Guidelines May Still Affect German Children of Today', *Scientific American*, 4 January 2019, www.scientificamerican.com/article/harsh-nazi-parenting-guidelines-may-still-affect german-children-of-today1/

Fruit Six: Peace

M Manoukian, 'The Real Reason This Buddhist Monk Set Himself on Fire', Grunge, 11 August 2021, www.grunge.com/484621/the-real-reason-this-buddhist-monk-set-himself-on-fire/

D P Fry ed., *War, Peace, and Human Nature: The Convergence of Evolutionary and Cultural Views*, Oxford University Press, 2015

K Endicott, 'Peaceful foragers' (2013) In: D P Fry, *War, Peace, and Human Nature*

M L Butovskaya, (2013) 'Aggression and conflict resolution among the nomadic Hadza of Tanzania as compared with their pastoralist neighbors' D P Fry, *War, Peace, and Human Nature*

V Frankl, *Man's Search for Meaning*, Rider, 2004; 1946

Y N Harari, 'Yuval Noah Harari: the theatre of terror', *Guardian*, 31 January 2015 www.theguardian.com/books/2015/jan/31/terrorism-spectacle-how-states-respond-yuval-noah-harari-sapiens

www.nytimes.com/2020/03/05/opinion/location-tracking-children.html

P Bronson, 'Web Exclusive: The New Science of Siblings', ABC News, 31 August 2019 abcnews.go.com/GMA/Parenting/story?id=8449624

Daily Mail, 'Had a row with your partner today? That'll be one of the 2,455 you will have this year', MailOnline, 20 May 2011 www.dailymail.co.uk/news/article-1389002/Fallout-Couples-argue-average-seven-times-day.html

P Lincolne, 'How often do kids and parents argue? Science has the answer', Babyology babyology.com.au/parenting/family/research-tells-us-how-often-parents-and-kids-argue-and-the-figure-seems-low/

G Music, *Nurturing Natures*, Routledge, 2016

T Hübl, *Healing Collective Trauma: A Process for Integrating Our Intergenerational and Cultural Wounds*, Sounds True, 2020

M F Bettencourt, 'The science of forgiveness: "When you don't forgive you release all the chemicals of the stress response"', Salon, 24 August 2015 www.salon.com/2015/08/24/the_science_of_forgiveness_when_you_dont_forgive_you_release_all_the_chemicals_of_the_stress_response/

Root Seven: Hopelessness

C Polihronis et al, 'What's the harm in asking? A systematic review and meta-analysis on the risks of asking about suicide-related behaviors', *Archives of Suicide Research*, 25 July 2020

The National Center for Health Statistics in the US released data in 2018 showing that, between 1999 and 2017

'Aldous Huxley Took LSD While Dying' www.youtube.com/watch?v=4NGT05sXvz8

R R Griffiths et al, 'Psilocybin produces substantial and sustained decreases in depression and anxiety in patients with life-threatening cancer: A randomized double-blind trial', *Journal of Psychopharmacology*, Vol 30, Iss 12, 2016

M Pollan, *How to Change Your Mind: The New Science of Psychedelics*, Allen Lane, 2018

R Ebert, 'The Day after Tomorrow', rogerebert.com, 28 May 2004 www.rogerebert.com/reviews/the-day-after-tomorrow-2004

C Ryan, *Civilized to Death: The Price of Progress*, Simon and Schuster, 2019

M Greenspan, *Healing through the Dark Emotions: The Wisdom of Grief, Fear, and Despair*, Shambhala Publications, 2004

J Bendell, 'Deep Adaptation: A Map for Navigating Climate Tragedy', jembendell.com, 27 July 2020 lifeworth.com/deepadaptation.pdf

Z Tsjeng, 'The Climate Change Paper So Depressing It's Sending People to Therapy', Vice, 27 February 2019 www.vice.com/en/article/vbwpdb/the-climate-change-paper-so-depressing-its-sending-people-to-therapy

M J Wheatley, 'Restoring Hope to the Future Through Critical Education of Leaders', margaretwheatley.com, 2001 www.margaretwheatley.com/articles/restoringhope.html

Fruit Seven: Hope

Bhagavata Purama archive.org/stream/bhagavata-purana-vol-2-ramesh-menon/Bhagavata%20Purana%20Vol%202%20-%20Ramesh%20Menon_djvu.txt

C G Jung, *The Archetypes and the Collective Unconscious*, Routledge, 1991

historycollection.com/wp-content/uploads/2017/07/Children-playing-with-Gas-Masks.-Tumbler.jpg

G Eisen, *Children and Play in the Holocaust: Games Among the Shadows*, University Massachusetts Press, 1990

M Spinka et al, 'Mammalian play: training for the unexpected', *Quarterly Review of Biology*, Vol 76, Iss 2, 2001

G Music, *Nurturing Natures*, Routledge, 2016

R Carson, *The Sense of Wonder*, HarperCollins, 1998

C Letheby and P Gerrans, 'Self unbound: ego dissolution in psychedelic experience', *Neuroscience of Consciousness*, Vol 2017, Iss 1, 2017 2017, academic.oup.com/nc/article/2017/1/nix016/3916730

M Seligman, *The Hope Circuit: A Psychologist's Journey from Helplessness to Optimism*, Nicholas Brealey Publishing, 2019

S B Kaufman, 'Review of Learned Hopefulness: The Power of Positivity to Overcome Depression', *Scientific American*, 5 June 2020 blogs.scientificamerican.com/beautiful-minds/review-of-learned-hopefulness-the-power-of-positivity-to-overcome-depression/

R Solnit, ' "Hope is an embrace of the unknown": Rebecca Solnit on living in dark times', *Guardian*, 15 July 2016 www.theguardian.com/books/2016/jul/15/rebecca-solnit-hope-in-the-dark-new-essay-embrace-unknown

X Luo et al, 'Reasons for living and hope as the protective factors against suicidality in Chinese patients with depression: a cross sectional study', *BMC Psychiatry*, Vol 13, 2020 www.ncbi.nlm.nih.gov/pmc/articles/PMC4955123/

ACKNOWLEDGEMENTS

Even though it is my name and my mugshot on the cover of this book, and even though, yes, I did do most of the work (well done Louis, pat on the back), the truth is that I have received so much support and encouragement from so many people from the time this book was just a seed of an idea to now.

My family have been a constant support to me, and I am very grateful to them for keeping me grounded and reminding me of the importance of not being too earnest. I am especially grateful to my wife Laurey, who has been very patient during this process and is simply an amazing mother to Rose. It is such a joy to me when, early in the mornings, I go up to my office to write and I can hear Laurey and Rose laughing hysterically downstairs.

My daughter Rose is my heart inspiration for this book, and I want so deeply for her to experience a future world where human beings are more peaceful and compassionate. I especially appreciate the moment a year ago when Rose decided she was going to write her own book, and started to bash a random soup of letters on the keyboard, before asking me 'what does it say daddy?', eventually asking to print her 'book' out and showing it proudly to visitors: 'Look, I wrote a book!'

I also want to thank all the children I have worked with over the last 20 years (and all the grown-ups with beautiful, frightened, confused, innocent, playful children inside of them) who have made me laugh, made me cry, made me feel really angry with the world and how it is damaging their minds, but also – most importantly – who have reminded me to stay connected to the precious qualities of childhood, like being silly and free from the conditioning of this mad world.

Tamsin Olivier is the person who inspired me to be a therapist. She was my supervisor when I was running the therapeutic school on behalf of Kids Company, and in one session she gave me a life-changing experience of being instantly free from suffering, and I decided I simply had to learn how to share that gift with others. I went to train at CCPE where Tamsin taught; Angela Gruber accepted me on to the training and I am grateful to her.

Then there are a bunch of amazing people who helped me to create and shape the book. Valeria Huerta is my super-agent, who made me jump through several hoops to get signed with a great publisher. I resented all this extra work at the time, but she was spot on and is also just a beautiful soul. She connected me with Brigid Moss who is a great editor, not afraid to say it as it is, and really helped me transform my meanderings into something much more pragmatic. Thank you.

Sam Jackson is the editor at Vermillion who took a chance on this lesser-spotted first-time author with zero social media following. Thank you for having faith in me. And thank you to the team at Vermillion for all your support in pulling this project together.

Dave Rock is a genius coach who guided me to write from a place of heart-felt truth. Shelley Sperry gave generous advice on how to weave narrative into a non-fiction book. And Stuart Laird is one of my oldest friends whose sharp and tough critiques I love and fear in equal measure. I'm so glad to have a friend in my life who is consistently, and lovingly, willing to call BS on things.

Then there are the people I interviewed for the book, who kindly gave their time and wisdom. David Lancey for his anthropological wisdom; Meg Wheatley for reminding me not to sugar-coat anything; Michael Ungar for his radical views on resilience; Craig Chalquist for his encyclopaedic knowledge of myths and a deep understanding of how our minds are more connected to the natural world than we realise; Jude Currivan for her understanding of how the inner worlds interface with the outer worlds in magical and empowering ways; Darcia Narvaez for her integrated understanding of what human children need to thrive; René Veugelers for a unique and playful approach to helping children and grownups stay connected to their bodies; Jennifer Murphy for helping me understand how our capacity for interoception develops; Michael Rexman for challenging my understanding of the differences between humans and other animals; Andrew Cook for his deep understanding of trauma and the body; Nicholas Tampey for a compassionate and political lens on why concepts like 'resilience' and 'grit' can do more harm than good; Lisa Marchiano for helping me dig into the deeper ways in which a Victim complex can manifest in families and the wider world; Barbara Horowitz for guiding me to understand adolescence as a unique biological stage that we can learn a lot about from the animal world; Laura Kerr for bringing an extra degree of sensitivity to what parents need to heal from trauma and dissociative states; Thomas Dixon for his advice on the history of emotions and for helping me shape the chapter on Happy-Washing. Wow that was a long paragraph. I'm so grateful to all these people who shared their knowledge and guidance with me.

There are a number of people who read chapters, and some who even read the whole book. Thank you to Matt Williams and Alex Evans and Phillipa Perry for reading the whole book from start to finish and giving me a big and much-needed boost of encouragement. I really appreciate you. Thank you Yemisi Mokuolu and Justyna Parada for helping me see my biases and making the text more inclusive. Thank you Odilia Mabrouk for giving simple practical advice around what kids need to stay in their bodies. Thank you Roma Norris for helping me be more sensitive to the impact of infant trauma. Thank you Louisa MacInnes for reviewing the chapters in Scarcity and Abundance, highlighting areas where more compassion was needed and helping me with the cover copy. Thank you Sara Magalhaes for your clinical wisdom and lived experience on parenting and emotions. Thank you Pamela Alexander for reviewing the chapter on Happy Washing and giving much needed reassurance on that. Thank you Robin Prospect for reviewing the chapter on Victim with a keen and critical eye on diversity, inclusion and truth. Thank you to Jessie Brinton for helping reduce the doominess and adding some more light to the cover copy. Thank you to Sara Weston, Nick Sunderland, and Miguel de Lara for your guidance on all things design related, and to Phil Volkers for taking photos.

I stayed in a beautiful writing cabin called Ty Twt while writing the chapter on Hopelessness. Built by Rina and Tim Clarke, managed by our dear friend Lowri Clarke, it is a beautiful spot to go deeper into your writing.

I also want to thank anyone who has ever given me encouragement, even just by being there, and all those who have helped me feel less alone, especially through the dark times. Encouragement is hugely underrated. It is an energy that fills our hearts. We all need it, and I am grateful for all those beings visible and invisible who have encouraged me on this path.

Finally, sending thanks out there into the cosmos for my dear friend Dan who would be so proud of me writing this book, and who always gave me encouragement and – more than that – unconditional love. We both believed in the power and magic of synchronicity, and so it feels appropriate to sign off here with our favourite quote from a taxi driver in Goa who helped us find our way home one night when we were feeling a little dazed and confused, and as we stumbled out of the taxi he serenely pointed to the vast sky with a twinkle in his eye and said: 'This no accident.'

INDEX